# Improving
# Reading
# Through
# Individualized
# Correction

# Improving
# Reading
# Through
# Individualized
# Correction

## Second Edition

**Delwyn G. Schubert**
California State College at Los Angeles

**Theodore L. Torgerson**, Emeritus
University of Wisconsin

WM. C. BROWN COMPANY PUBLISHERS
Dubuque, Iowa

Printed in U. S. A.

# Preface

*Improving Reading Through Individualized Correction* represents a complete revision of the earlier and highly successful book, *Improving Reading in the Elementary School*, by the authors. The general organization of the book and its emphasis on diagnosis and individualized self-correction has been enthusiastically supported by those hundreds of individuals who evaluated the previous edition.

The authors have retained their emphasis on diagnosis and individualized correction by using self-directed instructional material. Twenty-one new topics are discussed, including visual discrimination, brain injury, dominance, programmed learning and in-service reading programs. All discussions are fully documented. The appendix has been expanded to include a glossary, an author index, a subject index, a letter to parents, a reading readiness check list and several new reading tests.

To the teacher who uses this book it will be a handy reference for the use of instructional material and equipment designed to implement a program of individualized correction. Diagnosis of reading difficulties followed by the use of self-directed corrective material forms the basis for an effective improvement program in reading at all instructional levels.

Teachers found the first edition a valuable source book for ordering material and equipment in the field of reading. The present edition provides a more extensive list accompanied by up-to-date prices. Although prices continue to change, the knowledge that an article is, for example, in the one- to five-dollar category rather than the ten- to fifteen-dollar category proves very helpful when contemplated purchases are subject to budgetary limitations.

The authors are confident that instructors will find this volume a useful guide in teaching prospective elementary and secondary teachers.

# Contents

# Introduction

What percentage of children in our schools have a reading disability? Many investigators, including Durrell, McCallister and Witty (see references) have provided an answer to this question. Their estimates vary between ten to twenty-five per cent. Such percentages mean that fifty to one hundred twenty-five of every five hundred school children are in need of corrective reading.

A reading disability can have disastrous consequences. Often it results in failure in the primary grades. In the intermediate and upper grades, it makes effective reading in content fields impossible. Since reading is a process permeating the entire curriculum, success in all subject matter areas, even arithmetic, becomes difficult for the seriously disabled reader.

The frustration and consequent emotional tension generated by a reading disability can warp and distort young personalities. The resultant personality maladjustment constitutes an impediment to scholastic progress. Those who somehow manage to struggle through high school with a reading handicap find it impossible to succeed in college. As a result, human resources are lost and society suffers.

Who must bear the onus of this situation? The answer is obvious: the school. This may seem to be unfair because we know certain causal factors of reading disability (an impoverished home environment reflected in neglect and rejection, for example) may appear to be beyond the jurisdiction of the school. But in such cases, the school has the obligation to provide a compensating environment, one that will enable the child to experience success and the thrill of learning.

1

The causes of reading disability are complex; usually a constellation of interacting factors is responsible. Little can be accomplished by blaming the child, the home or hereditary factors for the difficulty. *The authors believe it is important to place emphasis on those factors over which the school has direct control.* This volume, therefore, will delineate hazards and causal factors of reading disability that stem from conditions and practices within the school. It will set forth techniques of diagnosis accompanied by methods and materials useful in implementing a program of correction.

A number of widely employed but inefficient or unwholesome practices that are found in many schools and contribute to frustration and failure in reading are listed below. These are discussed in some detail in Chapter 1.

1. Beginning formal instruction in reading before a child has acquired readiness;
2. Accepting a low level of mastery of word recognition during the primary grades;
3. Promoting pupils to the fourth grade who have not gained independent reading habits and skills;
4. Failing to follow a systematic program of detecting hazards to reading progress;
5. Assuming that reading can be taught effectively as an isolated communicative skill;
6. Relying on group instruction to meet the reading needs of all pupils;
7. Requiring retarded readers to pursue instructional material in reading on a frustration level of difficulty;
8. Failing to estimate the true capacity of poor readers;
9. Failing to employ a balanced program in reading;
10. Considering reading as a mere mechanical process;
11. Assuming that retardation is nonexistent when the class average on standardized reading tests reaches or exceeds the norm;
12. Using instructional material on only one level of difficulty;
13. Failing to motivate children to read widely;
14. Assuming that the curricular content covered and the instructional effort expended are criteria of instructional effectiveness;
15. Assuming that skill learning does not differ from information learning;
16. Failing to eliminate weaknesses in reading when they first appear;
17. Failing to recognize and promote wholesome teacher-pupil relationships as a prime-learning prerequisite;
18. Failing to limit the size of classes;
19. Inadequate training of teachers in the intermediate grades in primary reading methods;
20. Inadequate utilization of cumulative records.

The foregoing practices are closely related to meeting individual differences, the latter being a concept familiar to teachers for more than four decades. In an attempt to come to grips with the problem of instruction geared to individual needs, various experiments in individualized instruction have appeared on the educational scene. The Winnetka plan, the Dalton plan, individualized reading and countless interclass and intraclass grouping plans, are a few of the many approaches that have evolved.

The importance of attending to individual learning problems when teaching reading is evident when one considers that a normal fifth grade will show a range in reading achievement from second grade to seventh grade. Educational growth in terms of individual potential is more readily attained when differentiated instruction is geared to individual needs.

Learning to read effectively demands systematic developmental instruction and individualized correction. Basal readers form the core of most developmental instructional programs. Basal readers are, however, frequently criticized for having a limited and repetitious vocabulary which provides an unimaginative, uninteresting and frequently deadly content. The authors contend that while this is sometimes true, instruction will not be dull when in the hands of a skillful teacher who provides meaningful practice in terms of interesting and attainable goals.

The reading program advocated by the authors recommends employing basal readers for systematic developmental reading in the first four grades and encourages supervised recreational reading. But it does not stop at this point. *It employs individualization as a supplement to group instruction. It upgrades the reading level of all children by employing diagnosis of reading difficulties and an individualized approach for corrective instruction.* The authors make simple clinical procedures an essential and integral part of classroom teaching. The diagnostic, developmental and corrective procedures described are the result of many years of experience on the part of the authors in directing a reading clinic and helping teachers in the field to improve reading programs.

This book sets forth conditions and practices which are essential to successful learning. It delineates conditions essential to a flexible program of instruction designed to prevent, correct and eliminate reading failure. It shows elementary teachers how to determine individual needs and how to meet those needs with a minimum of time and effort. It clarifies the problem of how to modify group instruction to meet the needs of the retarded reader without using out-of-school time for individual tutoring. It resolves the questions teachers raise, "Do I dare neglect the bright children by giving extra time for the less able?"

The authors recognize that in spite of the presence of many unwholesome conditions and inefficient practices, from fifty to sixty per cent of the pupils in the average school attain a so-called normal status in reading. This book describes an improvement program in reading which has as its objective the attainment of true reading potential for all pupils.

Classroom teachers can streamline their corrective work by moving from individual tutoring into a program of individualized correction utilizing self-directive instructional material. When this is done pupils can work independently in overcoming their difficulties. The required high-level mastery of the basic reading skills of word recognition and word analysis can then be attained. Such mastery will give rise to independent fourth-grade readers, readers who can cope with the many new and unfamiliar words that are introduced at that level with machine-gun rapidity. The authors contend that a primary grade program which insures total mastery of the basic reading skills of word recognition and word analysis will preclude, in a large measure, later reading failures. Mastery of these basic skills provides a sound foundation for the successful mastery of the vast hierarchy of new reading skills (using the dictionary, finding central thoughts of paragraphs, skimming, summarizing), which is developed at the fourth-grade level and beyond.

Another essential of reading improvement involves a carefully planned recreational reading program for all pupils. Daily fun reading of this type permits individual choice of books and other reading material under teacher guidance. In order to find the right books for the right children, materials which vary widely in interest appeal and difficulty level must be provided. Pupils do not profit from books that are uninteresting or too difficult.

In summary, the authors emphasize the following essential aspects of an effective program in reading: (1) systematic developmental instruction in the reading skills in the first four grades (The instructional material utilized for this purpose will be determined largely by the training and experience of the staff. Teachers who are competent to provide systematic instruction which results in a mastery of the reading skills by employing materials other than basal readers should be encouraged to do so.), (2) periodic and systematic parent and pupil interviews and the use of screening tests to discover hazards to learning in the areas of health, hearing, vision and adjustment, (3) periodic and systematic evaluation of each child's reading efficiency as a part of the teacher's instructional program so that reading difficulties can be discovered as soon as they develop, (4) total mastery of the reading skills maintained at all levels, the frustration level of instruction avoided and all instructional material adapted to the reading level of the pupil, (5) a diagnosis of individual reading problems utilizing school records, oral and silent reading tests of a formal and informal nature and intelligence tests, (6) corrective instruction following diagnosis to be individualized through the use of self-directed instructional material, (7) a systematic program of recreational reading for all pupils, permitting free choice of material selected from books adapted to the reading competence of the individual in his fields of interest.

The unwholesome conditions and school practices previously listed are discussed in some detail in Chapter 1. The essential aspects of an improvement program in reading already set forth are discussed and described in the remaining chapters. Individualized correction in reading that utilizes self-directed material is emphasized throughout the book with an extensive listing of teacher-made and commercial reading material. The discussions direct the teacher and administrator to the sources in the appendix which will aid the school in implementing an individualized diagnostic and corrective reading program.

The chapters discuss limitations of group instruction and point out the important role of individualization in corrective reading. They set forth procedures for diagnosing reading difficulties and selecting, adapting and preparing materials for individualized correction. They also discuss the organization, administration and evaluation of the reading program at all grade levels from one through eight. Behavior inventories useful in observation appear at the end of Chapter 2. Chapters 4 and 6 provide record forms for organizing and interpreting the data obtained from a study of a child's reading difficulty. The reading inventory at the end of Chapter 4 also permits the inclusion of an objective record of individual progress in the corrective program. Chapters 5, 7 and 9 include more than three hundred items describing commercial and teacher-made instructional materials, most of which are self-directive and self-corrective. These constitute a source from which the teacher can evolve a reading improvement program geared to the needs of the individual. Chapter 9 discusses an over-all evaluation of the current school program in reading and indicates specific elements to be studied as a basis for an in-service improvement program. Questions and problems listed at the end of most chapters will assist students and teachers in applying the diagnostic and corrective procedures set forth in the text.

In the Appendixes are found a listing of certain phonetic aids, a summary of the kinesthetic method, an annotated list of group intelligence tests, oral and silent reading tests and a classified list of professional books in reading, together with names and addresses of publishers.

The writers wish to state that this book does not attempt to delineate a complete elementary grade program in the teaching of reading. It does, however, focus attention on unwholesome conditions and inefficient practices that prevail in elementary schools and indicates how they may be improved. The volume pinpoints the limitations of group instruction and indicates that developmental instruction alone does not attain for all pupils a required mastery of reading skills. This goal cannot be realized without an accompanying program of discovery and correction of individual reading difficulties. The organization and detailed workings of such a program of individualized correction are described in subsequent chapters.

## REFERENCES

D. D. DURRELL, *Improvement of Basic Reading Abilities* (New York: Harcourt, Brace & World, Inc., 1940), p. 281.

J. M. MCCALLISTER, *Remedial and Corrective Instruction in Reading* (New York: Appleton-Century-Crofts, 1936), p. 4.

P. A. WITTY, *Reading in Modern Education* (Boston: D. C. Heath and Company, 1949), p. 178.

# 1

# Conditions and Practices Which Tend to Produce and Aggravate Reading Disabilities

"When I was a boy," writes an editorialist "we all learned how to read. Of course, we didn't have to contend with those new-fangled methods." Statements such as these are found daily in newspapers and magazines throughout the United States. They infer that a return to "the good old days" is the panacea for all educational ills.

Teachers do not share this opinion. Many of them would explain reading problems in terms of out-of-school hazards. They feel that poor readers often are the products of homes where the intellectual, physical and emotional needs of children have been ignored. Parents, of course, admit no shortcomings and believe that the school alone is responsible for all reading problems. "If the teacher would devote more time to my child, he would be a better reader."

Needless to say, research shows that both home and school can contribute to reading failure; however, when the stigma of reading failure does fall on the school, an honest appraisal of the situation leads to the inevitable conclusion that only a small percentage of handicapped readers are products of schools where teachers did not give them sufficient attention. Most poor readers have received a lion's share of the teacher's time — time which likely as not included individual as well as group attention. How, then, was the school inefficient?

The school was remiss if it failed to provide wholesome conditions for learning — conditions which, with few exceptions, could have been improved or eliminated by the school. Some of these unwholesome conditions are as follows:

## Beginning Formal Instruction in Reading
## Before a Child Has Acquired Adequate Readiness

Reading readiness has been defined as "the level of maturity a child must reach before he can succeed in formal reading under normal instruction. A chronological age of six years and a minimum IQ of 100 is usually implied, with normal health, hearing, vision, etc." (1)

Although reading readiness is of great significance at the first-grade level, it is not a concept that should be limited to beginning reading. Reading readiness pertains to all levels: third grade, sixth grade and even high school. Subject matter teachers need to concern themselves with special kinds of reading readiness. A science teacher, for example, knows that a chapter in a textbook may be rather meaningless if students lack an appropriate background of experience. In short, all teachers at all levels and in all subject matter areas must concern themselves with reading readiness.

Reading readiness for beginning reading grows out of multiple maturities. When a school relies primarily on chronological age as the determining factor for entrance to first grade (six years six months is a widely used criterion), serious errors may result. Some children are a few weeks over the minimal age; others have not quite reached the cutoff age. As a result, the latter group enters first grade almost a year older. Such a difference may be quite significant in certain cases since children may show rapid physical, intellectual and emotional growth during their early years.

The number of years and months a child has lived does not tell us with any degree of assurance the amount and quality of his experiential background, how much native ability or intellectual maturity he possesses, his powers of visual and auditory discrimination, his emotional and social maturity and a host of other factors. We cannot, therefore, consider a child's sixth or seventh birthday as optimum to initial reading instruction.

Unfortunately, many parents feel their children are ready to read as soon as they reach school age. Often parents are so ambitious for their children that they will initiate instruction at home at very young ages. Newspaper advertisements and books have added fuel to the fire by advocating the formal teaching of reading to children at two, three or four years of age.

Most specialists in early childhood education are opposed to early reading instruction. (2, 3) They do not feel very young children are sufficiently mature physically and emotionally to take formal reading instruction without undesirable side effects. They believe childhood is the time for many learnings that are needed before formal instruction in reading begins. Lastly, they feel that a premature introduction to reading might give rise to permanent antagonism or distaste for the reading process.

A good kindergarten experience is of inestimable value to children who might otherwise lack readiness for beginning reading. (4) In a study by Fast it was shown that there is a definite relationship between attending kindergarten and reading progress in the first grade. Children who have had the benefit of kindergarten experiences are better able to sustain attention, follow directions and adjust to group situations in the primary grades. (5) Such training is particularly vital to the child who comes from a home that has failed to provide needed verbal stimulation and an appropriate background of experiences.

Better schools of today employ sensitive screening procedures to detect children who lack the requisite readiness for reading. Informal day-by-day observations by kindergarten and first-grade teachers, combined with reading readiness and intelligence tests, yield valuable data in determining a child's readiness for reading. (See Appendix for a description of readiness tests.)

Although some forms of immaturity such as myelination of nerve fibers require time and time alone, teachers need not sit back and wait for readiness to develop. Often, as in the case of culturally deprived children, the situation can be helped by taking trips and excursions, listening to stories, telling stories, guessing rhyming words, repeating words and expressions, seeing and participating in puppet shows and using reading readiness workbooks. To help immature children develop the motor skills that underlie perceptual ability, teachers will want to acquaint themselves with the unique approaches described by Radler and Kephart (6) and Getman and Kane. (7) (See pages 37-38 for a discussion of their concepts.)

Immature children can be the bane of a first-grade teacher's existence. It is difficult if not impossible to teach reading to children who cannot give sustained attention, cannot get along with others in group situations, cry easily, have temper tantrums and cannot and will not remain seated. One can appreciate why research has shown it is better to err on the side of waiting too long for reading readiness to develop than to force a child into reading before he profits from it. (See Appendix D for a Reading Readiness Check List.)

## Accepting a Low Level of Mastery of Word Recognition During the Primary Grades

The majority of children come to school with a wide speaking and meaning vocabulary. Since, as one child stated it, "Reading is nothing more than talk writ down," the first-grade teacher's job is primarily one of encouraging and aiding associational learning. The child must learn to match "those little scratches on paper" with their familiar auditory counterpart.

Although reading in its most elementary form involves synthesizing sight and sound, mature reading goes much further. One must never lose sight of the fact that reading is a meaningful process. A child who recites all the words but when asked what he read says "he wasn't listening" is not reading. Reading is a cerebral process that requires comprehension and critical thinking.

There are times when a child's background or experiential maturity is so meager that he can't bring proper meaning to the printed page. He is not ready to comprehend what he is reading. Too often, however, teachers put the cart before the horse by stressing high-level skills of comprehension and interpretation before a child has evolved an adequate sight vocabulary. The first step in learning to read involves mastering word perception. Nothing is more fundamental to all reading skills than an adequate sight vocabulary.

With the help of pictures, charts, filmstrips, preprimers and storytelling, most pupils are able to bring proper meaning to printed symbols. They read many stories that provide maximum repetition of a limited vocabulary. When they learn to recognize and recall familiar words without hesitation, a sight vocabulary is born.

Of course, individual differences in rate of learning soon become apparent. Some pupils are able to recall words with a minimum of practice. They read stories fluently with few, if any, errors. Other pupils fail to recognize many of the words even though they have been exposed to them innumerable times. Faulty word recognition results in slow word-by-word reading. This, in turn, raises havoc with comprehension and destroys interest in learning to read better.

Basal readers in the primary grades contain a controlled vocabulary based on the spoken and hearing vocabularies of children in these grades. Investigations reveal that six-year-old children who do not have a language handicap have a speaking vocabulary of at least three to five thousand words. A first-grade reader containing a vocabulary of a thousand words or less, therefore, does not present a problem in comprehension to the vast majority of children. In this connection, it is significant that problems of comprehension which seem apparent when children read orally or silently are usually nonexistent when the same material is read aloud to the children by the teacher. In the lower grades problems of comprehension during silent and oral reading usually are the result of an inadequate sight vocabulary coupled with an inability to attack new words.

When a child experiences sight vocabulary problems, he is in distress. An immediate halt should be called. He should not be exposed to more difficult readers until he can demonstrate at least a ninety-five per cent mastery of the words listed in back of his present reader. Daily and weekly evaluations of word mastery are essential. The teacher can help a child acquire this mastery by giving him other books and materials of parallel difficulty and by employing suitable individualized corrective procedures. If a child is exposed to a new and more difficult reader before he has acquired the requisite sight vocabulary, his reading ceases to be meaningful and enjoyable. Independent reading habits and skills become an unattainable goal.

It is true that a few stories entail settings that may be foreign to the experiential backgrounds of some pupils. When these stories are involved, a resourceful teacher provides appropriate learning experiences. By taking pupils on field trips, using pictures, films and the like and by employing oral discussion, the teacher can furnish the orientation needed.

## Promoting Pupils to the Fourth Grade Who Have Not Gained Independent Reading Habits and Skills

The skills of word analysis emphasized in grades two and three become the open sesame whereby a child continues to acquire an extended sight vocabulary of new and unfamiliar words when he reaches the fourth grade. This is evident when one learns that of the 2,000 words the average pupil can identify readily at this level, one half of them are gained through the skills of word analysis. For example, one representative reading series presents 1,778 different words in its basal readers for the primary grades. Of these 1,778 different words, 863 are to be learned as a sight vocabulary and the remaining 915 through the skills of word analysis.

The fourth-grade pupil who is an independent reader has acquired an introduction to dictionary usage. His stock of sight words prepares him for recognizing and understanding almost all words except new technical ones. Pronunciation of unfamiliar words is accomplished independently through his knowledge of word analysis. The dictionary is of further assistance in arriving at the correct pronunciation of the most difficult words and proves an authoritative source for checking their meaning.

Students who have an adequate sight vocabulary and possess independence in word-analysis skills are ready to do recreational reading. They are eager to use these skills as tools in exploring new and interesting content. In guiding the reading growth of such pupils, teachers should shift instructional emphasis to comprehension skills since unfamiliar words and concepts are encountered more frequently by these students.

The fourth-grade pupil who lacks mastery of word perception skills cannot use reading as a tool in the content areas. Since the uncontrolled vocabulary he meets includes many words foreign to his own speaking and listening vocabularies, he readily becomes confused. Limitations of time make it extremely difficult for his teachers to help him overcome his deficiencies. The problem is further complicated by the pupil's resistance to corrective work involving lower-grade materials.

Students with I.Q.'s between 70 and 80 are found in regular classrooms. If these slow learners are promoted to the fourth grade (a rigid grade standard of achievement is not tenable in such cases), teachers must continue to strive for high levels of sight vocabulary mastery and word-analysis skill. The slow-learning child who is introduced to fourth-grade material before these foundational skills are well in hand will experience a hopeless sense of failure.

A basic cause of failure in reading in the intermediate grades stems from promoting a child from the third grade into the fourth when his basic sight vocabulary is at a level of mastery of ninety per cent or less. Teachers in the primary grades should strive for one hundred per cent mastery of word-recognition and word-attack skills. Similarly, intermediate grade teachers should give retarded readers corrective work of this kind before moving into more difficult material. Reading progress would take place more rapidly and there would be considerably less failure if teachers adhered religiously to this basic principle.

## Failing to Follow a Systematic Program
## of Detecting Hazards to Reading Progress

"I don't know exactly what it is, but something is definitely wrong with that child." An examination by a physician revealed that the teacher who had made the foregoing statement was right. Something was wrong. The child had a visual impairment that had gone unnoticed for years. How could this be? Why didn't the child complain? Why hadn't his parents discovered the condition?

A child does not know that he is different from others. He supposes, for instance, that all children see fuzzy letters when reading or that everyone's eyes get tired after looking at books for a while.

Parents see their own child week after week, year after year, in more or less isolation. They become accustomed to his peculiarities. And because of this, they often are completely oblivious to aberrations which are readily evident to a teacher who works with several dozen children daily and has an opportunity to make comparisons.

Because screening procedures for detecting physical defects in general are woefully inadequate in many schools, teachers must be doubly alert. In addition to observing children with a jaundiced eye (see behavior inventories on pages 51-56), they should avail themselves of cumulative records and hold conferences with parents. Once physical defects are detected, steps should be taken to alleviate or correct them. The school doctor and nurse should be consulted and their services enlisted. On occasions, the teacher's concern, via the school administrators, should be brought directly to the attention of parents.

The well-known proverb, "A stitch in time saves nine," is directly applicable to the prevention and correction of reading difficulties. Too often small difficulties are overlooked, the assumption being that they are unimportant or that the pupil will cope with them on his own. Since advanced and more complex skills are dependent on simple and foundational ones, crises soon arise. To avoid such situations, remedial or corrective steps using appropriate self-directive materials should be provided to help the child strengthen the specific reading skills in which he is deficient as soon as they are uncovered.

## Assuming that Reading Can Be Taught Effectively as an Isolated Communicative Skill

Successful teaching of reading must be related to all phases of the language arts. Listening, speaking, writing and reading have a great deal in common. All are means of social communication involving ideas, concepts and emotions. Children express themselves through writing and speech while they interpret the expressions of others through listening and reading. A close relationship between the language arts is inescapable. As a matter of fact, one authority stresses the great similarity between speaking and reading in his definition of the reading process.

> Psychologically, the processes of speech and reading are quite similar, the difference being mainly in the sense avenues through which the verbal stimuli are received. . . . The essential difference between knowing how to understand oral speech is the substitution of visual perception of printed verbal symbols for the auditory impression of the same symbols when spoken. The thoughts expressed are the same, the vocabulary is the same, and the word order is the same. The new problem in reading is to learn to recognize the visual symbols with accuracy and reasonable speed. (8)

As a child gains proficiency in one communicative skill, all language skills benefit indirectly. This is reflected in high correlations between reading and spelling, reading and composition. The majority of poor readers are inaccurate spellers. By the same token, the child who reads little is not likely to write well. The language-experience approach popularized by Van Allen capitalizes on such interrelationships. The basic premise being, "What they can say, they can write, and what they can write, they can read."

There is no doubt the language-experience method is a valuable approach to reading growth. It is highly desirable for teachers to emphasize the relationship between speaking, writing, listening and reading.

## Relying on Group Instruction to Meet the Reading Needs of All Pupils

Undifferentiated group instruction, a common practice in the intermediate and upper grades, tends to be inefficient since all children do not thrive on the same educational diet. When instructional material is of optimum difficulty for the average reader, it is too difficult for some and too easy for others. What results? Poor readers invariably are stymied while superior readers become bored because they are not challenged. As the superior readers stagnate, reading difficulties continue to accumulate for the disabled reader and resistance to instruction becomes increasingly acute. If this situation persists, all motivation, self-direction and satisfaction in work well done withers away.

Undifferentiated group instruction also fails to take cognizance of factors that inhibit learning. In addition, resistances to learning which develop are treated frequently as discipline problems rather than attitudes and behavior to be understood and improved through proper guidance.

It is evident that undifferentiated group instruction provides but a partial answer to the multiplicity of learning problems facing the classroom teacher. Only when group practices are augmented by diagnosis and individualized corrective instruction can children's unique needs be met and only then can effective learning be achieved.

## Requiring Retarded Readers to Pursue Instructional Material in Reading on a Frustration Level of Difficulty

One cannot develop his biceps with weights that are too heavy to manipulate. By the same token, a poor reader cannot improve his reading skill when books are too difficult. With books of optimum difficulty, however, practice becomes meaningful and improvement results. Relying on practice with materials of the grade at which the student is experiencing failure is largely a waste of time. The students involved experience failure, frustration and loss of interest that impedes further progress.

Teachers who wish to locate the right book for a child's instructional or free reading programs* should be aware of the significance of each of the following levels.

*Independent Reading Level*: This is the highest reading level at which a child can read easily and fluently, without help, with few word-recognition errors and very good comprehension and retention. At this level, word-recognition errors do not exceed more than one per one hundred words of running text and comprehension scores are ninety per cent or higher.

*Instructional Reading Level*: This is the highest level at which a child reads satisfactorily, provided he receives teacher preparation and supervision. At this level, word-recognition errors do not exceed more than five per one hundred words of running text and comprehension scores are seventy per cent or above.

*Frustration Reading Level*: This is the lowest level at which a child's reading skills break down. Fluency disappears, word-recognition errors are common, comprehension is defective, retention is poor and evidence of emotional tension and discomfort manifests itself. At this level, word-recognition errors exceed ten per one hundred words of running text and comprehension scores are fifty per cent or below.

---

*See Appendix F2 for a list of publications containing bibliographies of books for retarded readers.

*Capacity Reading Level*: This is the highest level at which a child can comprehend seventy per cent of what is read aloud to him.

## Failing to Estimate the True Capacity of Poor Readers

Teachers sometimes are prone to consider poor readers dull. "I do a good job of teaching," they say. "If a child doesn't learn, he's just dumb." The truth is that approximately ninety per cent of all poor readers have intelligence quotients in excess of 80 with some reaching well into the 130s and above. In most cases, the poor readers do have potential to do better.

It is unfortunate if teachers believe pupils are working up to capacity because distributions of reading and mental ability in a class are similar. Based on this premise, it is assumed that the poor reader is a slow learner. The school, they feel, is therefore absolved of any responsibility for improving the reading status of its pupils. Needless to say, intelligence tests scores are often cited to bolster this contention.

Group intelligence tests should be interpreted warily since many such tests above the third grade are heavily weighted with items involving reading. This means the intelligence quotient of a poor reader on a verbal intelligence test usually underestimates his true mental ability. It therefore is always important to secure a nonlanguage or performance I.Q. and M.A. along with verbal aspects of a poor reader's intelligence. When this is done, it is not rare to find that for poor readers most verbal I.Q.'s are markedly below nonverbal I.Q.'s. This discrepancy has been widely reported in the educational literature. Records kept at the University of Wisconsin Reading Clinic, where the California Test of Mental Maturity was given to two hundred sixty-six intermediate grade children who entered the clinic, revealed an average verbal I.Q. for this group of poor readers of 92 and an average nonverbal I.Q. of 99. Twenty-eight per cent of the group had verbal I.Q.'s of 100 and above while forty-one per cent had nonverbal I.Q.'s of 100 or above. Almost half (forty-eight per cent) had verbal I.Q.'s that were five or more points below their nonverbal I.Q.'s.

When group intelligence tests are employed, results may be invalid. A poor reader who has suffered through years of failure often works at an intelligence test as he would any other school assignment; that is, he guesses or does it in a very perfunctory way. Such a give-up or I-don't-care attitude may result in a low score. The most valid measure of a retarded reader's intellectual capacity can be obtained by the school psychologist who administers an individual test such as the Stanford-Binet or the Wechsler Intelligence Scale for Children.

Another avenue of appraisal open to the teacher is to read aloud for a child and then quiz him on what was heard. If the child can comprehend material at or above his reading grade level in difficulty, the teacher can be assured that the pupil has normal reading potential. Commercial tests such as the Durrell-Sullivan Reading Capacity Tests and Spache's Diagnostic Reading Scales use this same approach to ascertain a student's potential reading ability.

Underestimating a poor reader's capabilities usually results in neglect of the child. This may prove disastrous to the individual and often results in a distinct loss to society.

## Failing to Employ a Balanced Program in Reading

Many reading programs fail to furnish a sufficient variety of materials. A well-balanced program should include several sets of basal readers to provide systematic instruction in basic reading skills and the techniques of reading. Workbooks accompanying these readers also are needed to minimize the time-consuming activity of creating suitable follow-up work. Commercially made and teacher-made reading games and activities are valuable in making provision for pupils who need additional practice in word recognition and word-analysis skill. A classroom library of books and magazines together with picture dictionaries should be found in all primary classrooms. Above the primary grades reference books such as a world atlas and almanac also have an important place. Other accessories needed to balance a reading program include filmstrips, slides, recordings and movies.

A functional reading program never overemphasizes one aspect of the reading process at the neglect of another. When it does, children's reading skills suffer. Too much emphasis on phonics, for example, tends to destroy interest in reading and results in slow and laborious word calling. On the other hand, too little emphasis on phonics weakens word-attack skill and makes independent reading difficult. Other aspects of the reading program, such as study-type reading versus recreational reading and oral reading versus silent reading also require a similar balance. It should be remembered that all readers must have their reading programs fit their individual needs.

If we wish all children to develop into well-rounded and independent readers with a lifetime interest in reading, constant vigilance must be given to both group and individual balancing of the reading program.

Going to extremes cripples the program and disables the readers involved.

## Considering Reading a Mere Mechanical Process

Reading is more than a process of eye movements and word recognition skill. Reading is more than "barking at the print." Proper meaning must be brought to printed symbols to insure their understanding and enhance interpretation. Too often students lack the concepts needed to make words live. A student's ability to call words accurately doesn't mean in itself that he comprehends the material. One third grader read beautifully before the class, but when asked to tell in his own words what he had just read, hesitated a few moments and said, "Gee, I guess I wasn't listening to myself."

One of the best ways for a teacher to make reading a vital thinking process is to ask stimulating questions that enable the child to project himself into and identify himself with the characters in a story. Teachers who ask questions such as, "What is the color of Mary's hat?" are not encouraging a child to think. Reading should not be done for the purpose of regurgitating facts. Reading should be an idea-getting and an idea-stimulating process. Teachers who view reading as a thinking process can do much to help children by employing more questions of the "how" and "why" variety. For example, rather than, "What is the color of Mary's hat?" the question, "Why would or wouldn't you like to wear a hat the color of Mary's?" would be preferable. This could encourage the child to evaluate what he is reading in terms of himself. In the final analysis, all the meaning a child ever finds in a story comes to him only in terms of his own particular experiences.

Unless we encourage a child to think about and evaluate what is read, he will be unable to evaluate contradictory points of view in the numerous newspapers, magazines and books to which he is exposed later on in life. (See pages 152-153 for a discussion of critical reading.)

## Assuming that Retardation Is Nonexistent When the Class Average on Standardized-Reading Tests Reaches or Exceeds the Norm

Norms on achievement tests are averages of the performance of pupils in each of several grades throughout the nation. What is true of the country at large isn't, however, always applicable to an individual grade or class. What is more, national norms do not constitute standards of excellence or even satisfactory achievement. Most students fail miserably to measure up to their full potential.

The teacher who consults norms is dealing with averages. It must not be overlooked that fifty per cent of the scores fall below the norm. In a typical fourth grade, for example, approximately one third of the children are reading on third-, second- and even first-grade levels. By the same token, approximately one third of the children in the average fourth grade are reading on the fifth-, sixth- and seventh-grade levels.

The teacher who accepts norms as the standard for her grade and expresses satisfaction with the results, overlooks the retarded readers in her class who are in dire need of corrective instruction. A teacher should convert individual scores on a standardized reading test to grade scores and group these scores in a way that highlights those children who are retarded one, two, three or more years in their reading skills. She should make a similar tabulation of those who are accelerated. The teacher thus becomes aware of the retardation and acceleration in her grade. This gives her a more realistic view of the problems to be faced in terms of the number of atypical readers in the class and the nature of their problems.

## Using Instructional Material on Only One Level of Difficulty

Sometimes teachers attempt to avoid responsibility for helping severely retarded readers and markedly accelerated ones by saying that they are fourth-, sixth- or eighth-grade teachers. When only the textbooks assigned to the grade are used, there is failure to provide for individual differences and poor readers, and accelerated readers are overlooked.

Teachers who do concern themselves with pupils as individuals usually encounter problems. They may be told that the administration furnishes books designed only for the grade. The administration may feel that teachers have the responsibility of getting all students "to read up to grade" and that this can be done by forcing all students to "measure up" to books written for the grade in question.

When a teacher uses only books assigned to the grade, individual differences are ignored, and readiness as a basic principle of learning is violated. The poor reader in the class encounters constant frustration as he attempts to learn from books that are too difficult, books he cannot read or understand. The superior reader vegetates and occasionally develops bad habits which may result in later retardation.

Teachers at all grade levels should have an ample supply of basal and supplementary readers. These should cover several levels of difficulty in order to correspond to the reading abilities in their classrooms. Pupils cannot be expected to build their reading skills if instructional materials fail to conform to their level of reading ability.

## Failing to Motivate Children to Read Widely

Educational psychologists tell us that purposeful practice is essential to the mastery of any complex skill. The pupil who reads only a basal reader and is not induced to any additional reading usually does not develop his reading skill to maximum potential. Likely as not, such a student's reading activities outside of school are virtually nonexistent. Without sufficient practice it is difficult for him to develop or even maintain skills taught in the earlier grades. Sooner or later he becomes a nonreader in fact as well as theory.

Since motivation is the indispensable ingredient of all learning activity, a wise teacher should be a good merchandiser of reading material. Often a child is fascinated by a story in the basal reader and wishes he could read more stories like it. The teacher should be able to "strike while the iron is hot" by immediately supplying him with additional stories dealing with the same subject. This can be done by using the school library which is always a most valuable adjunct to the classroom.

Teachers should surround children with reading stimuli. A classroom library with books of all kinds and descriptions should be provided. Poor readers should be furnished books adapted for them and superior readers should be given books having a wide variety of content at grade level and above. In this connection, the special motivational appeal of paperbacks should not be overlooked.

Paperbacks are inexpensive and have other advantages as well. Unlike hard-cover books, they are not associated as readily with study, examinations and other unpleasantries. Since they are not bulky, they can be slipped into a purse or pocket for ready accessibility whenever opportunities for reading present themselves.

One ingenious teacher used paperbacks in connection with the initiation of a familiarization period for twenty nonreaders. Attractive paperbacks were distributed and after each two-minute interval, a whistle was blown. The blowing of the whistle was a signal for the pupils to exchange paperbacks. After it had been blown three or four times, several students gave the teacher unfriendly looks. (Already they had found a book they wished to read.) But the whistle blowing continued until the class period ended. At that point, the teacher informed the students that the paperbacks with which they had become familiar were available for checkout. Within a few short minutes all paperbacks disappeared.

Stereotyped and laboriously detailed book reports destroy reading interest. Imaginative teachers are capable of devising book-reporting procedures that are both enjoyable and motivational. For example, a California teacher* has great success employing a bimonthly book-court session which she describes as follows:

> We hold court session in our room every other Friday. The court consists of a judge, the defendant (the person who is making the book report), and a jury, consisting of class members who also have read the book being reported on.
>
> The defendant who is seated to the left of the judge is sworn in with his hand on a dictionary. After he is sworn in, the judge asks some leading questions about events in the story, about the characters, etc. During this examination, the judge and defendant are very serious. When the questioning is concluded, the jury decides whether the defendant has read and understood the book, or was trying to bluff. If the jury decides he was just bluffing, the judge sentences him to read the book and to appear in court in two weeks to report on it again.
>
> "Next case!" The gavel bangs on the desk, and a new defendant and a new jury take their places for the next book report. All is done in good spirit, and no one becomes angry. As a matter of fact, the children love this form of book reporting and look forward to it avidly.

Another teacher had book reports take the form of a "Tell the Truth" panel. This is based on the television show bearing the same name. A moderator introduces three students who are seated behind a table as numbers one, two and three. The name and author of the book in question is then introduced by the moderator. Class members ask questions of the panel members by addressing them by number. Each member is supposed to pretend he has read the book or, conversely, each member can fabricate vague replies so the class wonders if anyone has read the book. After a few minutes of questioning, the moderator asks the class, by a show of hands, to decide who is the real reader of the book. The person who really read the book then stands and gives the rest of his report.

Many students enjoy supplementing the reading of a book by writing a follow-up story of their own. Other students can be encouraged to write a letter to the author of the book read. By addressing the letter to the author in care of the publisher, an answer is very often assured. (It

---

*Mrs. Leah Rawson, Grendel School, Azusa, California.

is important, however, not to write to authors who are no longer living.) The author's reply can be posted on the bulletin board for all to see.

Students who are artistically inclined should be encouraged to design posters or book jackets as a form of book reporting. Other pupils can model clay figures or dress dolls in costumes to depict characters in stories.

It is evident that book reports can be used to motivate and stimulate pupils to read. They need not incur negative reactions. If handled properly, book reporting can be a rewarding experience serving to interest all students in the joys of reading.

A systematic recreational reading program is essential for the reading improvement of all pupils. Children in the elementary grades should be given some time to read for fun every day. This makes learning to read worthwhile and can do more than anything else to inculcate children with a lifetime interest in reading.

Recreational reading is a tremendous boon for superior readers. They are not forced to follow, in lock-step fashion, a standard curriculum. Free reading permits superior readers to move ahead as fast as they wish and gives them the opportunity to develop rapidly along the lines of their special interests and talents.

Care must be exercised when selecting books for poor readers. These pupils will not benefit from books that are too difficult. On the other hand, they do not like baby books. They must be given books that are especially adapted so as to have high-interest appeal and a difficulty level that facilitates easy reading. Preferably, grade markings or designations should be absent.

## Assuming that the Curricular Content Covered and the Instructional Effort Expended Are the Criteria of Instructional Effectiveness

Many teachers never evaluate their teaching in terms of learning or desirable changes in their pupils. These teachers are prone to say, "I do a good job of teaching. I work hard with my students, real hard. I have presented the required curricular content. What more can I do?"

Teaching does involve a generous expenditure of time and energy, but it is important that attention be devoted to what is appropriate. The teacher should consider himself successful only when all the children with whom he works are progressing. This criterion of good teaching calls for continuous testing, diagnosing, teaching, testing and more diagnosing. It calls for individualizing instruction in terms of pupils' levels of achievement, peculiar strengths and weaknesses, rates of learning and learning potential. The answer, then, is not a need to work harder but to work more effectively.

When a teacher can see students forging ahead in the acquisition of reading skills, when he can see interest sparkle, when he can see a noticeable improvement in scholarship, when these changes are taking place in his classroom, then, and then alone, can he say with satisfaction "I am doing a good job of teaching."

## Assuming that Skill Learning Does Not Differ from Information Learning

Many teachers fail to recognize that learning of skills differs from learning information or developing concepts. Methods of instruction must differ in each instance. For example, information can be imparted orally by a teacher, but improving reading skills is something only the student can do through practice. It is a perfect example of learning through doing.

Demands on the learner are very exacting when skills are being learned. A pupil may acquire new information readily if he has an eighty per cent mastery of previously related information; but an eighty per cent mastery of the sight vocabulary of a given reader does not provide a student with the readiness he needs to succeed with the more complex comprehension skills and the more challenging vocabulary of a subsequent reader. Word-perception skill must entail at least a ninety-five per cent mastery of the sight vocabulary before a student is ready to move into more difficult material.

## Failing to Eliminate Weaknesses in Reading When They First Appear

It should be recognized that prevention is the key that will insure normal progress in reading. The teacher who is keenly aware of the importance of preventative measures will be alert to individual difficulties when they first arise. She will correct these difficulties immediately by providing suitable instruction. She will not introduce new and more difficult material until the child is prepared for it. When difficulties first arise they are few in number and a minimum of correction is needed to overcome or eliminate them. When inadequate or partial learning is permitted to go unheeded and uncorrected, the cumulative effect results in frustration, failure and feelings of inadequacy characteristic of retarded readers.

The golden era for prevention is in the primary grades. In these grades the teacher should adopt a goal of complete mastery of reading skills taught at each level. This is the key to prevention. Introducing new and more difficult material to a primary grade child before he has mastered the current sight vocabulary ignores the first step in a program of prevention. This common practice results in a rapid accumulation of difficulties which causes loss of interest, absence of growth, lowered mastery and ultimate failure.

## Failing to Recognize and Promote Wholesome Teacher-Pupil Relationships as a Prime Learning Prerequisite

Perhaps no condition for learning in the elementary school is more important than wholesome teacher-pupil relations. The child who likes his teacher is the child who likes to learn. Strong emotions of insecurity, hate, fear or resentment inhibit learning. Motivation must come from within rather than be imposed from without. Pupils resist learning if the teacher exhibits traits of unfairness, sarcasm or ridicule. When the teacher shows partiality, when she is autocratic and disregards the rights and privileges of her pupils, she destroys confidence, security and social acceptance. As a result, learning is replaced by loss of interest, emotional tensions and disciplinary problems.

Mental health, a basic condition of learning, is best fostered in a classroom by a teacher who is warm and understanding, a teacher who has a genuine interest in children. These are teacher qualities that always have and always will have a magical effect in a learning situation.

## Failing to Limit the Size of Classes

It is very doubtful if any teacher, regardless of her capabilities, can do a good job of teaching with a classroom of fifty or more children. Even smaller classes on the primary grade level can prove an impossibility since children in these grades have short attention spans and find it difficult to work independently.

A positive relationship exists between reading growth among students and provision for their individual needs. When classes are too large it is a physical impossibility for a teacher to become well acquainted with the reading needs of all her pupils. Students who develop difficulties go unheeded. And when they are brought to the attention of the teacher, she is so harrassed by demands on her time that corrective work is not attempted. There is little doubt that large classes are fertile breeding grounds for poor readers.

## Inadequate Training of Teachers in the Intermediate Grades in Primary Reading Methods

Many teachers in the intermediate and upper grades have little or no training in primary reading methods. They feel frustrated in their attempt to provide correction for their severely retarded readers because they are unable to discover the nature or the extent of their reading difficulties. Further handicaps stem from a lack of suitable instructional materials.

In some instances, intermediate and upper grade teachers place the blame on primary teachers by accusing them of not doing a thorough job of teaching. Passing the buck solves no problems and is not commendable professionally.

All teachers would be better teachers if they availed themselves of professional courses in corrective reading. Such courses are offered by universities and colleges during their academic year and during summer sessions as well. In some school systems, in-service training courses in corrective reading are offered by reading specialists drawn from a neighboring college or university.

When courses at colleges or universities are not obtainable, teachers should turn to some of the many books available on the subject. (See Appendix F1.)

## Inadequate Utilization of Cumulative Records

Above the primary grades all pupils will have attended school for three or more years. A number of teachers will have had extensive opportunities to observe, confer and evaluate their growth in learning. Perhaps too, certain physical, emotional and intellectual problems impeding the success of normal progress will have been detected. All this information together with the results of developmental and corrective programs should be recorded on cumulative school records. When this responsibility is faithfully discharged by each teacher, a gold mine of useful information about each child can be made readily available when needed.

All teachers should study cumulative records very carefully at the beginning of each school year. They should add additional information to these records whenever anything of significance arises. The dividends resulting from this practice would be tremendous. The gap that too frequently exists because of the yearly break in continuity of instruction as a child moves from one teacher to another would disappear.

## Summary

While the school recognizes that the home must share in the responsibility for reading failure, it sometimes fails to recognize the serious consequences of certain practices and conditions over which it has control. When first-grade pupils are exposed to formal reading before they have attained the necessary maturity, disinterest and subsequent failure result. When classes, especially in the primary grades, are large, teachers find it difficult and frequently impossible to discover individual needs and to prevent an accumulation of reading difficulties. When reading errors are overlooked and allowed to accumulate, frustration and failure follow. When accelerated readers receive little or no guidance, books soon become a boring rather than a challenging experience.

Undifferentiated group instruction using the same basic reader for all pupils makes no provision for individual differences and violates the principle of readiness. Many pupils in the lower grades who are subjected to this practice become victims of a low level of mastery in the skills of word recognition and word analysis. This prevents their becoming independent readers when they reach the intermediate grades. Unless a comprehensive diagnosis is made of individual reading difficulties followed by intensive corrective instruction, these pupils soon become severely retarded readers or even nonreaders.

A basic shortcoming of many schools is an inadequate program of evaluation. A knowledge of a pupil's level of readiness must precede selection of appropriate instructional material. Identifying and correcting reading errors requires formal as well as informal evaluation. The use of grade norms on a standardized reading test as the only criterion of reading performance in a classroom overlooks and fails to identify retarded and accelerated readers.

Many individuals vary in their attainment of reading goals in spite of a balanced developmental program of instruction for the class. Unless the corrective and recreational reading program is adjusted to individual idiosyncracies in learning, reading difficulties multiply, learning is inhibited and scholarship suffers.

SUPPLEMENTARY PROBLEMS FOR ORAL AND WRITTEN DISCUSSION

1. Consult current professional magazines in education for data revealing wide variance in reading skill among elementary school pupils at different grade levels.
2. In what way is heterogeneity in reading achievement a problem in group instruction?
3. What is reading readiness and why is it of significance in the first grade?
4. Discuss prevention as an important principle in the teaching of reading.
5. Consider the unwholesome instructional practices discussed in Chapter 1 and name the five you consider most prevalent.
6. Why is the fourth grade a most critical year in school for most children?

## REFERENCES

1. DELWYN G. SCHUBERT, *A Dictionary of Terms and Concepts in Reading* (Springfield, Ill.: Charles C Thomas, Publisher, 1964), pp. 200-201.
2. S. MOSKOWITZ "When Should Reading Instruction Begin?" *IRA Conference Proceedings* (1963), pp. 218-222.
3. N. B. SMITH, "Shall We Teach Formal Reading in the Kindergarten?" *The Compass* (February, 1964).
4. M. C. ALMY, *Children's Experience Prior to First Grade and Success in Beginning Reading*, contributions to Education, No. 954, Bureau of Publications, Teachers College, Columbia University, 1949.
5. R. FAST, "Kindergarten Training and Grade I Reading," *Journal of Educational Psychology* (January, 1947), pp. 52-57.
6. D. H. RADLER and N. C. KEPHART, *Success Through Play* (New York: Harper & Row, Publishers), 1960.
7. G. N. GETMAN and E. R. KANE, *The Physiology of Readiness* (Minneapolis: P.A.S.S., Inc.), 1964.
8. G. T. BUSWELL, "The Process of Reading," *The Reading Teacher* (December, 1959), p. 108.

## SELECTED READINGS

DEBOER, JOHN and MARTHA DALLMAN, *The Teaching of Reading* rev. ed., New York: Holt, Rinehart & Winston, Inc., 1964, chs. 5A, 5B.
DECHANT, EMERALD, *Improving the Teaching of Reading*, Englewood Cliffs, N. J.: Prentice-Hall, Inc., 1964, ch. 4.
HARRIS, ALBERT, *Effective Teaching of Reading*, New York: David McKay Co., Inc., 1962, pp. 317-340.
HEILMAN, ARTHUR, *Principles and Practices of Teaching Reading*, Columbus, Ohio: Charles E. Merrill Books, Inc., 1961, ch. 1.
SCHUBERT, DELWYN, *Readings in Reading: Practice-Theory-Research*, New York: Thomas Y. Crowell Company, 1968, selections 12-14.
SPACHE, GEORGE, *Toward Better Reading*, Champaign, Ill.: Garrard Publishing Co., 1963, ch. 1.

Chapter

2

# The Child and His
# Learning Difficulties in School

How can one identify those children who are most likely to benefit from special help in reading? This is an important question which perennially plagues teachers. As Harris states it: "Attempting to serve all usually means giving the right kind of help to none. Lavishing time and energy on the wrong pupils also leads to disappointing results." (1)

Criteria widely accepted in determining a pupil's reading expectancy or potential are as follows.

*Mental Ability.* The criterion used most universally in selecting poor readers for special help involves a comparison of reading and mental maturity. When the difference between a student's mental age and reading age favors the former, he is felt to be a disabled reader who can profit from help: the greater the discrepancy, the greater the promise for improvement. Harris suggests the following minima in this regard: ". . . six months in the first three grades, nine months for children in grades four and five, or a year for children above the fifth grade." (2)

There is little doubt that mental maturity and reading skill are positively related. With children in the elementary grades, the following correlations between reading test scores and the California Test of Mental Maturity have been reported.

language factors with Thorndike-McCall Reading Test ........ .824
nonlanguage factors with Thorndike-McCall Reading Test .... .557

language factors with Gates Silent Reading Test, type A .... .805
nonlanguage factors with Gates Silent Reading Test, type A .. .359

language factors with Gates Silent Reading Test, type B ........ .799
nonlanguage factors with Gates Silent Reading Test, type B ... .413

language factors with Gates Silent Reading Test, type D ........ .844
nonlanguage factors with Gates Silent Reading Test, type D.... .514 (3)

From these and other investigations, it is obvious that although the correlation between reading comprehension tests and group intelligence tests is positive, a one-to-one ratio does not exist. No two abilities are perfectly correlated. What is more, reading and intelligence test scores invariably are standardized on samples drawn from different populations, a factor making valid comparison impossible.

Care must be exercised in selecting an intelligence test for a poor reader. Many group intelligence tests are largely verbal and therefore not valid for the retarded reader. These intelligence tests (in reality they are reading tests in disguise) should not be employed with poor readers if one wishes to use the results as a reading-expectancy criterion. Nonverbal or performance tests are preferable. Representative group intelligence tests which have nonverbal sections are *California Test of Mental Maturity, Pintner-Durost Elementary Test, Pintner Intermediate Test* and the *Lorge-Thorndike*.

Another factor worth considering is that a poor reader often becomes completely discouraged because of continued failure and frustration. He develops a defeatist attitude which easily can invalidate intelligence test scores. Many disabled readers with this attitude take tests in a perfunctory manner. This is particularly true when group measurements are used; therefore, pupils with intelligence quotients of 75 or lower, and those showing a variability of 10 or more points on successive administrations, should be given an individual intelligence test by a trained examiner.

Even with individual intelligence tests like the Stanford-Binet and Wechsler Intelligence Scale for Children, caution is still necessary. Bond and Fay report that retarded readers do considerably poorer on the Stanford-Binet than do children of equal ability who have no reading problem. (4) Notwithstanding this indictment, Clymer's study suggests that the best measure of mental ability to be used with retarded readers is the Stanford-Binet. (5)

A discrepancy between mental and reading levels (the former being based on nonverbal scores) is widely used to determine the progress and degree of a child's reading retardation. For example, if a child possesses a mental age of ten and reads as well as an eight year old, a retardation of two years is evidenced. Since reading scores are most often expressed as grade placement scores, it is helpful to transmit a mental age into a grade placement score. This can be done by subtracting five from the mental age. (The assumption is that a child is six years of age when in the first grade.) Thus, a child with a mental age of twelve has the mental level of an average seventh grader. Should he possess a reading grade placement score of five, it is estimated that he is reading two grades below his mental level or potential reading level.

The use of mental age as a reading expectancy index leads to an awkward situation when very bright or dull students are considered. Many studies show that bright students do not achieve academically on a level commensurate with their mental age. Dull students, on the other hand, overachieve in this regard. To handle such cases, and others as well, Bond and Tinker suggest calculating a reading expectancy score by the following method: Multiply the student's I.Q. by the number of years he has spent in school and then add 1.0. (6) For a student with an I.Q. of 150, halfway through the seventh grade, his reading expectancy score would be $6.5 \times 150 + 1.0$, or 10.75. Investigation has shown that calculations based on this formula are far more realistic than those using mental age alone. (7)

Some school systems use a combination of chronological age and mental age in arriving at an expectancy age. (8) Usually this is contingent on the belief that the older student has a greater apperceptive mass and should be expected, therefore, to read on a level above that of a younger one. Harris is of the opinion that the method is too complicated for school use and is of questionable value. (9)

*Listening Comprehension.* The level at which a student can comprehend material read aloud to him (his auding level) is one of the most valuable indexes of reading potential. (10) Commercial tests based on this premise are available and include the Spache *Diagnostic Reading Scales* (California Test Bureau), *Durrell-Sullivan Reading Capacity Test* (Harcourt, Brace & World, Inc.) and the *Brown-Carlsen Listening Comprehension Test* (Harcourt, Brace & World, Inc.).

One can develop his own test of aural comprehension by utilizing duplicate forms of a suitable reading-comprehension test. One form should be given orally to the pupils while the other is administered as a silent reading test. The poor reader with marked potential will score higher on the form he was given orally: the greater the discrepancy, the greater the promise of reading potential.

When using listening comprehension as a criterion of reading potential, the examiner should remember that the retarded reader's opportunity for acquiring a good vocabulary, as well as an understanding of written material, is considerably poorer than that of the good reader. The language the student may have heard seldom includes the unusual words encountered on vocabulary tests. What is more, written prose is often more complex structurally than that which is spoken. As a consequence, a poor reader may be bewildered by the unusual language and organization of paragraphs read aloud from a silent reading test.

*Success in Arithmetic.* Success in a nonlanguage area such as arithmetic is sometimes used as an index of reading potential. Terman has defined intelligence as the ability to deal with abstractions. Thus, there is some basis for believing that the poor reader who handles arithmetic fundamentals successfully has the mental ability needed for successful performance in reading. Sometimes, however, a poor reader with much potential does miserably in arithmetic because habitual frustration growing out of failure in reading results in hatred for school and all subjects associated with it.

Locating retarded readers who will profit most from help in reading is not a simple matter. Since each criterion for selection has its advantages and disadvantages, its strengths and weaknesses, the conscientious teacher will use a suitable combination of criteria to arrive at individual reading-expectancy levels.

## Probing the Causes of Reading Difficulties

When retarded readers who are most readily salvageable have been determined, a teacher must become an accomplished sleuth. She must ferret out the many causes of reading failure which often are expressed in overt pupil behavior. It is unusual to find only one factor responsible for a child's learning problem or reading dilemma. Readiness for learning in general, and reading in particular, is influenced by a host of factors and conditions within the home, the school and the child as well. The child's constitutional handicaps, emotional and mental immaturities are hazards to learning that must be recognized by the teacher. Through the aid of specialists in their respective fields, handicaps may be corrected or ameliorated while the school, by providing a compensating environment, can enhance learning by minimizing the effect of existing hazards. (11)

A teacher's detective work and sensitivity to the meaning of a child's behavior must be objective, impartial and untiring. Some important areas of concern are as follows.

### INTEREST

"No" is the answer a retarded reader invariably gives when asked if he enjoys reading. Needless to say, pupils who are not interested in reading read few books. Any child who curtails his reading activities becomes more and more retarded in reading skill. Just as it is impossible to become a good swimmer without swimming, it is not possible to become a proficient reader without extensive reading. This fact undoubtedly is fundamental to many cases of reading retardation.

Why do so many children become uninterested in reading? It is much like the well-known fact that mixing cod-liver oil with a child's orange juice is a sure way to bring about an aversion for the latter. The child who experiences frustration and displeasure when he reads soon begins to avoid the process. Sometimes this Pavlovian conditioning is a direct outgrowth of being forced into first-grade reading before adequate readiness has been developed. Often, too, instructional material chosen for the child throughout the grades is far above or below (usually the former) his reading level. Still another explanation could be overemphasis on isolated word drill and old-fashioned phonics which result in a "reading isn't fun" attitude. In any event, one is forced to conclude that failure to adjust material and instructional approaches to meet individual needs is undoubtedly a primary factor in reading disabilities. It is a cause that often dwarfs all others.

The interest factor also relates to the limited experiential background characterizing many poor readers. After the primary grades much of a child's background of experience is acquired vicariously through reading. These vicarious experiences stand the child in good stead when he is attempting to read new material. The printed page is always more meaningful when proper concepts are brought to the word symbols involved. The retarded reader often has great voids in his experiential background because he has not read a great deal. These voids make successful reading comprehension difficult.

Although a teacher can find many studies that do an excellent job of furnishing him with a knowledge of the general trends of children's interests (12, 13, 14), he finds no rule of thumb for determining the exact interests of specific children. This requires detective work, the most fruitful of which involves observation, questionnaires and interviews. (See Witty's *Reading in Modern Education*.)

## MATURATION*

Superficially, seven-or eight-year olds in a group look very much alike. But a little scrutiny soon reveals differences. Children enter every school grade showing wide disparities in their mental, emotional and

---

*See pp. 8-9, 34-35 for additional information pertaining to the subject.

physical maturities. The reasons for these variations are multiple. They involve inheritance, parental training, school environment, the child's chronological age and his sex. Although it is not fair to blame reading retardation on sex, it is a known fact that two and three times as many boys as girls are found in reading disability groups.

Some authors (15) have tried to explain the difference in terms of hormones. There probably are simpler explanations, however. Boys are far more active physically than girls and find it difficult to adjust to sedentary classroom activity. Besides, they are interested in cowboys, Indians and jet airplanes. Dick, Jane and the little red hen prove lifeless and unstimulating. On a Saturday afternoon, it is not unusual to find a group of little girls playing school. But little boys — they would sooner be caught embroidering than playing school. As a matter of fact, many boys feel strongly that reading is sissy stuff. Add to all these explanations the basic fact that boys at age six lag behind girls about six months in physical maturity, and we have some good reasons why the distaff side of life fares so well in reading.

Schools which abide by research findings often require a minimum mental age of six to six and one half for beginning reading. Of course, children with much lower-mental ages can be taught to read when conditions are favorable. It is well known, however, that most children taught by an average teacher in an average classroom using conventional material need mental ages of six to six and one half if they are to prove successful in learning to read. Schools which base entrance solely on chronological age therefore expose many first-grade children to inevitable failure.

Although intelligence tests are not without error, intelligence quotients and mental ages derived from them have value if one bears in mind that a child's reading ability can be expected to approximate his intelligence only when all conditions are optimum. It must be recognized that intelligence test scores are influenced by a child's experiences, language development and interests.

Teachers should recognize that a retarded reader (one reading below grade level) who has an intelligence quotient below 90 may be doing as well as can be expected for an individual of limited-mental ability. When a child's mental grade placement is below his actual grade placement, he cannot be expected to attain the grade status of his class; however, it must not be assumed that all handicapped readers are mentally slow. Retarded and disabled readers are found at every level of intelligence. The child whose reading grade placement is below his mental grade placement should be considered a disabled reader. Such a reader is achieving below his potential and will profit from appropriate remediation.

## VISION

Approximately eighty per cent of the children in a typical school have normal vision. The remaining twenty per cent can be expected to suffer from visual anomalies such as farsightedness and nearsightedness, astigmatism and faulty fusion. While many children who have visual defects are not retarded in their reading, poor vision is never an asset and in many cases proves inimical to reading progress. There are instances when teachers can minimize a child's visual handicap by proper seating. A nearsighted child, for example, should be seated in the front of the room so blackboard viewing is facilitated.

Of the various types of immaturity that relate to reading success or failure, there is strong evidence that visual immaturity is highly significant. (16, 17, 18, 19) A sizable percentage of six- and seven-year-old children have eyes that haven't had sufficient time to develop fully. Such eyes are likely to be so farsighted that seeing objects like printed words on a page proves troublesome. Another problem stems from the inability of some children's eyes to work together as a team. When near-point binocular vision is not properly developed, a child sees printed words that are fuzzy and indistinct. Needless to say, such a situation does not augur well for reading success.

The well-known optometrist and educator, Dr. A. M. Skeffington, advocates the use of convex spherical lenses in the first grade. (20) These "learning lenses," as he terms them, would protect the vision of young children and would make it easier for them to engage in near-point work. According to Harmon, near-point tasks give rise to an avoidance response: a physiological urge to escape. The use of convex spheres "allows the organism to continue at the near-centered visual task; but it provides satisfaction of the avoidance urge, that of avoiding or getting away from the containing task. Thus, the organism can 'achieve' and 'avoid' at the same time." (21)

Apropos, here is the reported success of the New Castle, Pennsylvania system of teaching reading in the first grade. (22) The New Castle approach minimized near-point reading and used filmstrips intensively. All first graders (even some with low I.Q.'s) are reported to have learned how to read and to have achieved unprecedented reading scores on standardized tests at the end of the year.

Another solution to the problem of visual immaturity is to omit formal reading from the programs of children who demonstrate this shortcoming.

Although some children may feel excluded and suffer emotionally when this is done, it is more desirable than forcing them into near-point activity before they are ready.

It is well known that practice lags behind research a decade or two in most areas. It nevertheless is unfortunate that many schools fail to recognize the relationship between visual immaturity and first-grade reading failure. Schools should employ the proper near-point tests or seek cooperation of visual specialists who can do a competent job of determining which children are visually immature.

All screening tests for vision used by the schools have shortcomings. This is particularly true of the Snellen chart. It is important to recognize that this test checks vision only at far point and fails completely to detect severe cases of poor fusion and muscular imbalance. It also fails to detect most cases of astigmatism and farsightedness. Nearsightedness is the only defect adequately screened by the Snellen chart and this defect, ironically, is the one most often associated with good reading and good scholarship.

More effective visual screening is taking place in many schools through the use of devices employing stereoscopic cards. These devices are the Orthorater (23), Keystone Visual Survey Tests (24) and the Sight Screener. (25) They measure near-point as well as far-point vision and give attention to fusion, depth perception and binocular and monocular acuity. School systems that have the funds should replace their outdated Snellen chart with one of these machines. If this is financially impossible, then the Eames Eye Test (26) should be purchased. This inexpensive test, although not as refined as the aforementioned equipment, is capable of detecting a greater number of visual defects than the Snellen chart.

The most valuable vision-screening technique is known as the Modified Clinical Technique. According to The Orinda Study, it is by far the most efficient means of identifying children who are in need of professional vision attention. (27)

Some modern school systems enlist the cooperation of vision specialists who employ the Modified Clinical Technique. These specialists provide complete and competent visual-screening testing for all children at a very nominal cost. One such program is conducted by the Los Angeles College of Optometry in Los Angeles, California.*

The Los Angeles College of Optometry conducts visual screening in various Los Angeles County school districts. Approximately seven- to

---

*The writers are indebted to Frank A. Brazelton, O. D. Visual Survey Director, Los Angeles College of Optometry, for information about the College's vision-screening program.

eight-thousand children are examined yearly. In the typical school where testing takes place, all first graders, all referrals, all new transfer students and all children placed in a borderline category the previous year are tested.

The screening team consists of fourteen to fifteen students in their clinical year together with two faculty members who are licensed optometrists and hold Health and Development Credentials.

The tests given are essentially those of the Modified Clinical Technique and include the following:

1. Skiametry (retinoscopy) to determine the refractive state of the eye;
2. Visual acuity using the illiterate E test;
3. Phoria tests at 20 feet and 16 inches to measure muscle imbalance or binocular coordination;
4. The Cover Test or objective and quantitative determination of binocular coordination;
5. Convergence and vision tests to determine ocular motility;
6. Internal (ophthalmoscopic) and external inspection for pathology or organic anomalies.

All children are given all tests. These are performed by the student clinicians, and the record is then evaluated by one of the supervising staff before a disposition is made. The dispositions are pass, borderline, fail and under care. The record is given to the nurse, and consultation on individual cases is held at the time of testing. If necessary, retesting is done. The nurse then makes the referral by notifying parents of the results. Since the teachers are usually present while their classes are screened, it is frequently possible to correlate the visual test results with teacher observation and/or scholastic achievement. This often results in more accurate and meaningful referrals.

Programs such as the foregoing are very successful and pay unprecedented dividends to the school districts employing them.

The teacher, because of his opportunity to view children in reading and study situations, is in a strategic position to detect visual defects which otherwise might pass unnoticed. If he has any proclivities of a Sherlock Holmes and is alert, he will look for symptoms such as frequent rubbing of the eyes, closing or covering one eye while reading or watering of the eyes when doing close work (see page 52 for a listing of symptoms of visual defects). Observation of any symptoms such as these should be reported to the school nurse or doctor for further visual screening. If no school nurse or doctor is available, the matter should be brought to the attention of the parents who have the responsibility of taking their child to the proper medical specialist for an examination.

In certain instances, the school nurse may report negative findings while the teacher continues to feel great concern about the child's vision because of a chronic symptomatology. When this happens, school principals should inform the parents of the teacher's concern. On occasions, well-meaning nurses fail to detect a visual problem because their skill in specialized areas is limited or because the instruments and tests at their disposal are not sufficiently refined. Sometimes only a thorough examination by a competent visual specialist can pinpoint the problem.

## VISUAL PERCEPTION

A child may have perfect vision but imperfect visual perception or understanding. Just as a baby is surrounded by a conglomeration of stimuli for which he has no experiential guide by which he can combine them into meaningful units, the reader without perceptual skill is unable to integrate parts of a pattern (letters) into meaningful whole words.

According to Radler and Kephart, a child's ability to discern similarities and differences between words that are alike in configuration depends on his previous success in more concrete perceptual settings. (28) As an infant, a child manipulates and explores his body and objects in his immediate environment. Once the abiltiy to recognize shapes and forms is developed, he evolves a knowledge of space relationships, for example, distances between objects and the right and left and top and bottom of them. Awareness of space relationships is dependent on muscular movements. A child's eyes and hands work together until eye-hand coordination is assured. Then slowly, as he continues to mature, visual skills begin to take over. No longer must he reach out to touch an object by way of determining its location in space. Eye movement alone takes the place of hand and eye movement together.

With some children the foregoing sequence is interrupted and difficulties arise. When this happens, remedial steps are needed. The Winter Haven Lions Research Foundation has sponsored an evaluative and training program for improving hand-eye coordination. (29) Kephart and Getman describe training procedures that develop perceptual motor skills underlying reading readiness. (30, 31) Suggestions for training procedures involve the following:

1. Practice in general coordination as a means of helping children develop an awareness of their body parts and the coordinations of head, arms, torso and legs;
2. Practice with the walking board, balance board and trampoline to help children explore and develop the interrelationships of the sides of their bodies and the combinations of movements involved in balance;

3. Chalkboard practice in eye-hand coordination to help children use their hands in a coordinated manner and give opportunities to use eyes and hands as a team;
4. Practice in form recognition to help children in their perception of forms, a prerequisite to the manipulation and interpretation of symbols;
5. Practice in visual memory as a means of developing skill in the recall and accurate visualization of previous experiences;
6. Practice in eye movements, both pursuit and saccadic, to help children develop the control and accuracy needed in making ocular fixations, lateral sweeps and other movements of the eyes required in the reading act.

## HEARING

Most hearing losses fall into two categories: perceptive (nerve) loss and conduction loss. The latter is a loss in loudness due to sound that is blocked in its transmission to the inner ear. Examples of the causes for conduction losses are wax in the ear, otitis media damage and otosclerosis. Nerve loss is the result of deterioration or lesions within the inner-ear structure. Vowel sounds usually are heard when a nerve loss is present, but many or all the voiceless consonants are not heard. These include *f, h, th, p, t, sh* and *ch*. Difficulties with voiced consonants also are likely. These involve *b, d, g, v, th, z, zh, j* and *w*. Lastly, the nerve-deaf child tends to confuse nasal sounds such as *m, n* and *ng*.

Since learning to read involves making visual auditory associations, the student having a hearing loss is readily confused and is at a distinct disadvantage. (32, 33) He sees letters which he has been unable to hear and finds that words which sound the same to him have different letters in them.

The degree to which a given auditory loss impedes a child's progress in reading is dependent on many facts. These include the age at which the child suffered the loss, the extent and configuration of the loss, the extent of language development and comprehension prior to the loss and the level of the child's intelligence. It should also be remembered that a constellation of factors usually is involved in reading retardation. A child with a marked visual problem, for example, would be more encumbered by a hearing loss than a child who had normal vision.

Children who cannot detect the presence of sound are said to lack *auditory acuity*. Some children, however, can hear the presence of sound but have great difficulty discriminating between sounds that are similar. These children lack powers of *auditory discrimination*. They might find it impossible, for example, to hear the differences between the words *bat, bet, bit, but.* Their inability to discern small differences between sounds often manifests itself in their speech and spelling. Phonic training proves difficult and word recognition skill fails to develop at a normal rate. Some writers consider poor auditory discrimination an important cause of reading deficiency. (34)

Spache states that poor auditory discrimination is often associated with pitch discrimination, recognition of auditory rhythms and beat, discrimination of tonal quality, timbre and loudness. (35) If this is true, it would appear obvious that children with poor auditory discrimination would not show normal musical aptitude. The administration of the Seashore Musical Aptitude Test to such a group might prove interesting.

Regardless of causation, it would seem valuable to expose children with poor auditory discrimination to simple poems and nursery rhymes as well as commercial games such as Consonant Lotto and Go Fish. Such exposure would bring to their attention both alliteration and rhyme and would motivate them to sharpen their auditory discrimination.

Once the presence of a hearing defect is known, classroom teachers at all levels can take measures to minimize its effects. Some of these are listed:

1. Assign a front seat to the child which favors his better ear and give him a roving-seat privilege so that he may always move close to the source of sound.
2. Liberally repeat oral directions.
3. Write directions being given orally on a small card or piece of paper and place it in front of the child.
4. Give the child additional speech clues by letting him see your face in good light when you speak.
5. Summarize the day's happenings periodically.

The most valid test of hearing is an audiometric test. When no audiometer is available the teacher can employ, as a last resort, several rough screening tests. A description and discussion of these follows.

*Whisper Test.* A series of unrelated words or two digit numbers is whispered by the examiner with residual breath. A quiet room should be used for testing. The child being tested usually stands at a distance of 20 feet from the examiner, although this distance may be changed if the acoustical properties of the room warrant it. (When this is done, it is necessary to determine the proper distance by noting how far the average person must be in order to hear the whisper.) The child who is being tested stands with his side toward the examiner and responds with one ear occluded, then the other. If the child does poorly, the examiner moves closer. Should the child fail to respond as well as a normal child would at the standardized distance, a hearing loss may be suspected.

*Watch Tick Test.* Ordinarily a loud ticking watch which the average person can hear at a distance of 48 inches is used for this test. When other watches are employed, it is necessary to standardize them on a number of children. Any time pieces other than the watch being used by the examiner should be removed. The child then stands at right angles to the examiner with his finger in the ear not being tested. The youngster also should be required to hold a small card beside his head so he cannot see the watch when he is being tested. The examiner begins by placing the watch close to the child's ear. He withdraws it slowly until the child no longer hears it. He then moves the watch slowly toward the child until it is heard. An average of the two distances is taken. If a child fails to respond as a normal child would at the standardized distance, a hearing loss may be suspected.

*Coin Click Test.* The coin click test, like the watch tick test, is a test of high frequency. To the extent that it can be standardized for a given room and given coins, the coin click test is a useful supplement to the whisper test.

Some school systems do not provide adequate hearing testing. Instead of employing an audiometer periodically, they rely on the rough screening tests described. Davis feels, however, that these tests will continue to have their place since they are easily given and no expensive equipment or elaborate surroundings are required. (36) He points out that the whisper test checks frequencies in the speech range extending from three hundred to three thousand cycles per second. The coin click and watch tick test reach frequencies above this range. Since hearing loss often begins with high-frequency difficulties, the coin click and watch tick tests prove to be valuable supplementary tests.

There is no doubt that the whisper, watch tick and coin click tests are better than no tests at all. But a word of warning. There are many hearing losses that may escape detection when these tests are used. It is essential, therefore, that teachers develop a seismographic sensitivity to any manifestations of auditory impairment so intelligent referrals to an otologist can be made.

## EMOTIONAL STABILITY

"I don't feel so good," the child said when a strange and inexperienced therapist asked him to begin reading an oral reading test.

"Try, please try," repeated the therapist.

"Gee, I don't feel so good in my stomach, I'm real sick."

"Read this!" the examiner insisted.

Minutes later, it was too late for regret. The child had meant it. The session was at an end.

Pathological illness such as this is not unknown among retarded readers. Some children complain of nausea when faced with a reading situation; others suffer pains, headaches or dizziness. These psychosomatic manifestations are used by the child to escape or temporarily avoid a disagreeable situation.

Pathological illness is one of the many symptoms of personality maladjustments shown by poor readers. Gates has catalogued the symptoms manifested by one hundred cases of reading disability in the following way:

1. Nervous tensions and habits such as stuttering, nail biting, restlessness, insomnia, and pathological illness — ten cases;
2. Putting on a bold front as a defense reaction, loud talk, defiant conduct, sullenness — sixteen cases;
3. Retreat reactions such as withdrawal from ordinary association, joining outside gangs and truancy — fourteen cases;
4. Counterattack such as making mischief in school, playing practical jokes, thefts, destructiveness, cruelty, bullying — eighteen cases;
5. Withdrawing reactions including mind wandering and daydreaming — twenty-six cases;
6. Extreme self-consciousness, becoming easily injured, blushing, developing peculiar fads and frills and eccentricities, inferiority feelings — thirty-five cases;
7. Give-up or submissive adjustments as shown by inattentiveness, indifference, apparent laziness — thirty-three cases. (37)

The full import of the relationship between emotional disturbances and reading problems is evident when one considers its frequency. Over two decades ago, Witty reported that about half the children coming to the psychoeducation clinic at Northwestern University suffered from "fears and anxieties so serious and so far-reaching that no program of re-education could possibly succeed which did not aim to re-establish self confidence and to remove anxieties." (38) Gates' estimate was still higher. He believed that seventy-five per cent of poor readers show evidence of personality maladjustment. (39) More recently, Harris stated that close to one hundred per cent of the children seen in the Queens College Educational Clinic show some kind of emotional difficulty. (40)

Many reading authorities concur in the belief that most of the emotional disturbance seen among disabled readers is a result of reading failure rather than the cause of it. The child who reads poorly not only feels inadequate because he knows he is not doing as well as his classmates but often is subjected to numerous social pressures. Teachers may unwittingly remark, " I don't think you'll ever learn" or "Why must you be so lazy?" Classmates don't hesitate to label him a dumbbell and his parents may make home life intolerable by their unsympathetic reactions to his failure. Preston, for example, reports that parents of one hundred poor readers of normal intelligence called their children lazy, stupid, dumb, boob, dunce, simp, bonehead, big sissy, blockhead, fool, idiot and feebleminded. (41) Certainly it is not difficult to see why disabled readers become emotionally disturbed.

Although most disabled readers are emotionally disturbed because of their frustrations and failure, one must not overlook those children whose emotional difficulties came from other sources. For example, (42) a child who is labeled lard, fats, slats or beanpole because of his physical stature is subjected to stress. Worse still is the emotional scarring suffered by the youngster born with crooked teeth, facial birthmarks or strabismus. These conditions and many others can have an adverse effect on the emotional health of a child.

Those of us who have sat through a movie when the picture was out of focus can appreciate the emotional disturbance children with visual defects experience when they constantly have to contend with distorted images. On occasion, all of us have heard a defective sound track that proved intolerable after only a few minutes of unintelligibility. Think of what the auditorily impaired child experiences.

Endocrinologists tell us that hyperthyroidism frequently manifests itself in nervousness and emotional instability. Similarly, it is not unusual to find irritability and irascibility accompanying brain damage. Certainly a child suffering from undernourishment, lack of rest, chronic infections and the like finds nothing in his poor health to improve his disposition.

Many emotionally disturbed children are victims of unfortunate home conditions. A child may be rejected because he was unwanted. Such a child may fail in reading as a means of securing attention from parents who otherwise are indifferent to him. On the other hand, a child may be the victim of oversolicitousness. Since busy teachers are not able to give undivided attention to a child who was babied and pampered, reading failure is inevitable. Certain children do not want to learn how to read since they realize that learning how to read is associated with growing up. The last thing they want to do is grow up.

Youngsters who come from broken homes or homes in which dissension and inconsistent discipline are prevalent, are in a perpetual state of emotional turmoil. Very often unwitting parents subject children to invidious comparisons. If a child is forced to compete with a superior sibling or neighborhood prodigy, he frequently develops feelings of inferiority resulting in a give-up or submissive attitude which spells defeat before he begins.

Because the home plays such an important role in the emotional life of a child, teachers of emotionally unstable children will want to visit with parents. Once a teacher pinpoints a possible cause or causes of the problem, he should not hesitate to talk to the parents about it. More often than not, parents will initiate changes if they believe their children will benefit. (See Appendix E for a letter of suggestions which can be given to parents.)

Teachers, too, may be guilty of some of the same shortcomings characterizing parents. They may reject certain children or make unfavorable comparisons between brothers and sisters. Sarcastic remarks by the teacher, such as, "How can you be so stupid?" and "I don't know why I waste my time on you" may have traumatic effects on a child. An unpleasant teaching personality accompanied by uninspired teaching and the use of deadening drills have driven many children into maladjustment. Other children suffer maladjustment because they are forced into reading before they have the requisite readiness. Frustration and failure do not augur well for future mental health.

There are many ways for classroom teachers to detect emotionally disturbed children. Perhaps the most simple and practical is daily observation of the child's overt behavior. In this connection the teacher would find a listing of the symptoms of emotional difficulty helpful. (See pages 53 to 54 for this listing.) When employing such a list, however, the teacher should realize he is dealing with a whole child. Consequently, each symptom must be considered in light of the child's total personality.

A question employed by Paul A. Witty which frequently helps in uncovering the causes of an emotional problem is: "If you had one wish which might come true, what would be your wish?" (43) Older students can be asked to write responses to questions such as, "What Bothers Me" and "Things I Worry About."

Psychologists are trained to employ a number of methods and techniques for studying personality. Most clinical psychologists give projective tests such as the Rorschach and the Thematic Apperception Test. Other tests that may be given include the Michigan Picture Test, the Children's Apperception Test and the Fehrenbach Sentence Completion Test.

Certain personality tests can be used by classroom teachers who wish to supplement their subjective judgment of children's personality patterns. These include Mental Health Analysis Test, (44) California Test of Personality (45) and Aspects of Personality. (46) When employing such tests teachers should realize that children often answer questions in a way they feel will be pleasing to parents or teachers. Teachers also should consider that poor readers may misinterpret questions. Reading the questions aloud for the child is not recommended either since tests are not standardized in this way and the norms would be inapplicable.

## HEALTH

Part of a teacher's detective work must concern children's general health. Research in reading has shown that, to a degree, the ancient Greeks were right in believing that a good body and a good mind go hand in hand. (47, 48, 49)

Freedom from disease, proper rest and good nutrition give rise to the alertness and attention-sustaining power conducive to good reading. Children who are ill are more likely to react phlegmatically to intellectual tasks or easily become irritable and tense when things do not go well. Many times too, children who are ill miss out on basic reading instruction because of excessive absence. When such children do attend school they often lack the zest and enthusiasm to profit from instruction.

Teachers will want to remain alert to the symptoms of poor health at all grade levels. They should be aware of symptoms indicative of underactivity and overactivity of the thyroid gland as well. (See pages 52-53 for appropriate list of symptoms.)

## SPEECH

Most investigations show that speech defectives are more prevalent among poor readers than one would expect to find in the general population.

Sometimes children with speech defects suffer from actual malformation of the speech organs. In most instances, however, the causal factors of the disorder are almost identical to those which give rise to reading problems. Emotional problems seem particularly potent as a cause of speech defects. This is especially true of stuttering. It must be remembered that a child with a speech defect is often embarrassed when reading by real or imagined laughter from his classmates and teacher. In subsequent reading situations greater feelings of insecurity and a flooding of the emotions build up inside of him. This in turn results in more articulatory difficulty, and a vicious circle is perpetuated.

Children with speech problems (see pages 54 to 55 for a suitable inventory) should be referred to a speech specialist if possible. The teacher will want to do what is possible, however, to prevent the emotional difficulties that accompany speech defects from spreading to reading. Scott and Thompson's book will prove valuable to the teacher who is unable to get help from a speech specialist. (50)

## DOMINANCE

The terms *dominance* and *laterality* refer to the consistent choice or superior functioning of one side of the body over the other. This is believed to result from a dominant cerebral hemisphere which is on the side opposite the preferred hand, eye or foot.

Those who relate dominance to reading skill believe that not being completely one sided in handedness, eyedness, and footedness constitutes a condition wholly or partially responsible for reading disability.

A number of theories involving dominance have been evolved through the years to explain reading disability. Two of the better known are by Orton and Dearborn.

Orton believed that visual records, or engrams found in the dominant hemisphere of the brain are used in making symbolic associations. (51) Engrams in the nondominant hemisphere, he reasoned, would be opposite in sign, or mirrored in nature. Most often these mirrored engrams are elided or unused in the language function. When, however, an individual fails to develop consistent dominance, these latter engrams evince themselves in the form of reversals. Since, according to Orton, the making of reversals was the foremost characteristic of the poor reader, he suggested the word *strephosymbolia*, meaning twisted symbols, as a suitable label for the difficulty.

Dearborn believed that movements away from the center of the body are more easily made than those in the opposite direction. (52) The right-handed and right-eyed individual would find it easier, therefore, to write and read since both skills necessitate left to right progressions. Sinistrads and those with a mixed or inconsistent preference for either side would be prone to make reversals and in general experience word-recognition confusions.

A current proponent of unilateral cortical control is Delacato. He states that "Right-handed humans are one sided, i.e., they are right eyed, right footed and right handed, with the left cortical hemisphere controlling the organism." (53)

What Delacato and other theorists in this area fail to recognize is that *anatomically eye preference and handedness are unrelated.* (54, 55) Although the nerve fibers pass from each hand to the opposite hemisphere of the brain, *both hemispheres are involved in the control of each eye.*

(56) When the nerve fibers from each retina pass through the optic chiasma, they decussate. Fibers from the nasal side of the retina pass onto the opposite hemisphere, while the others terminate on the same side. Crider found that individuals who were right handed had retinas which were more sensitive on the right side. (57) Since the right hemisphere is involved in controlling the right side of the retinal field, one would expect such individuals to be left handed. It is neurologically sound, it would seem, to be right handed and left eyed or vice versa. Ironically, this is a condition deplored by Dearborn, Orton and Delacato.

Delacato's use of occlusion to change eyedness and his advocacy of the Stereo-Reader (a device designed to encourage suppression of vision in one eye which in itself is considered by specialists in vision to be an unhealthy condition) would seem fruitless. As stated by Flax: "Since neither eye can send all of its incoming visual information to a single side of the brain, attempts to equate uniocular function with unilateral cortical dominance are incompatible. The success reported by Delacato must stem from factors other than visual dominance." (58)

Spache, a leading reading authority, states that reading disability cannot be cured or prevented by imposing one-sided motor preferences on an individual. (59) In reference to dominance tests, he says:

> The time spent in futile tests of these functions might better be devoted to discovering children whose perceptual-motor development is inadequate. These children exhibit problems of confusion in left-right orientation, in directionality, in form perception and spatial perception and in concepts of body image. Their lack of development results also in ocular inco-ordinations and lack of hand-eye co-ordination with consequent difficulties in reading and writing. (60)

Since we live in a right-handed society, left-handed children are subjected to many pressures and sometimes develop emotional problems which may account for confusions thought attributable to left handedness per se. There have been instances, for example, where teachers and parents, with misplaced zeal, have tied a child's left hand behind his back so he would be unable to use it.

Another frustration is that a left-handed child often is forced to use a desk designed for right handers. Under these circumstances, writing proves a chore even though the child slants his paper in the appropriate direction. One elementary school principal has spent much time observing and studying left handedness. He himself is a sinistrad. He believes left-handed children, on the average, write more slowly than right-handed children. This is because a left-handed child must push rather than pull his pencil across the paper when writing from left to right. The latter, he contends, is easier.

In summary, the evidence that left handedness or mixed dominance is directly involved in bringing about reading disability is insufficient to warrant such a conclusion. Dramatically new research approaches are needed before a definite relationship between laterality and reading disability can be established. Secondary conditions such as those described in the two foregoing paragraphs undoubtedly may contribute to a left-handed child's maladjustment and should not be overlooked.

## Brain Injury and Word Blindness

There is no doubt that severe injury to the brain can cause loss of reading ability. For example, some individuals who are victims of an apoplectic stroke lose the ability to read. Dattner, Davis and Smith (61) tell of a fifty-year-old coast guard officer who lost his ability to read as the result of an accident. The man was able to write, however, and showed no other loss in the area of language. This kind of aphasia is usually referred to as word blindness, or acquired alexia.

The man to whom use of the terms "word blindness" and "acquired alexia" is often attributed was an English ophthalmologist named Hinshelwood. (62) Hinshelwood examined children who had not succeeded in learning how to read. Since the symptoms of these young nonreaders were similar to those who were victims of acquired alexia, he hypothecated the presence of a congenital variety of alexia. This was due, he said, to an abnormality of the angular and supramarginal gyri of the dominant hemisphere. (63)

Evidence that word blindness stems from an abnormality of a localized area of the brain (specifically the occipital lobe) isn't conclusive. Hallgren feels that reading difficulty resulting from a localized lesion in the dominant hemisphere is exceedingly rare. (64) Goldstein views every mental performance as a dynamic process which involves the entire cortex. (65)

Gesell placed emphasis on minimal brain damage as a cause of reading disability and singled out birth injuries as frequently responsible. (66) In support of Gesell's views, several studies employing electroencephalography report that abnormal EEG's appear in high concentration in children with reading disabilities. (67, 68)

Because of increased concern about cerebral dysfunction as a correlate of reading deficiencies, we find new tests are being developed to help specialists in this realm. One such index is the Illinois Test of Psycholinguistic Abilities (University of Illinois).

Bond and Tinker state that there seems to be a tendency during recent years to place an increasing amount of emphasis on brain injury. They have said, "It is likely that there is an overemphasis upon brain damage as a cause of reading disability." (69)

A number of books in the medical field have employed the terms "congenital word blindness," "dyslexia," or "specific reading disability" to describe a certain group of reading disability cases. (70, 71) In reviewing Hermann's book, Spache expresses concern over the labels "congenital word blindness" or "congenital alexia" because of the fact that "the group is clearly identified in Dr. Hermann's mind despite his recognition that there is not 'one single symptom nor one straight forward objective finding on which to base the description.'" (72) In a similar vein, Spache says the following about Money's designation of a group of readers as dyslexic.

> It is difficult for this reviewer to recognize clearly the small group of severely retarded readers who are assumed to be dyslexic. This is particularly true since, as repeated frequently in these papers, there is *not a single*, consistent symptom or reading behavior which distinguishes the syndrome called "specific reading disability," from among the clinical population of severely retarded readers. Perhaps it is naive to expect that a recognizable syndrome would be composed of a group of interrelated symptoms or behaviors which collectively have diagnostic significance and aid in differential diagnosis and treatment. Symptoms of dyslexia are mentioned by the dozens in these various papers, but no coherent or distinguishing syndrome appears. In fact, every symptom or behavior mentioned as characteristic of this "specific reading disability" has been observed in many retarded readers by this writer and other reading clinicians, who then, in naive ignorance of the incurability of the condition, proceeded to repair the retardation and restore the clients to apparent normalcy. We cannot help but wonder what the course of clinical reading would have been during the past three or four decades if this pessimistic theory had been offered earlier. (73)

From the evidence available at the present time, it would seem prudent for teachers to be cautious about attributing reading disability to brain damage. They should be careful, too, about labeling a child "word blind," or "dyslexic." It is obvious that there is no concensus as to what is meant by such terms and the application of an imposing label is not synonymous with diagnosis.

## A NEUROCHEMICAL THEORY

According to Smith and Carrigan symptoms which are most characteristic of severe reading disability are blending deficiency, slow reading rate and deficient discrimination of sounds and visual symbols. Underlying these symptoms lies perceptual inefficiency which is related to neural transmission. (74)

To make it possible for impulses to travel from one neuron to another, a transmitter agent is needed to bridge the junction (synapse) between neurons. The substance permitting this is acetylcholine (ACh). Once activated by (ACh), repetitive firing of a neuron persists until neutralized by another chemical, cholinesterase (ChE). The latter acts as a circuit breaker. When a functional balance between (ACh) and (ChE) exists, perceptual behavior is normal. If a network of nerve cells is involved, too much (ACh) makes it impossible for an individual to change his fixation point. This results in slow and methodical reading and an inability to blend phonemes. Too much (ChE) makes it difficult for an individual to continue fixation and causes rapid shifts of attention. The latter results in inaccurate reading characterized by many substitutions of one sound or letter for another.

Smith and Carrigan also believe that endocrine functioning has a bearing on synaptic transmission. They advocate the use of appropriate medication to help children who are metabolically insufficient.

Although the organic approach to reading difficulty advocated by Smith and Carrigan remains unproved at the present time, it warrants serious consideration and continued evaluation.

## Summary

The causes of reading failure are many and complex. Almost always a matrix of factors is involved. Good teachers, as a result, must be good detectives. They must be alert to any and all symptoms indicating the presence of factors that are inimical to learning. Questions such as the following provide teachers with the proper orientation. Are these children sufficiently mature to be exposed to formal reading instructions? Do my pupils have the interest that is essential to reading growth? Do they have normal vision and hearing? How is their general health? Are they alert and full of life? Are they suffering from any emotional disturbances?

The teacher must always do what he can to minimize any hazards to learning as soon as he uncovers them. He makes, for example, special seating arrangements for a nearsighted or auditorily impaired child. He provides special understanding and warmth when an emotionally disturbed child is involved. He often calls on other school specialists for help. Perhaps the school has a speech therapist, a psychologist or doctor who can render valuable assistance. When these measures are not sufficient, parents should be alerted and the assistance of out-of-school specialists solicited.

## Causal Factors in Reading Disability

In order to resolve problems in reading, the teacher must have an understanding of the reading process and the possible causal factors underlying reading disabilities. Following is a brief outline of some of the causal factors of reading disability.

| *Hazards* | *Some Possible Results* |
|---|---|
| A. Constitutional | Introversion |
| 1. Impaired hearing | Defective speech |
| | Language and reading retardation |
| | Intellectual retardation |
| 2. Impaired vision: myopia, hyperopia, astigmatism, poor eye coordination | Cannot see blackboard clearly |
| | Blurred and confused images of letters and words |
| | Headache and fatigue, slow rate of reading |
| 3. Neurological problems: faulty motor coordination | Faulty handwriting |
| | Faulty concentration |
| | Eye coordination difficulties |
| | Excessive reversals and repetitions |
| | Gait difficulties |
| | Slow rate of reading |
| 4. Poor health | Listlessness, fatigue, irritability, nervousness |
| B. Intellectual retardation | Lack of readiness for reading |
| | Faulty grade placement |
| | Faulty comprehension |
| | Slow rate of reading |
| C. Emotional factors | Recessive behavior, aggressive behavior, negativism, inadequacy, inferiority, nervous mannerisms, block on reading |
| D. Instructional inadequacies* | Nonreading |
| Formal reading started before readiness is attained | Word-by-word reading |
| Adequate sight vocabulary not acquired | Faulty word recognition |
| Skills of word analysis not mastered | Faulty word analysis |
| | Reading disability |
| | Behavior problem |

*See Introduction (p. 2) for more extensive listing.

Inadequate practice on easy
   reading material
Lack of individualization
Failure to instruct pupils on
   their level of readiness

E. Environmental hazards
   Faulty parent-child relationships
   Faulty parent-teacher relation-
     ships
   Home insecure emotionally
   Home insecure economically
   Low cultural status

Unwholesome adjustment
Social and emotional immaturity
Language handicap
Lack of interest in reading
(See also "Emotional factors")

## Behavior Inventories*

The following inventories will facilitate child study by providing the observer with lists of significant symptoms of overt pupil behavior in the areas of hearing, vision, health, social and emotional behavior and speech. The use of these inventories will awaken teachers to a greater awareness of the existence of learning problems and provide a record of systematic observational data.

The Home Environment Inventory highlights significant factors in the child's out-of-school life that should be recognized and ameliorated by the school program.

Intelligent use of these inventories, coupled with a sympathetic understanding of childhood problems, will serve to make observation more objective and impartial and help provide a constructive mental health program in the school.

HEARING

### *Acuity*

1. Questions must be repeated
2. Imitates other pupils
3. Seems confused
4. Daydreams
5. Faulty speech
6. Unintelligible speech
7. Speaks in a monotone
8. Voice abnormally loud or soft
9. Symbolic gestures in lieu of words
10. Language handicap
11. Strained expression on face when listening

---

*All inventories and forms appearing in this book may be reproduced by teachers for their own use.

12. Ignores verbal directions
13. Reads lips
14. Tilting or turning head as if to favor better ear
15. Cupping a hand behind the ear
16. Blank expression on face

## Ear Trouble

1. Spells of Dizziness
2. Noises in the ears
3. Excess of wax in ears
4. Discharge from ears
5. Earaches or mastoid pains
6. Previous middle-ear problems

### VISION

1. Squinting when reading from or looking at the blackboard
2. Excessive blinking, scowling or facial distortion when reading at nearpoint
3. Holds book too close to eyes
4. Holds head too close to desk
5. Confuses words and letters
6. Tilts head to one side
7. Closes or covers one eye when reading
8. Irritability evidenced when reading
9. Has inflamed, swollen eyelids
10. Has inflamed eyeballs
11. Has discharge from eyes
12. Pain in and about eyes
13. Pain in the back of the neck
14. Has headaches after reading, seeing a movie or viewing television
15. Eyes sensitive to light
16. Eyes tire when reading
17. Unwilling to wear glasses prescribed
18. One eye turns in (squint)
19. Eyes tremble or twitch
20. Frequent rubbing of the eyes
21. Watering of the eyes with close work
22. Dizziness or nausea after much close work

## Observable Pupil Behavior Symptomatic of Underlying Problems When Frequently Displayed

### PHYSICAL DEVELOPMENT

1. Obese, overweight
2. Thin, underweight
3. Excessive height
4. Retarded stature

HEALTH

1. Mouth breather
2. Frequent severe colds
3. Frequent sore throat
4. Chronic cough
5. Poor teeth
6. Sore gums
7. Swollen or enlarged neck glands
8. Dry, scaly skin
9. Protruding eyeballs
10. Frequent itching
11. Convulsions, fits
12. Blank spells
13. Fainting spells
14. Frequent headaches
15. Persistant pain
16. Nervous mannerisms, tics
17. Puffiness of eyes and face
18. Swollen hands or feet
19. Sallow complexion
20. Flushing of the skin
21. Listless, tired
22. Falls asleep in school
23. Frequent absence due to illness

HANDICAPS

1. Faulty posture
2. Awkward gait
3. Crippled, physical handicap
4. Partially paralyzed
5. Has had scarlet fever
6. Has had rheumatic fever
7. Not immunized against disease

SOCIAL AND EMOTIONAL BEHAVIOR

*Aggressive*

1. Angers easily
2. Temper tantrums
3. Uncooperative
4. Sex irregularities
5. Uncontrolled bladder or bowels
6. Enuresis (bed wetting)
7. Truancy, unexcused absences
8. Cheats
9. Resents correction
10. Destructive
11. Overcritical of others

12. Irresponsible
13. Impudent, defiant
14. Quarrelsome
15. Cruel to animals
16. Irritable
17. Belligerent, bossy
18. Bully
19. Vindictive
20. Steals
21. Dishonest, untruthful
22. Marked change in personality
23. Negativistic

### *Recessive*

1. Runs away from home
2. Seeks attention
3. Overconscientious
4. Emotionally inadequate
5. Overexuberant
6. Whiner
7. Pessimistic
8. Suspicious
9. Plays by himself
10. Avoids others, unfriendly
11. Shunned by others
12. Overreligious
13. Daydreams, preoccupied
14. Plays with younger children
15. Physical coward
16. Selfish
17. Feigns illness
18. Too submissive
19. Depressed
20. Overdependent
21. Sullen
22. Nervous tensions, ties
23. Bites fingernails
24. Fearful, timid, shy
25. Worries
26. Jealous
27. Cries easily

## SPEECH

### *Vocal*

1. Remains silent because of his speech handicap
2. Speaks too loudly
3. Has to be reminded frequently to speak louder
4. Quality of voice annoying

5. Voice lacks variety
6. Inflections of voice are tiresomely repetitious
7. Voice suggests a person of different age or sex

## Articulatory

1. Speaks too slowly
2. Speaks too rapidly
3. Omits or slides over sounds
4. Adds superfluous words
5. Difficult to understand pronunciation of certain words
6. Clumsy speech
7. Speech requires undue effort
8. Speech is accompanied by distractive movements of the lips or tongue

## Rhythmic

1. Speech is blocked at times
2. Speech is blocked by stopping the air flow
3. Speech is blocked by restricting movements of the tongue or lips
4. Repeats certain sounds unnecessarily
5. Distractive movements of head, face or hands during speech block

## Linguistic

1. Shows difficulty in understanding simple oral directions
2. Although words are clear, difficult to understand the meaning of his thought
3. Resorts to signs and gestures to express his wants
4. Has difficulty in recognizing simple words when spelled for him orally

## HOME ENVIRONMENT

## Parental Relationship

1. Parents are incompatible
2. Parents quarrel
3. Broken home
4. One or more relatives live in the home

## Child Training

1. Parents disagree on methods of child training
2. Parents dominate the child
3. Parents are inconsistent in disciplining the child
4. Parents are too severe in their discipline
5. Parents are overindulgent or oversolicitous
6. Parents are neglectful
7. Child's spending money is inadequate or excessive
8. Child has no home duties or responsibilities

9. Child's food habits are undesirable
10. Child's rest is inadequate
11. Child's moral and ethical training is inadequate

## Parent-Child Relationship

1. Parents reject the child
2. Father seems unconcerned about the child's problem
3. Father seems unconcerned about the child's future
4. Father disapproves of the child's choice of a career
5. Father shows no concern for the child's education
6. Mother seems unconcerned about the child's problem
7. Mother seems unconcerned about the child's future
8. Mother disapproves of the child's choice of a career
9. Mother shows no concern for the child's education

## Child-to-Child Relationship

1. Children are quarrelsome in the home
2. Child is jealous of a sibling
3. Child is an only child
4. Child has too few contacts with other children

## Socio-Economic Status

1. Parents do not speak English
2. Parents have few if any cultural interests
3. Parents do not read to the children
4. Parents do not use the public library
5. There are no worthwhile books or magazines in the home
6. There are no books for children in the home
7. Father tends to be shiftless
8. Mother tends to be shiftless
9. Family is insecure economically
10. Home is inadequate

## Community

1. Neighborhood is undesirable
2. Companions are undesirable
3. Playgrounds are lacking or unsupervised
4. Home-community relationship is unwholesome

### REFERENCES

1. ALBERT HARRIS, *How to Increase Reading Ability* (New York: Longmans, Green and Co., 1961), p, 299.
2. *Ibid.*
3. RUTH STRANG, CONSTANCE MCCULLOUGH and ARTHUR TRAXLER, *Problems in the Improvement of Reading* (New York: McGraw-Hill Book Company, 1955), pp. 74-75.

4. Guy Bond and Miles Tinker, *Reading Difficulties: Their Diagnosis and Correction* (New York: Appleton-Century-Crofts, 1967), p. 90.
5. Theodore Clymer, *The Influence of Reading Ability on the Validity of Group Intelligence Tests* (Unpublished Ph.D. thesis, University of Minnesota, Minneapolis, 1952).
6. Bond, *op. cit.*, p. 92._
7. *Ibid.*, p. 93.
8. Harris, *op. cit.*, p. 300.
9. *Ibid.*, p. 301.
10. George Spache, *Reading in the Elementary School* (Boston: Allyn & Bacon, Inc., 1964), p. 170.
11. Theodore Torgerson and Georgia Adams, *Measurement and Evaluation for the Elementary School Teacher* (New York: Holt, Rinehart & Winston, Inc., 1954), ch. 1.
12. George Norvell, *The Reading Interests of Young People* (Boston: D. C. Heath and Co., 1950).
13. Herbert Rudman, "The Informational Needs and Reading Interests of Children in Grades IV Through VIII," *Elementary School Journal* 55: 502-512, 1955.
14. Robert Thorndike, *Interests* (Bureau of Publications, Teachers College, Columbia University, 1941).
15. George Park et al., "Biologic Changes Associated with Dyslexia," *Archives of Pediatrics* 72: 71-84, 1955.
16. Luella Cole, *The Improvement of Reading* (New York: Farrar and Rinehart Inc., 1938), p. 282.
17. George Berner and Dorothy Berner, "Reading Difficulties in Children," *Archives of Ophthalmology* 20: 830, 1938.
18. George Park and Clara Burri, "Eye Maturation and Reading Difficulties," *Journal of Educational Psychology* 34: 538-539, 1943.
19. O. Nugent, and Vivienne Ilg, "Newer Developments in Orthoptics with Reference to Reading Problems," *Archives of Physical Therapy* 22: 225-232, 1941.
20. A. M. Skeffington, "What 'Learning Lenses' Mean in the Beginning School Grades — and Why," *The Optometric Weekly* (September 6, 1962).
21. Darell Harmon, *Notes on a Dynamic Theory of Vision* (Privately published, 1958).
22. Glenn McCracken, "New Castle Reading Experiment," *Elementary English* 30: 13-21, 1953.
23. Bausch and Lomb Optical Co., 730 Fifth Ave., New York, N.Y.
24. Keystone View Co., Meadville, Pennsylvania.
25. American Optical Co., Southbridge, Massachusetts.
26. World Book Co., South Broadway & Sunnyside Lane, Tarrytown, New York.
27. Henrik Blum, Henry Peters, and Jerome Bettman, *Vision Screening for Elementary Schools. The Orinda Study* (Berkeley: University of California Press, 1959).

28. D. RADLER and NEWELL KEPHART, *Success Through Play* (New York: Harper & Row, Publishers, 1960).
29. *Perceptual Achievement and Training Forms*, Winter Haven Lions Research Foundation, P.O. Box 1045, Winter Haven, Florida.
30. NEWELL KEPHART, *The Slow Learner in the Classroom* (Columbus, Ohio: Charles E. Merrill Books, Inc., 1960).
31. G. N. GETMAN and ELMER KANE, *The Physiology of Readiness* (Minneapolis P.A.S.S., Inc., 1964).
32. DOROTHEA EWERS, "Relations Between Auditory Abilities and Reading Abilities," *Journal of Experimental Education* 18: 239-262, 1950.
33. MIRIAM FIEDLER, "Teachers' Problems with Hard of Hearing Children," *Journal of Educational Research* 42: 618-622, 1949.
34. SPACHE, *op. cit.*, p. 43.
35. *Ibid.*, p. 43.
36. HALLOWELL DAVIS, *Hearing and Deafness* (New York: Murray Co., 1947), p. 126.
37. ARTHUR GATES, "Failure in Reading and Social Maladjustment," *Journal of the National Education Association* 25: 205-206, 1936.
38. PAUL WITTY and DAVID KOPEL, *Reading and the Educative Process* (Boston: Ginn and Company, 1939), p. 231.
39. ARTHUR GATES, "The Role of Personality Maladjustments in Reading Disability," *Journal of Genetic Psychology* 59: 77-83, 1941.
40. HARRIS, *op. cit.*, p. 264.
41. MARY PRESTON, "The Reaction of Parents to Reading Failure," *Child Development* 10: 173-179, 1939.
42. Parts of this section are drawn from D. G. SCHUBERT's "Understanding and Handling Reading-Personality Problems," *Elementary English* (December, 1960), pp. 537-539.
43. WITTY and KOPEL, *op. cit.*, 339.
44. CALIFORNIA TEST BUREAU, Monterey, California.
45. *Ibid.*
46. *Ibid.*
47. GEORGE PARK, "Dyslexia from a Physical Viewpoint," *Illinois Medical Journal* 97: 30, 1950.
48. THOMAS EAMES, "Incidence of Diseases among Reading Failures and Non Failures," *Journal of Pediatrics* 33: 615, 1948.
49. THOMAS EAMES, "Physical Factors in Reading," *The Reading Teacher* 15: 427-432, 1962.
50. LOUISE SCOTT, and J. THOMPSON, *Talking Time* (Manchester, Mo.: Webster Publishing, 1951).
51. SAMUEL ORTON, *Reading, Writing and Speech Problems in Children* (New York: Norton, 1937).
52. WALTER DEARBORN, "Structural Factors which Condition Special Disability in Reading," *Proceedings of the American Association of Mental Deficiency* 38: 266-283, 1933.
53. CARL DELACATO, *The Treatment and Prevention of Reading Problems* (Springfield, Ill.: Charles C Thomas, Publisher, 1959).
54. DELWYN SCHUBERT, *The Doctor Eyes the Poor Reader* (Springfield, Ill.: Charles C Thomas, Publisher, 1957).

55. Lois Bing, "A Critical Analysis of the Literature on Certain Visual Functions Which Seem to Be Related to Reading Achievement," *Journal of American Optometric Association* 22: 454-463, 1951.
56. Blake Crider, *Ocular Dominance: Its Nature, Measurement, and Development* (Unpublished doctor's dissertation, Western Reserve University, reported by H. Robinson in *Why Pupils Fail in Reading,* Chicago: University of Chicago Press, 1946).
57. *Ibid.*
58. Nathan Flax, "The Clinical Significance of Dominance," *American Journal of Optometry* 43: 566-580, 1966.
59. George Spache, *Toward Better Reading* (Champaign, Ill.: Garrard Publishing Co., 1963, p. 117.
60. *Ibid.,* p. 116.
61. Bernhart Dattner, Vernam Davis and Charles Smith, "A Case of Subcortical Visual Verbal Agnosia," *Journal of Nervous and Mental Disorders* 116: 808-811, 1952.
62. James Hinshelwood, *Congenital Word Blindness* (London: Lewis, 1917).
63. *Ibid.*
64. Bertil Hallgren, *Specific Dyslexia* (Copenhagen, Denmark: Munksgaard, 1950), p. 53.
65. Kurt Goldstein, *Aftereffects of Brain Injuries in War* (New York: Grune and Stratton, Inc., 1942), p. 82.
66. Arnold Gesell, and C. Amatruda, *Developmental Diagnosis: Normal* and *Abnormal Child Development* (New York: Hoeber, 1947), p. 248.
67. J. Hughs, R. Leander, and G. Ketchum, "Electroencephalographic Study of Specific Reading Disabilities," *Electroencephalographic and Clinical Neurophysiology* 1: 377-378, 1949.
68. Margaret Kennard, Ralph Rabinovitch and Donald Wexler, "Abnormal Electroencephalogram," *Canadian Medical Association Journal* 67: 332, 1952.
69. Bond, *op. cit.,* p. 118.
70. Knud Herman, *Reading Disability: A Medical Study of Word-Blindness and Related Handicaps* (Springfield, Ill.: Charles C Thomas, Publisher, 1961).
71. John Money, *Reading Disability: Progress and Research Needs in Dyslexia* (Baltimore: John Hopkins Press, 1962).
72. George Spache, "Interesting Books for the Reading Teacher," *The Reading Teacher* 11: 374, 1962.
73. George Spache, "Interesting Books for the Reading Teacher," *The Reading Teacher* 18: 239, 1964. Reprinted with permission of the author and the International Reading Association.
74. Donald Smith, and Patricia Carrigan, *The Nature of Reading Disability* (New York: Harcourt, Brace & World, Inc., 1959).

### Selected Readings

Bond, Guy and Miles Tinker, *Reading Problemss Their Diagnosis and Correction,* 2nd ed., New York: Appleton-Century-Crofts, 1967, chs. 4-6.

DECHANT, EMERALD, *Improving the Teaching of Reading,* Englewood Cliffs, N. J.: Prentice-Hall, Inc., 1964, chs. 2, 3.

HARRIS, ALBERT, *How to Increase Reading Ability,* 4th ed., chs. 9, 10. New York: Longmans, Green and Company, 1961.

OTTO, WAYNE and RICHARD MCMENEMY, *Corrective and Remedial Teaching,* Boston: Houghton Mifflin Company, 1966, ch. 2.

ROBINSON, HELEN, *Why Pupils Fail in Reading,* Chicago: University of Chicago Press, 1946.

STRANG, RUTH, *Diagnostic Teaching of Reading,* New York: McGraw-Hill Book Company, 1964, ch. 9.

# 3

# Individualized Instruction
# in Reading

There is one question uppermost in the minds of conscientious teachers everywhere: "How best can I teach boys and girls who are reading far above or below their grade placement?"

This question is particularly pressing because the problem of variability in achievement is always with us. A retardation of twenty-five per cent or more and an acceleration of a like amount in reading is prevalent in elementary classrooms everywhere. Third- and fourth-grade teachers encounter a range of talent covering five or more grades. And disconcerting though it may be, the situation becomes worse in this regard as one moves up the educational ladder. Fifth- and sixth-grade teachers are likely to find a still greater range. What is the answer to the chronic problem imposed by extreme heterogeneity in every grade?

## Limitations of Group Instruction

The answer cannot be found in having all children use the same reader, cover the same pages and answer the same questions. The school that prescribes or encourages a program for all children consisting of the same methods and the same curricular experiences is destined to defeat its purposes. Such a school is setting the stage for a human drama of failure and discouragement for some of its pupils and boredom and disgust for others. In such a system, scholarship difficulties and behavior problems are sure to flourish.

Group instruction, the prevailing method used in today's schools, consists of maximum teacher direction and minimum pupil motivation and participation. At its best, group instruction may provide differentiated assignments, individual projects and special activities. Even then, however, it leaves much to be desired in terms of the systematic and sequential learning experiences required for developing better readers.

It is well to remember that instruction is not an end in itself. Learning is the end product, and instruction is but a means to this end. Learning involves changes that take place in individuals, and this is the goal of all instruction.

Although learning is an individual experience, it should not be assumed that all instruction must be individualized. Group instruction proves quite effective when all the learners in a class have attained the necessary state of readiness. Children with good listening vocabularies and normal experiences in auding can acquire information and develop concepts just by listening to the teacher. Oral presentation by the teacher, then, proves an effective medium for imparting information. Similarly, when a teacher employs visual aids, all children usually are able to profit. Their learning is limited, of course, by the degree of their native intelligence, experiential background, attitudes, interests and other conditioning factors.

The story is quite different, however, when a teacher requires that all children read the same material. Proficiency in reading skills is now the all-important factor. Those who are retarded in their reading skills find the text too difficult and suffer confusion and frustration. They fail to profit from this kind of group instruction until they have attained a facility with written language (reading) that is comparable to their facility with spoken language.

The most glaring deficiency of group instruction grows out of its failure to provide adequately for retarded and accelerated readers. It also fails to provide for average readers who have a special handicap or disability.

Group instruction tends to be teacher directed, employing extrinsic rather than intrinsic methods of motivation. Frequently, the child feels he is working for the teacher. With individualized correction he soon discovers he is working for himself at his own rate to overcome his deficiencies.

Recitation during group instruction is frequently wasteful since each child actually participates for only a fractional part of the class period. Individualized instruction gives each child an opportunity to work independently and to function effectively every moment of the instructional period.

## Individualized Instruction and Corrective Reading

How can a teacher turn the independent listener into an independent reader? Can she do it by straight oral instruction? The answer is an obvious "no." The child must attain mastery of basic reading skills through systematic developmental instruction plus individualized corrective practice. Only then will he acquire a mastery of the reading skills needed to become an independent reader who can profit from book learning.

*Individual instruction* in common practice is not the same as *individualized instruction*. Individual instruction usually fails to meet the unique needs of the individual. It merely involves doing with one child what ordinarily is done with the other thirty or forty. Sometimes, it is true, the material utilized by the teacher is simplified, but usually the techniques and materials of instruction are essentially the same as those used with a group.

The two approaches also differ in terms of the time and effort demanded of the teacher. Individual instruction with a single pupil conceivably could consume a teacher's entire time. An individualized approach with materials that are *self-directive* will enable the teacher to meet the needs of all handicapped readers in the class and still enable him to supervise or work with the remaining group.

Since reading difficulties of specific pupils differ in number, type and severity, the corrective must be *individualized*. If it is not, the unique array of problems peculiar to each individual cannot be met. This is why teacher-directed instructional material that has been employed with groups is limited in use to only a few pupils.

Individualized instruction increases the efficiency of readers experiencing difficulty because the self-directed material is geared to their readiness, interests and needs. Recreational reading with its provisions for self-selection provides unlimited opportunities for improving the reading proficiency, tastes and attitudes of average and superior readers as well.

By utilizing *self-directed* material which provides practice in those skills and abilities each child has failed to master, corrective instruction can be *individualized* and made available to all who need it. When the instructional materials are of an appropriate level of difficulty, each pupil can work independently and successfully at his own rate. Consequently, pupils become motivated as they progress. As they become proficient at working independently, they gain skill in evaluating their own performance. Their teacher is relieved of the time-consuming activity of working individually with each child in need of corrective work and is able to direct group and individual projects simultaneously.

Severely retarded readers in the intermediate and upper grades usually are deficient in the basic reading skills of word perception. A reading difficulty at these levels can best be met through *individualized instruction* following a sound diagnosis. When the principles of this approach are understood and appropriate *self-directed* materials employed, reading problems will be minimized. As a result, scholarship problems will be resolved.

Chapters 5, 7 and 8 contain lists of commercial and teacher-made instructional materials that are *self-directive* or can be made *self-directive*.

## PRACTICES AND CONDITIONS ESSENTIAL TO INDIVIDUALIZED CORRECTION

The following practices and conditions are considered basic to a program of individualized correction.

1. Learn all you can about the nature of each child and his specific reading problem. As part of the diagnosis, consult his cumulative folder and catalogue all important aspects of his growth. This involves valid measurements of his mental maturity, oral and silent reading levels and proficiency in various subject matter fields. Other essentials entail awareness of the child's interests, hobbies, attitudes and personality pattern. Work habits, too, should be scrutinized. General health and physical fitness with particular emphasis on vision and hearing must not be overlooked. Be alert to manifestations of sensory defects. In short, all facets of the child's reading readiness and hazards to learning must be considered. (The reader is referred to Chapter 2 for more information pertaining to this section.)

2. Do not assume that an awareness of difficulties and hazards to a child's progress is enough. Appropriate ameliorative or corrective measures must be initiated if anything worthwhile is going to be accomplished. If, for example, a child with a physical defect is encountered, he should be referred to the proper specialist. Thus, a child with a visual problem would be brought to the attention of an optometrist or oculist for fitting of suitable corrective lenses. Only after correction is made can one be confident that this impediment to learning no longer exists.

3. Build a warm relationship with each pupil and recognize that this relationship is basic to his mental health and academic achievement. The child who likes his teacher is more highly motivated to overcome handicaps than the child who is indifferent to his teacher. One way to establish the kind of rapport essential to success is through personal conference. Convince the child by what you do, and tell him you are his friend. Usually, a child who repeatedly has met failure in reading needs

a sympathetic and understanding adult who can help him rebuild feelings of adequacy. Be optimistic about the possibilities of improvement by showing the child you have confidence in his ability to achieve. Help the child understand the nature of his reading problem and provide him with the tools that will enable him to improve.

4. Acquire and develop corrective instructional materials that allow children to work *independently* in overcoming their weaknesses and consolidating their strengths. Such materials provide simple directions for doing specific exercises and should be accompanied by answers. *Self-directive materials* which permit *individualized corrective instruction* might include reading games, programmed learning materials, workbook exercise files, tape recordings, magic slates and electric boards. (See Chapters 5, 7 and 8 for a more detailed discussion of these and many other self-directive approaches to learning.)

5. To facilitate individualized corrective work, provide each child with a small activity notebook on which his name appears. All such notebooks are kept by the teacher and are made available to pupils during those periods when the group engages in corrective work.

Each notebook lists by date corrective activity which the instructor feels is most appropriate for the child. A sample activity sheet from a notebook might be as follows:

---

May _____ , 19 _____

a. In SRA Laboratory 3a, read selection _____ and answer questions _____ . Check your answers. If you miss more than three, read the selection again.

b. Get Exercise 28 from the workbook file. Complete it and then check your answers.

c. Work with Harry on card _____ , level _____ . (Durrel's Word Analysis Practice.) Ask your teacher for help if you get stuck on any of the words.

d. Work with Flash-X level _____ , card _____ .

e. On Table 2, you'll find many books on your reading level. Find one you like and start reading it.

---

6. Since we know that nothing succeeds like success, one must be sure to use instructional material that is geared to the child's intellectual and educational levels. By beginning at the learner's level of accomplishment (with retarded readers it often is wise to begin slightly below this level), further failure, frustrations and discouragement can be avoided. When in doubt as to the difficulty level of an ungraded book, it is very helpful to have the child "try it on for size" by having him read several passages orally.

7. Capitalize on the reader's interests by introducing or encouraging pupils to select books and materials through a recreational reading program which coincides with these interests. In this way, reading becomes a vital and worthwhile experience for the child. "Here is something," he says to himself, "that I really want to know about."

8. Implicit in the foregoing conditions is the need for a great variety of reading materials. These materials must vary not only in difficulty but in content and interest appeal as well. Helping the right books come in contact with the right children is foundational to an individualized reading program. In this connection, it is important for a teacher to provide guidance in the choice of books. Some children are prone to choose books that are too difficult. Remember that the ultimate goal of any reading program is to develop in the child a love of reading.

9. Developmental instructional material should be designed to unfold gradually and systematically a logical sequence of skills or concepts to be mastered. It must be of optimum difficulty for the learner. A child should not be introduced to more difficult material until he has thoroughly mastered all that is foundational or prerequisite to it.

10. Evaluate both developmental and corrective instruction at frequent intervals to determine their effectiveness. An inventory of individual reading difficulties prepared by the teacher will serve as a useful guide. If what you are doing isn't paying learning dividends, renovate your approach. Keep in mind that learning and not teacher-dominated instruction is the goal.

11. Help each pupil evolve charts of various types and descriptions as a means of recording achievement in a dramatic way. Such charts, particularly if constructed by the pupil rather than forced on him by the teacher, are valuable incentives to improvement in learning and useful guides for the teacher in planning individual instructional programs.

## FEASIBILITY OF AN INDIVIDUALIZED READING PROGRAM

"Impractical and impossible" say those teachers whose experiences have been limited to group instruction. "How can you individualize a program for thirty students?"

*The teacher should be reminded that an individualized approach to reading is not in addition to but in place of a large portion of the time devoted to group instructional practices. A redistribution of time previously devoted exclusively to teacher-directed group instruction now emphasizes an early diagnosis to discover individual reading difficulties, followed by self-directed corrective instruction. The teacher discovers that while supervising the activities of the normal and accelerated readers, retarded readers are successfully pursuing self-administering corrective material independently.*

The teacher begins by acquiring basal readers and supplementary books on several grade levels. These include a good classroom library of books suitable for retarded, average and superior readers. In addition, the teacher must have an array of workbooks, informal tests, exercises, reading games and activities which are self-directional in nature. (The reader is referred to Chapters 5, 7 and 8 for descriptions of suitable material.)

Assuming a twenty-five per cent retardation in reading with a class of thirty, a teacher will have seven or eight pupils in need of remediation. Individualized instruction for these pupils will vary from individual activities to group activities, depending on the skills to be mastered and the materials and techniques used by the teacher. If, for example, the entire group demonstrates a basic sight vocabulary deficiency of service words, a group game such as Look might be employed. On the other hand, if a single child in this group did not know his initial consonant sounds, specific pages from a workbook or specific exercises or games might be assigned individually to help overcome the deficiency.

It is important that the teacher design and acquire materials that are *self-directive*. This will enable her to do developmental work with normal and accelerated readers, while the retarded readers are pursuing individualized self-directive activities independently, without frustration or loss of attention to the tasks at hand. When the normal and accelerated readers are engaged in recreational reading, the teacher is free to extend any needed help to the retarded group.

## Developmental Instruction in Reading

In the introductory chapter the reader was reminded that this volume does not promote a specific developmental program in reading; however, the authors do point out inefficient and unwholesome practices frequently found in the developmental program and recommend that it be augmented by a correctional program consisting of self-directed instructional material. When optimal conditions for learning prevail and the developmental offering is highly efficient, many reading problems are prevented, disabilities disappear and the need for correction is reduced to a minimum. The present status of retardation in reading was discussed briefly in the introductory chapter and the need for preventive and corrective measures is abundantly clear. Unwholesome conditions in the school together with inefficient instructional practices are discussed in Chapters 1 and 2. These chapters clarify the need for and the nature of a program of prevention and diagnosis in reading for every school.

Efficient developmental programs in reading, individualized or otherwise differentiated, are dependent on an ample supply of appropriate instructional material utilized to the fullest by teachers who promote wholesome classroom practices. An enumeration of some of these essential items follows.

1. A classroom library containing an ample supply of materials such as the following:
   a. basal readers of several series and grade levels
   b. an extended list of books of high interest and low level of difficulty
   c. a variety of trade books and pamphlets as well as books the children may have made
   d. children's newspapers and magazines
   e. a variety of reading games
   f. a variety of workbooks in reading
   g. a teacher prepared file of self-directed instructional material
   h. an atlas and encyclopedias
2. Supplementary material as listed:
   a. a variety of standardized test material
   b. cumulative records
   c. collections of films, filmstrips and recordings
   d. projector and rate controller
   e. a school library of current professional books in reading
   f. a personal library of up-to-date professional books in reading
3. Classroom practices involving the following:
   a. the development of reading readiness and its acceptance as a prerequisite to formal reading instruction
   b. individualized oral reading
   c. use of oral reading in an audience situation
   d. use of individual pupil interviews or conferences to locate difficulties, evaluate, motivate and direct recreational reading
   e. use of flexible grouping
   f. use of self-directed correctional material
   g. systematic evaluation and early correction of difficulties
   h. consistent promotion of individual mastery of reading skills
   i. systematic discovery, analysis and correction of individual reading problems
   j. wholesome teacher-pupil relationships

The ensuing chapters of this volume are devoted to showing the teacher how to select, prepare and apply individualized activities in developmental and corrective teaching. Extensive sources of materials, methods and tests will be set forth in detail.

## Summary

Variability in achievement at all grade levels is a serious problem for teachers and one which cannot be met through undifferentiated group instruction. Undifferentiated group instruction is inefficient because it fails to provide correction or challenging activities to meet the needs of the atypical learner. It violates the principle of individual readiness and results in frustration and failure for the poor reader.

Individual instruction or tutoring also proves unrealistic in solving the problem of heterogeneous achievement within a classroom since the excessive time and effort involved make it impossible to provide for more than one or two pupils.

Individualized instruction proves practical and feasible for both developmental and corrective reading when the teacher employs self-directive material of appropriate difficulty and challenging content. With this approach all pupils are able to pursue appropriate differentiated instructional material while the teacher is free to assist individuals with unique problems.

The materials and techniques of individualized instruction must encompass the following in order to be highly successful:

1. Determination of the child's learning and reading problem by making a careful diagnosis;
2. Introduction of ameliorative and corrective measures to eliminate impediments to learning;
3. Building a warm relationship with the child;
4. Development of corrective materials that are self-directive so pupils can work independently in overcoming difficulties;
5. Using activity notebooks to individualize corrective work when a group of children is involved;
6. Employing instructional materials of the appropriate difficulty for each pupil;
7. Capitalizing on reader interest by encouraging children to select books which coincide with their interests;
8. Providing a variety of reading materials in terms of interest and difficulty levels;
9. Providing ample corrective materials which will result in a mastery of the reading skills;
10. Periodical evaluation of the instructional program;

11. Employing reading inventories as instructional blueprints and progress charts as a means of recording achievement in a dramatic way.

SUPPLEMENTARY PROBLEMS FOR ORAL AND WRITTEN DISCUSSION

1. Why is a comprehensive individual diagnosis an essential prerequisite to corrective reading?
2. In what way do the goals of instruction in information and in skills differ?
3. What are the essential criteria for effective self-directed instructional material in reading?
4. How does the use of self-directed instructional material for retarded readers differ from the use of teacher-directed material?
5. How does self-directed instruction compare with teacher-directed instruction in terms of pupil motivation and individual mastery?

SELECTED READINGS

BOND, GUY and MILES TINKER, *Reading Problems: Their Diagnosis and Correction* 2nd ed., New York: Appleton-Century-Crofts, 1967, ch. 3.

HARRIS, ALBERT, *How to Increase Reading Ability* 4th ed., New York: Longmans, Green and Company, 1961, ch. 11.

OTTO, WAYNE and RICHARD MCMENEMY, *Corrective and Remedial Teaching*, Boston: Houghton Mifflin Company, 1966, pp. 57-77.

SCHUBERT, DELWYN, *Readings in Reading: Practice-Theory-Research*, New York: Thomas Y. Crowell Company, 1968, selections 25-27, 42-43.

# Analyzing Difficulties in Word Recognition and Word Analysis

When pupils of comparable intelligence show a wide disparity in achievement it often can be attributed to a difference in their mastery of reading skills. Of these, basic reading skills (word-recognition and word-attack skills) are usually the most significant and critical.

In order to remedy the situation, a teacher must begin by discovering and analyzing the difficulties pupils are experiencing with these skills. General impressions will not suffice. Specific analytical data must be obtained and recorded in an organized manner if an effective instructional program is to evolve. (See the end of this chapter for a suitable form.)

Careful diagnosis, it is important to note, always precedes correction. When someone visits a physician and complains of chills and muscular aches, he isn't plunged into a tub of ice water to break his fever or given rubbing liniment to assuage his pain. A physician knows too well that the elimination of symptoms does not cure a disease. If he finds a syndrome that indicates bacterial invasion, antibiotics may be prescribed to attack the infection at its source and thereby restore good health.

A perusal of the literature on reading reveals that all too often corrective work in reading parallels the ice-water and rubbing-liniment analogy. Methods, techniques and gadgets are used which are primarily concerned with manifestations of symptoms rather than amelioration of causal factors.

Although diagnosis should precede prescription, it is not necessary to delay corrective work until absolutely all data about a child's problem are collected. Diagnosis and corrective procedures should be combined. As instruction continues and more testing and observation take place, the teacher gains additional insights into the problem. Diagnosis does not end until correction is completed.

Opportunities to make intelligent observations with respect to a pupil's competence and persistent difficulties in reading are many. The use of cumulative records and interviews with pupils, teachers and parents should serve to confirm or negate judgments the teacher may have formed. In making a systematic appraisal of individual competence and specific reading difficulties found in a classroom, answers to the following questions will prove helpful.

1. What learning problems, if any, does each pupil have? (See Chapter 2 for a discussion of learning problems.)
2. What are his oral and silent reading grade levels?
3. What is the nature of his reading problem? Do the difficulties encompass faulty word recognition, faulty word analysis or faulty comprehension?
4. What faulty reading habits has he acquired, and what specific reading skills and abilities has he failed to master?
5. Is the difficulty of the present developmental material on his frustration level, instructional level or independent reading level?
6. What grade level of difficulty is recommended for developmental instruction?
7. What is the pupil's present independent reading level?
8. What is his potential reading level?
9. What sequence of corrective instruction seems advisable?
10. What reading level should the pupil seek to attain this year?

Many of the foregoing questions can be answered by employing silent and oral reading tests. These tests (particularly the latter) will demonstrate objectively what deficiencies in the basic reading skills have led many pupils into scholastic doldrums. In order to eliminate the individual difficulties indicated by a detailed diagnosis, individualized self-directed corrective instruction must be provided.

Questions particularly relevant to an analysis of each pupil's weaknesses in word-recognition and word-analysis skills, most of which can be answered through the child's oral reading performance, are as follows:

1. What is the size of his sight vocabulary?
   a. Does he skip words?
   b. Does he add words?
   c. Does he substitute words?
   d. Does he repeat words?
   e. Does he reverse words?
   f. Does he read word by word?
   g. Does he point to words?
   h. Does he lose his place?

2. Does he know the names of the consonants and their sounds?
3. Does he know the sounds of common blends and consonant digraphs?
4. Does he know the long and short sounds of the vowels?
5. Is he aware of any generalizations or so-called rules pertaining to vowel sounds?
6. Does he utilize context clues?
7. Can he blend parts of a word into a whole?
8. Does he recognize common prefixes and suffixes?
9. Is he aware of word roots?
10. Can he break long words into syllables?

## Silent Reading Tests

Silent reading tests of the survey type often are limited to measures of comprehension and meaning vocabulary. Diagnostic silent reading tests include measures of such reading abilities as discovering central thoughts, locating related details, anticipating outcomes and following directions. Usually they do not provide sufficient information regarding sight vocabulary deficiency and word-analysis skill. In fact, there are times when the results of silent reading tests prove invalid in these regards. For example, a sixth-grade boy could recognize only two or three words on sight. His word-analysis skill was nonexistent. Yet, on a standardized silent reading test for the intermediate grades, he achieved a 2.7 grade score. Investigation revealed that this had been accomplished by filling in blanks at random.

## Oral Reading Tests

Filling in blanks at random is not possible when a pupil is given an oral reading test. Guessing or bluffing are quickly discerned and the teacher is able to locate specific difficulties in word recognition and word analysis. Faulty reading habits also become apparent.

Unlike silent reading tests, oral reading tests must be administered individually. From ten to twenty minutes is usually ample time for administration. Commonly used oral reading tests include the Gates (Bureau of Publications), Gray (Bobbs-Merrill) and Gilmore (Harcourt, Brace & World).

The teacher who uses an oral reading test soon becomes adept at employing a shorthand system for recording reading errors. A code such as the following (Gilmore Oral Reading Test) (1) can prove valuable when making assessments of a pupil's reading needs through informal reading tests. Teachers have many opportunities for informally evaluating children's oral reading in the classroom and through individual conferences.

| TYPE OF ERROR | RULE FOR MARKING | EXAMPLES |
|---|---|---|
| *Substitutions*<br>A sensible or real word substituted for the word in the paragraph | Write in substituted word. | black<br>The boy is back of the girl.<br>girl<br>See the girls. |
| *Mispronunciations*<br>A nonsense word which may be produced by (1) false accentuation; (2) wrong pronunciation of vowels or consonants; or (3) omission, addition, or insertion of one or more letters. | Write word in phonetically (if time permits) or draw a line through the word. | sĭm'-bŏl-ĭk<br>(1) symbolic (or)<br>symbolic<br>blĕs'-fŏol<br>(2) blissful (or)<br>blissful<br>blĕnt<br>(3) bent (or)<br>bent |
| *Words Pronounced by Examiner*<br>A word on which the subject hesitates for 5 seconds. (The word in then pronounced by the examiner.) | Make two checks above word pronounced. | It is a fascinating story. |
| *Disregard of Punctuation*<br>Failure to observe punctuation. | Mark punctuation disregarded with an "x." | Jack, my brother, is in the navy. |
| *Insertions (including additions)*<br>A word (or words) inserted at the beginning, middle, or end of a sentence or line of test. | Write in inserted word or words. | the<br>The dog and ∧ cat are fighting. |
| *Hesitations*<br>A pause of at least 2 seconds before pronouncing a word. | Make a check above the word on which hesitation occurs. | It is a fascinating story. |
| *Repetitions*<br>A word, part of a word, or group of words repeated. | Draw a wavy line beneath word (words) repeated. | He thought he saw a whale. |
| *Omissions*<br>One or more words omitted. (If a complete line is omitted, this is counted as one omission error.) | Encircle the word (or words) omitted. | Mother does all of her work with great care. |

Most standardized oral reading tests are similar to the Gilmore. This test has two forms and consists of ten paragraphs of increasing difficulty which range from first grade to high school. A child taking the test reads from a booklet of heavy cardboard in which single paragraphs appear on individual pages. In a separate record booklet, the examiner records the errors made according to the code already described. He also records reading time in seconds and the answers to the five comprehension questions following each paragraph. A manual provides directions for errors, norms for accuracy, comprehension and rate of reading. Although designed for pupils in grades one through eight, it can be employed most profitably with disabled readers in high school.

Through the use of a tape recorder, teachers will learn how to score an oral reading test objectively.* An individual record sheet will enable the teacher to record errors made by the pupil as he reads. After the scoring has been completed, the significant errors should be entered on the pupil's reading inventory. (See inventory at the end of this chapter. A descriptive list of oral reading tests appears in Appendix C.)

## Diagnostic Reading Tests (Group)

Although most diagnostic reading group tests do not provide sufficient information regarding sight vocabulary deficiency and word-analysis skill, several tests are very helpful in these respects. One of these, *The Silent Reading Diagnostic Tests*,† is especially valuable because it can be administered and interpreted by a classroom teacher who has not had special training in clinical reading. By employing the test, a teacher can learn a great deal about pupils' word-recognition vocabulary and word-attack skills. The following description of the eleven subtests involved will give the reader an understanding of what kinds of information *The Silent Reading Diagnostic Tests* yield.

TEST I: Word Recognition. This test has 54 items. Each consists of a picture accompanied by five words. A line is drawn around the word that tells about the picture. The choices are arranged so a child can commit initial, middle, final or reversal errors.

---

*Teachers can get practice and become proficient in objectively scoring oral reading tests by listening to tape recordings of children who have taken such tests. When teachers agree as to errors made, they have acquired the necessary objectivity in their scoring.

†Authored by Bond, Clymer and Hoyt and published by Lyons & Carnahan. For a more complete description see Bond, G. L. and M. A. Tinker, *Reading Difficulties: Their Diagnosis and Correction* (New York: Appleton-Century-Crofts, 1967), pp. 221-227.

TEST II:      Recognition of Words in Context. The test consists of 28 items, each of which involves a child's choosing one of five words to complete a sentence.

TEST III:     Recognition of Reversible Words in Context. The list consists of a short story in which 23 words can be reversed, each of which involves the possibility of making a full or partial reversal.

TEST IV:      Word-Recognition Techniques, Visual Analysis, Locating Usable Elements. This is a 36-item test involving a picture that is accompanied by a long word containing the shorter word identified by the picture. For example, the word *addressing* would be accompanied by a picture of a dress.

TEST V:       Word-Recognition Techniques, Visual Analysis, Syllabication. This is a 24-item test requiring the child to draw lines between the syllables of lengthy words.

TEST VI:      Word-Recognition Techniques, Visual Analysis, Locating Root Words. A 30-item test consisting of words containing word roots around which the child draws a circle.

TEST VII:     Phonetic Knowledge, General Word Elements. A 30-item test which involves a child's encircling one of five word elements pronounced by the examiner.

TEST VIII:    Recognition of Beginning Sounds. A 30-item test which involves a child's encircling one of five words that begins with the same sound as the word pronounced by the examiner.

TEST IX:      Rhyming Words. A 30-item test which involves a child's encircling one of five words that rhymes with the word pronounced by the examiner.

TEST X:       Letter Sounds. A 30-item test which involves a child's encircling one of four letters that stands for the sound uttered by the examiner.

TEST XI:      Word Synthesis. A test which measures a child's ability to blend parts of a word into a whole, both visually and phonetically.

Although the Bond, Clymer and Hoyt tests just described were designed for use in grades three through six, they can be used to great advantage with disabled readers on the junior and senior high school levels.

Other group reading tests which provide diagnostic data relevant to sight vocabulary and word analysis include The California Reading Tests (California Test Bureau), Chicago Reading Tests (E. M. Hale), Doren Diagnostic Reading Test (Educational Test Bureau), Diagnostic Reading Tests (Committee on Diagnostic Reading Tests), Iowa Every-Pupil Test of Basic Skills (Houghton Mifflin Company). See Appendix C for additional information regarding these and other tests.

## In-Depth Tests

Several individually administered tests of a more detailed nature are available when such data are needed. One such test, a fairly recent one, is *The Diagnostic Reading Scales.** These scales provide the examiner with a wide range of diagnostic information.

The first unit of *The Diagnostic Reading Scales* is devoted to three word lists designed to test a pupil's skills at word recognition and analysis and to determine the level of reading passages to which he should be introduced. According to the author, these reading passages (they number twenty-two and are of graduated difficulty) simulate the type and range of material that might be found in classroom reading assignments at levels ranging from midfirst grade to eighth grade. The materials include narrative, expository and descriptive selections from the natural and physical sciences, social sciences and children's literature. The passages yield three levels for each pupil. These are the instructional level, independent level and potential level. The latter is determined by ascertaining the auding level.

The battery closes with six supplementary phonic tests which furnish information about a child's knowledge of consonant sounds, vowel sounds, consonant blends, common syllables, blends and letter sounds.

One of the authors has employed the foregoing test in a reading clinic setting with excellent results. Other tests which merit attention include the *Durrell Analysis of Reading Difficulty* and the *Gates-McKillop Reading Diagnostic Test.* (See Appendixes C and C1 for additional information regarding these tests.)

## Informal Testing

Teachers may acquire information about a child's sight vocabulary and word-attack skill by the use of informal tests. Selecting the fifteenth or twentieth word from several representative pages of a reader or textbook provides an effective word-recognition test. When this is done, two copies should be prepared. One is placed before the child and the other is used by the teacher for recording responses. A small card can be employed to expose words tachistoscopically. When a child misses a word that has been flashed, it can be presented a second time without any time limit. Such a procedure will give the teacher a useful insight into a child's word-analysis skill. Usually, a flash recognition vocabulary

---

*Authored by George Spache and published by the California Test Bureau.

of ninety-five per cent indicates an adequate sight vocabulary for fluent reading.

Teachers interested in formulating informal tests of word-perception skills should consult Kottmeyer, Chapter VII. (2) Kottmeyer's informal inventory consists of fourteen questions about a child's word-perception skill accompanied by exercises which help provide needed answers. Some of the questions are "Does he try to use context clues?" "Does he know the names of the letters?" "Can he blend letter sounds to form words?"

## Is There a Best Method?

As stated by one of the authors in an earlier publication, when the numerous methods of teaching words are pondered, many teachers are in a quandary. (3) Each specialist (Gates, Monroe, Dolch, Fernald, all renowned in the reading field), advocates a different method. What is the answer? What should be used? Is there a best method?

Basically, there are three methods for teaching words to disabled readers: the visual, the phonic and the kinesthetic. There is no best method per se. Only when a corrective program is based on individual needs can any method be cited as superior.

For example, Marion Monroe tells of a seven-year-old boy who suffered from a severe reading disability of a neurological origin. No matter how hard the child tried, he was unable to remember words when the usual sight method was employed. As soon as the cause was uncovered, he was taught by tracing large models of words while saying them out loud. (4) This was a kinesthetic approach. And it worked! Soon he was able to recognize words and began to show definite and competent progress.

Bond's research shows that children suffering from hearing losses are at a marked disadvantage in learning to read when a purely phonetic method is employed. On the other hand, he found that the "look and say method" does not penalize the child who has an auditory loss. (5) It is evident that if a child suffers from auditory or visual deficiencies, it is wise to choose a method of instruction that minimizes the handicap as much as possible.

It is also a mistake to assume that just because children are free from discernible sensory impairments they will learn just as easily with one method as another. Any teacher can convince himself of the falsity of this belief by checking the auditory and visual memory spans of a group of children. Not infrequently does one find that students with fine visual memories have much poorer auditory memories or vice versa.

For seemingly inexplicable reasons some children have great difficulty in making visual associations but show excellent phonic aptitude. In such cases, Monroe's phonetic approach of blending and forming word elements into whole words is to be recommended.

For the child who is adept at making visual associations but shows ineptitude when phonetic approaches are employed, Gates' method of stressing the general configuration of words as a basis for recognition is appropriate. Since it is not possible to tell which method will work best in an individual case, the teacher must be flexible and versatile. If Harry does not respond favorably to one method, another method must be tried.

In final analysis, if there is a best method, we are forced to term it eclectic. When an individual method is used to the exclusion of others, some children are doomed to failure regardless of how sincere, competent and enthusiastic the teacher. Today many teachers use the popular flash method. It is true that most children learn easily and quickly when this method is employed, but still there are needless fatalities. The number of failures could be reduced markedly if the teacher used several avenues of approach so the student could choose the particular method or combination of methods that seem to be best suited to his individual needs.

A simple yet ingenious test developed by Robert E. Mills provides a useful tool in studying this problem. *The Mills Learning Ability Test\** introduces groups of words in four ways: visual, phonic, kinesthetic and combined; it then checks retention after an interval of one day. By means of the test, an examiner can determine the particular approach for which a given child shows the most aptitude. It should be obvious that the test is a valuable tool in a reading diagnosis.

## General Procedures in Detecting and Diagnosing Word-Perception Difficulties by Using Standardized Tests

Earlier in this chapter, space was devoted to informal testing as a means of evaluating and diagnosing word-perception problems. In certain instances, observation and informal testing are all that is required. When, however, more complex cases are encountered, a formal evaluation based on the use of cumulative records, interviews and standardized

---

\*Available by writing to The Mills Center, 1512 Broward Blvd., Fort Lauderdale, Florida.

tests is needed. The following procedures suggest an approach to a more complete and objective analysis of difficulties in word perception.

1. In the primary grades, keep individual records of words not mastered which are part of the sight vocabulary of the readers used.

2. Use word-recognition tests or appropriate sight-vocabulary lists in all grades above the first. (For tests see Appendix C.) Employ these at the beginning of the year in order to discover the pupils who are weak in word-recognition and word-analysis skills. (See the list of sight-vocabulary tests which follows.)

3. In order to locate retarded readers, administer at the beginning of the school year a survey test in silent reading to all pupils above the third grade. Determine reading potential by comparing reading level with mental level on a nonverbal intelligence test or with an auding level. Do not overlook the disabled readers, that is, those reading below grade who have the potential to do better.

4. Administer, in grades above the first, a standardized oral reading test to all retarded readers who have potential. Do this early in the school year. Keep an individual record of the grade scores, reading errors and word-analysis deficiencies revealed. Transfer these to the reading inventory. (See Appendix C for a description of oral reading tests and record forms at the end of this chapter and Chapter 6.)

5. Administer one or more of the group tests in word recognition or word analysis listed in the Appendixes. Use this procedure in all grades above the primary with pupils who are retarded in six months or more on a silent reading test. From these data, determine individual grade levels of mastery in word recognition and word analysis. Record the skills in these areas that have not been mastered on the *Reading Inventory* and the *Individual Diagnostic Reading Summary*. (See end of this chapter and Chapter 6 for these forms.)

## Sight-vocabulary Lists

Botel, Morton, *Bucks County 1185 Common Words*. A list of 41 preprimer words, 67 primer words, 124 first-grade words, 359 second-grade words and 594 third-grade words. *How to Teach Reading*, Chicago: Follett Publishing Company, 1959, pp. 103-113.

Dolch, Edward W., *A Basic Sight Vocabulary*. A list of 220 words said to make up more than fifty per cent of the running words in elementary school reading materials. Printed cards useful in teaching these words are available from Garrard Publishing Co., Champaign, Illinois. *The Elementary School Journal* 36: 456-460, 1936.

————, *Ninety-five Nouns Common to the Three Word Lists*. A list of nouns common to three first-grade vocabulary lists. Picture word cards for teaching these are available from Garrard Publishing Co., Champaign, Illinois, 1941.

DURRELL, DONALD, A list of words according to intermediate grade levels: fourth, fifth, sixth. *Improving Reading Instruction,* New York: World Book Company, 1956, pp. 367-392.

FRY, EDWARD, "Teaching a Basic Reading Vocabulary." A list of 100 first-grade words, 100 second-grade words and 100 third-grade words. *Elementary English* 37: 38-42, 1960.

GATES, ARTHUR, *A Reading Vocabulary for the Primary Grades.* A list of 1,811 words, arranged in three levels of 500 words each and a supplementary list of 311 words. Bureau of Publications, Teachers College, Columbia University, 1935.

KEARNEY, NOLAN C., "An Analysis of the Vocabulary of First Grade Reading Material." A list of the 441 most common words found in 121 preprimers, primers, and first readers. *Journal of Educational Research* 43: 481-493, 1950.

KNIPP, HELEN, *Basic Vocabulary Phrases and Sentences for Early Reading Instruction,* Keystone View Co., Meadville, Pennsylvania, 1952.

KRANTZ, L. L., *The Author's Word List for Primary Grades.* A graded list of words based on the study of vocabulary of 84 preprimers, 69 primers, 84 first readers, 85 second readers and 47 third readers. Minneapolis, Minn.: Curriculum Research Company, 1945.

RINSLAND, HENRY, *A Basic Vocabulary of Elementary School Children.* A list of 14,571 words which is based upon words used in writing by children in grades 1-8. New York: The Macmillan Company, 1945.

STONE, CLARENCE, *Word Lists by Reading Levels.* A list of 100 preprimer words, 225 primer words, 455 first-reader words, 1,101 second-reader words and 1,916 third-reader words. Manchester, Mo.: Webster Publishing, 1950.

THORNDIKE, EDWARD L., *A Teachers Wordbook of 30,000 words.* A list based on a count of 10,000,000 words from both adult and children's books. Each word is categorized with a symbol denoting the thousand in which it belongs. Words in the first 5000 are designated as first half or second half of the thousand. Bureau of Publications, Teachers College, Columbia University, 1944.

## Reading Inventory and Progress Record

Following the diagnosis, the *self-directed corrective program* will be initiated. A systematic record of this program is made possible by utilizing the *Reading Inventory and Progress Record.* Errors, difficulties and faulty reading habits discovered in the reading diagnosis should be entered on the *Reading Inventory and Progress Record* by placing an X in the first column following each designated reading difficulty. This entry should be repeated in the succeeding columns at the end of each corrective period if no improvement is apparent. When improvement is made, a single diagonal line should be entered for each of the pertinent items. Absence of an entry after an item indicates the difficulty has been mastered. In this way, the Inventory provides a systematic record

| READING INVENTORY AND PROGRESS RECORD | | | | | | | | | |
|---|---|---|---|---|---|---|---|---|---|
| Disability present ⊠          Disability present but improved ◩ | | | | | | | | | |
| SPECIFIC READING DISABILITIES | | | | | | | | | |

| | Instructional Periods (weeks, months, etc.) | | | | | | | |
|---|---|---|---|---|---|---|---|---|
| | 1 | 2 | 3 | 4 | 5 | 6 | 7 | 8 |
| **A. READING HABITS** | | | | | | | | |
| 1. Omits words | | | | | | | | |
| 2. Adds words | | | | | | | | |
| 3. Substitutes words | | | | | | | | |
| 4. Repeats words | | | | | | | | |
| 5. Reverses words | | | | | | | | |
| 6. Reads word by word | | | | | | | | |
| 7. Vocalizes excessively | | | | | | | | |
| 8. Ignores punctuation | | | | | | | | |
| 9. Points to words | | | | | | | | |
| 10. Expressionless reading | | | | | | | | |
| 11. Faulty voice volume or pitch | | | | | | | | |
| 12. Poor book-body position | | | | | | | | |
| 13. Head movements | | | | | | | | |
| 14. Poor enunciation | | | | | | | | |
| **B. INADEQUATE SIGHT VOCABULARY** | | | | | | | | |
| 1. Configuration clues | | | | | | | | |
| 2. Contextual clues | | | | | | | | |
| 3. Phonetic analysis using | | | | | | | | |
| a. Initial sounds | | | | | | | | |
| b. Initial blends | | | | | | | | |
| c. Medial sounds | | | | | | | | |
| d. Final sounds | | | | | | | | |
| e. Final blends | | | | | | | | |
| f. Syllabication | | | | | | | | |
| 4. Structural analysis using | | | | | | | | |
| a. Root word | | | | | | | | |
| b. Compound words | | | | | | | | |
| c. Plurals | | | | | | | | |
| d. Prefixes | | | | | | | | |
| e. Suffixes | | | | | | | | |
| 5. Dictionary skills | | | | | | | | |
| **C. INADEQUATE MEANING VOCABULARY** | | | | | | | | |
| 1. Oral vocabulary | | | | | | | | |
| 2. General vocabulary | | | | | | | | |
| 3. Technical vocabulary | | | | | | | | |
| 4. Dictionary skills | | | | | | | | |
| **D. INADEQUATE COMPREHENSION AND STUDY SKILLS** | | | | | | | | |
| 1. Reading in thought units (phrasing) | | | | | | | | |
| 2. Retelling a story | | | | | | | | |
| 3. Following a sequence of events | | | | | | | | |
| 4. Following directions | | | | | | | | |
| 5. Locating central thoughts of paragraphs | | | | | | | | |
| 6. Detecting related details | | | | | | | | |
| 7. Reading maps, charts, tables, graphs | | | | | | | | |
| 8. Locating information | | | | | | | | |
| 9. Drawing conclusions | | | | | | | | |
| 10. Summarizing | | | | | | | | |
| 11. Outlining | | | | | | | | |
| 12. Rate | | | | | | | | |

of the effectiveness of the corrective program and the progress of the learner.

Suggested self-directed instructional material for word recognition and word analysis is listed and described in Chapter 5.

### SUPPLEMENTARY PROBLEMS FOR ORAL AND WRITTEN DISCUSSION

1. Summarize the descriptive evaluation of an oral reading test from Buros Mental Measurements Yearbook.
2. Summarize the descriptive evaluation of a survey test in silent reading from Buros Mental Measurements Yearbook.
3. Summarize the descriptive evaluation of a diagnostic test in reading from Buros Mental Measurements Yearbook.
4. Summarize an informal method of evaluating competence in reading.
5. How can a child's independent reading status be determined?
6. Administer an oral reading test to a pupil in the intermediate or upper grades and record the results obtained on the Reading Inventory.
7. What information in addition to the pupil's reading level can be gained through the use of an oral reading test?
8. What are some of the ways you can ascertain sight vocabulary mastery in the primary grades?
9. Why must competence in word recognition be determined in evaluating a silent reading test score?
10. What precautions must be taken in evaluating achievement in terms of grade norms?

### REFERENCES

1. *Gilmore Oral Reading Test. Manual of Directions.* Copyright 1952 by Harcourt, Brace & World, Inc., New York. All rights reserved. Reprinted by permission.
2. WILLIAM KOTTMEYER, *Teacher's Guide for Remedial Reading* (Manchester, Mo.: Webster Publishing, 1959).
3. DELWYN SCHUBERT, "Whose Brand of Reading Methods is the Best Buy?" *The Clearing House* (January, 1953), pp. 266-267.
4. MARION MONROE *Growing Into Reading* (Chicago: Scott, Foresman & Company, 1951), pp. 63-65.
5. GUY BOND, *The Auditory and Speech Characteristics of Poor Readers,* Teachers College Contributions to Education, No. 657, Teachers College, Columbia University.

### SELECTED READINGS

DEBOER, JOHN and MARTHA DALLMAN, *The Teaching of Reading* rev. ed., New York: Holt, Rinehart & Winston, Inc., 1964, ch. 6A.

BOND, GUY and MILES TINKER, *Reading Problems: Their Diagnosis and Correction* 2nd ed., New York: Appleton-Century-Crofts, 1967, ch. 9.

DECHANT, EMERALD, *Improving the Teaching of Reading,* Englewood Cliffs, N. J.: Prentice-Hall, Inc., 1964, pp. 223-233.

OTTO, WAYNE and RICHARD McMENEMY, *Corrective and Remedial Teaching,* New York: Houghton Mifflin Company, 1966, pp. 128-139.

SCHUBERT, DELWYN, *Readings in Reading: Practice-Theory-Research,* New York: Thomas Y. Crowell, Company, 1968, selection 46 by Mills.

STRANG, RUTH, *Diagnostic Teaching of Reading,* New York: McGraw-Hill Book Company, 1964, ch. 4.

Chapter

5

# Improving Word-Recognition and Word-Analysis Skills Through Individualized Correction

Pupils in the primary and intermediate grades who are deficient in word-recognition and word-analysis skills are in dire need of help. Teachers need more than basal readers to assist these pupils; they need supplementary instructional material that will provide individualized practice to overcome specific reading difficulties. The following instructional techniques and materials provide a useful approach to the problem.

## Emphasizing Wide Reading

Practice on common words and an introduction to new words take place most naturally when children engage in easy, pleasurable reading. Individualizing and personalizing a child's reading program requires knowing books and understanding the child and his interests. The teacher who is faced with the task of finding the right book for the right child should be guided by the following principles:

1. Utilize the child's present interests. No matter how immature his present interests are, it is essential to begin by introducing materials which are related to them. If the child is given material which he sees as vital and functional, interest becomes spontaneous.
2. Provide reading materials which are on or slightly below the pupil's level of reading ability. Easy material is essential for success. And success generates interest.
3. Acquaint yourself with book lists and bibliographies of children's books. These materials simplify finding the right book for the right child. Two excellent books in this regard are *A Place to Start* and *Good Reading for Poor Readers.* (1) For additional suggestions see Appendix F2.

85

## Utilizing Word Lists

The vocabulary lists described in connection with diagnostic procedures (see Chapter 4, pages 80-81) have considerable value in a corrective program for disabled readers. They help answer questions such as "What words are found most frequently in primary books?" "What words should be taught first when working with a disabled reader?" "What fourth-grade words should a pupil know on sight?"

Although compilers of word lists have rendered a great service, certain points should be considered by those who wish to use them. (2)

1. If a word list is based in part or in its entirety on the writing vocabulary of adults. it may not apply to the reading vocabulary of elementary school children.
2. Since a child's reading vocabulary is usually larger than his writing vocabulary. it is not wise to confine children's reading vocabulary to a list based on writing vocabulary.
3. Strict vocabulary control is likely to be debilitating to content. Content area subjects such as social studies and science will suffer if vocabulary control is too stringent. Remedial teachers should be cognizant of the fact that content field reading usually involves a heavier vocabulary burden.
4. Frequency of use, rather than word difficulty, is provided by vocabulary word lists.

When word lists are used for word study with pupils, attempts should be made to provide meaningful contextual settings. It is also advisable to employ a variety of approaches to help sustain interest. When possible have the child evolve a progress chart that will highlight his vocabulary growth in a dramatic way.

## Instructional Materials for Correcting
## Deficiencies in Sight Vocabulary

When individual pupils or groups of pupils are deficient in word-recognition skill, corrective practice can be individualized by using available commercial material such as:*

A. *Basic Sight Vocabulary Cards*: These instructional materials are for use with slow readers and include two hundred twenty words which constitute more than fifty per cent of all words encountered in ordinary reading. (For use with individual children or children working in pairs; $1.10; Garrard.)
B. *Durrell's Hand Tachistoscope*: A simple tachistoscope (quick exposure device) consisting of an oak-tag cover, an aperture, a shutter

---

*All games are designated by an asterisk.

and a series of word lists on strips of oak-tag board. (For use with individual children or children working in pairs; $1.30; World.)

C. *Educational Password Game*:* Based on the popular television show, this game uses basic sight and picture words found in primary and elementary readers. (For use with pairs of children or a group of children; $2.00; Milton Bradley.)

D. *Five First Steps and Pop Words*: These instructional materials involve one hundred fifty common sight or pop words printed in large, clear type on 4 by 6 inch cards. Consonant and vowel sounds are printed on colored cards and include sixteen easy consonants, four consonant digraphs, the sounds of *y* and the hard and soft *c* and *g* sounds, (For use with individual children, children working in pairs, or with a group of children under proper direction; $1.65; Kenworthy.)

E. *Flash Words* (Sets I and II): Two sets of flash cards that help the primary grade child learn words that cannot be mastered through the picture approach. A total of two hundred words are involved. (For use with individual children, children working in pairs, or with a group of children under proper direction; $1.00 a set; Milton Bradley.)

F. *Grab*:* A sight vocabulary game for remedial or classroom teaching. Three levels are involved: Grab Junior (Sets I and II); Grab Senior (Sets III and IV); Advanced Grab (Sets V and VI). (For use with two to four children, potentially self-directive; two sets on any level, $1.75; Teachers' supplies.)

G. *Group Word Teaching Game*:* A bingo-type game designed to teach the two hundred twenty basic sight words evolved by Dolch. (For use with two or more children, potentially self-directive; $1.59; Garrard.)

H. *Happy Bears Reading Game*:* A game in which children learn common nouns by matching pictures with words under them. Since the pairs of pictures differ, attention is drawn to the word under each picture. (For use with individual children, potentially self-directive; $.60; Garrard.)

I. *Jumble Jingle Flip Its*:* The flip-it device consists of a small, spiral-bound booklet attached to a paddle with a handle extension. The child holds the paddle and material with one hand while using his other hand to flip the pages. The Jumble Jingle Flip Its, a set of three flip its, self teaches one hundred twenty-two primer sight words drawn from lists evolved by Dolch and Gates. (For use with individual children, potentially self-directive; $3.75 for a set of three; Primary Playhouse.)

J. *Linguistic Block Series*:* The First Rolling Reader (primer level) consists of a set of ten blocks involving fifty pre-primer and primer words; The Second Rolling Reader (first-grade level) consists of a set of ten blocks involving fifty-four verbs, nouns and adjectives; The Third Rolling Reader (second-grade level) consists of a set of ten blocks involving fifty-four auxiliary verbs and negative constructions. (For use with individual children, children working in pairs, or a small group of children; $4.40 a set; Scott, Foresman.)

K. *Match*\* (Sets I and II). A reading game consisting of two sets of cards, each set containing half of the ninety-five commonest nouns evolved by Dolch. (For use with one or two children, potentially self-directive; $1.00 per set; Garrard.)

L. *Matchettes*: A set of ten inlay boards, $8\frac{1}{2}$" by $11\frac{1}{2}$", which provide experiences in identifying and matching illustrations and words. Removable pieces are printed on both sides for dual matching activities. Each board shows six objects and words that are in lower-case manuscript letters. (For use with individual children or children working in pairs; $4.50 per set of ten; Judy.)

M. *Picture Word Builder*: A training aid in which thirty-six familiar objects on heavy cards are die-cut so only the correct word can be inserted to complete the word and picture matching. (For use with individual children or children working in pairs; $.60; Milton Bradley.)

N. *Picture Word Lotto:*\* A game that teaches letter and word recognition. Played by matching picture to picture, word to picture and finally word to word. (For use with two or more children, potentially self-directive; $1.00; Garrard.)

O. *Picture Words for Beginners:*\* A matching game designed to help the primary grade child add over one hundred words to his vocabulary. The pupil learns to associate pictures with words found in first reading books. (For use with individual children, potentially self-directive; $1.00; Milton Bradley.)

P. *Popper Words* (Sets I and II): Popper Words, Set I contains the easier one-half of the two hundred twenty Basic Sight Vocabulary evolved by Dolch. Popper Words, Set II contains the harder one-half of this vocabulary group. (For use with individual children, children working in pairs, or with a group of children under proper direction; $1.00 per set; Garrard.)

Q. *Primary Reading Cards* (Beginning and Advanced): These instructional materials consist of two boxes of cards containing words appearing most frequently in primary books. The cards are three by four inches in size and are set in extra large manuscript for easy reading. (For use with individual children, children working in pairs or with a group of children under proper direction; $1.25 a box; Educational Card.)

R. *Probe:*\* A provocative game in which each player selects a word of twelve or fewer letters which he keeps secret. (He may use the dictionary in making his selection.) Other players try to guess it, letter by letter. Equipment includes four racks, four decks of letter cards, each of a different color and consisting of ninety-six cards and four letter card upright holders. The three hundred eighty-four cards in the game provide combinations for thousands of words. (For use with two to four children; $6.00; Parker.)

S. *Read-To-Read Puzzles*: A set of four puzzles that provide drill in matching word forms, associating words with pictures and building a sight vocabulary of common primer words. (For use with individual children or children working in pairs; $3.50 per set; Ben-G-Products.)

T. *Tumble Words:*\* A vocabulary building game consisting of lettered cubes and a shaker. The object of the game is to build as many words as possible from the letters appearing on the cubes after they have rolled from the shaker. A point system is described for recording the successes of the players. (For use with two children or a group of children, potentially self-directive; $1.00; Kohner Brothers.)

U. *Word Rummy:*\* A card game involving fifty-two cards on which appear twenty-six capital and twenty-six small letters in four different colors: red, green, blue and black. The object of the game is to form words or to regroup letters to form other words. The game has value in building an awareness of letter sounds, spelling skill and sight vocabulary. (For use with two or more children, potentially self-directive; $1.25; Educational Cards, Inc.)

When individual pupils or groups of pupils are deficient in word recognition skill, individualized practice can be provided by using teacher- or pupil-made materials such as the following:

A. *Bowling:*\* Make a bowling-pin tachistoscope (quick exposure device) of a bowling pin. At the center of the pin make an opening so words from tagboard by doing the following: Color and cut out the form which have been printed on strips of oak tag and slipped behind the structure can be exposed quickly, one at a time. If the child who starts can name ten words, he has made a strike and can try a new strip of words. (For use with two or more children.)

B. *Build-a-Train:*\* Engines and railway cars are cut from oak tag. Each piece has a word printed or written on it. Children who pronounce the words correctly build a train which becomes longer and longer. The object of the game is to see who can build the longest train. (For use with two or more children.)

C. *Card Method:* Each pupil is equipped with a small pile of cards (3 by 5 inch cards cut in half are fine). When an unknown word is encountered the pupil is instructed to write it on a card. The teacher, too, has cards in readiness at all times so any child in the reading circle who misses a word can be given an immediate written record of it. Several times a week the children are allowed to get together in groups of three for the purpose of quizzing each other on their cards. The chances are good that at least one of the three children will know a word. When all are uninformed, the teacher or an especially appointed assistant can provide the help needed. (For use with a group of children, potentially self-directive.)

D. *Carpenter:*\* Draw a picture of a house on a piece of heavy tagboard. Color all but the roof. Paste art corners on the roof, about 1½ inches apart in even rows. On small cards about one-half inch by 1¼ inches print the words for drill. Each card is a shingle. If a child can say the word, he can put it in the art corner and add a shingle to the roof. If he does not know it, it falls to the ground. More than enough cards are given the child so he can have reasonable success in completing the house. (For use with children working in pairs.)

E. *Checkers:** Buy a cheap checkerboard. Cut squares from masking tape that coincide in size with the checkerboard squares and place these on the squares where the checkers are to be placed or moved. Words are then printed on the masking tape (Dolch words frequently are used) right side up and upside down so both players can read any word appearing on the board. The game proceeds like regular checkers, but a child must be able to read the word or words if he is to complete a move. If he fails to call the word correctly, he is told what the word is. He must wait, however, until his next turn before attempting the move again. (For use with two children, potentially self-directive.)

F. *Classification:* Print in color on individual cards two or more words that constitute categories such as *home* and *farm*. Place these in an envelope along with many other cards bearing words such as *kitchen*, *stove* and *barn*. The latter must be categorized under the two words printed in color. By numbering the backs of the word cards, the exercise can be made self-corrective. (For use with individual children, potentially self-directive.)

G. *Color Match:* Words pertaining to various colors are printed on pieces of oak tag. Clothespins that have been colored are placed in an accompanying envelope. The child engaged in color match shows his understanding of the words by attaching the appropriately colored clothespins to the word cards. By coloring the backs of the word cards with the color named, this activity can be made self-corrective. (For use with individual children, potentially self-directive.)

H. *Cookie-pan Magnet Match:* Paste pictures of various objects on the inside surface of a shallow cookie pan. Design matching word cards on the backs of which are glued small pieces of a bar magnet. The pupil engaged in this activity places words in proper position. The word cards are held in position by the pieces of bar magnet which adhere firmly to the metal of the cookie pan. By numbering the pictures and the backs of the word cards, this activity can be made self-corrective. (For use with individual pupils, potentially self-directive.)

I. *Fishing:** Word cards are cut from tagboard in the shape of fish. A paper clip is slipped over each word card. Fishermen are equipped with a pole (short stick) a fish line (20 inches of store string) and a fish hook (small magnet). Each child gets a turn trying to catch a fish. If he can read the word attracted to the magnet, he may keep the fish involved. If he doesn't know it, he shows the word to the other children for a correct response and then returns it, face down, to the fish pond. (For use with two children or a group of children, potentially self-directive.)

J. *Jallopy Derby:** Make a five car race track on as large a piece of cardboard as you can find. Divide the track into three-inch spaces and mark a starting line. Let the children make little cars of paper or buy four little cars at a toy store.

On a small piece of tagboard print the words you want the children to learn. A die is tossed for order of beginning. Number One then tosses the die for his first move. He may move as many spaces as the number on the die if he can say the word on the card he draws. If he cannot say the word, he loses his turn and the next child may use his word or pick a new one. If he decides not to use the missed word, the next player may use it. If no one uses the missed word, it is put at the bottom of the pile. When the game is over, special help is given with the missed words at the bottom of the pile.

Each race is one lap. The winner is the one who comes out even with the finish line first. Should a potential winner throw a six and have only four or five spaces left, he may move just one space for the word he can say. Coming out even with the finish line adds excitement to the game. It gives each other child a chance to become a last-minute winner. (For use with one, two, three or four children.)

K. *Match-A-Picture*: An ingeniously designed self-corrective exercise can be made by pasting a picture on a piece of oak tag on which two matched and parallel columns of synonyms or antonyms have been written. The left-hand column is numbered from top to bottom so no difficulty can be experienced in arranging it properly at a later time. After this had been done, the oak tag is cut into individual word cards and the pieces are placed in a stiff manila folder. The pupil who engages in this exercise begins by arranging the left-hand column as numbered. He then arranges in a parallel column the matching pieces. All the pieces involved are put in position inside the folder. When the pupil is ready to check his work, he closes the folder and flips it over. Upon opening the folder a complete picture appears. Any error manifests itself in a jumbled picture. (For use with individual pupils, potentially self-directive.)

L. *Matching*: Print words that designate specific colors (*snow, fire engine, violets*, etc.) on a sheet of oak tag. Place small cards of different colors in an attached envelope. The child matches the colored cards with the words. By using an identification scheme on the backs of the color cards, this activity can be made self-corrective. (For use with individual children, potentially self-directive.)

M. *Old Maid*:* Print words on pieces of oak tag the size of playing cards. Complete twenty cards and then make a duplicate set so twenty pairs of words result. Print one Old Maid card or, if you wish, one word alone may be used to designate the Old Maid card. Distribute the cards and begin with the person to the left of the dealer who starts the game by drawing a card from the person at his right. As pairs are formed, the words are called and placed on the table. This continues until all pairs are matched and one person holds the Old Maid. (For use with two to four children, potentially self-directive.)

N. *One Look Game*:* The Dolch cards are used with this activity. Pupils work in pairs with one child acting as a helper. The pack of cards is placed before the learner who picks up one card at a time, calls the word and then hands it to the helper. The helper retains those cards called correctly and segregates those called incorrectly. Any marked hesitation constitutes an error. When all cards have been called, the number of words missed is calculated and recorded in chart form. The helper then calls each word for the player who repeats aloud each word he has failed. The entire pack is reshuffled and is made ready for another "one look" trial. (For use with children working in pairs.)

O. *Pairs*:† Pairs is a game similar to rummy and can be played by two to five children. Twenty-five words, each of which appear twice on oak-tag playing cards, make a fifty card deck. The object of the game is to get as many pairs as possible. When playing the game, five cards are dealt to each player and the remainder of the deck is placed face down on the table. The player to the right of the dealer begins by asking a fellow player for a specific card that will match one in his hand. If the latter has the card requested, he must give it up. If he does not have it, the asker draws one card from the pile and terminates his play. The player who gets the card for which he asks (should he not know the word he may solicit help from anyone present), either from another player or from the pile, gets a second turn. As soon as a player has a pair, he places it on the table. The player with the most pairs wins.

P. *Pick-A-Chip*:* Divide Dolch's Basic Sight Vocabulary Words into four sections of fifty-five words each. Type or write the words on pieces of masking tape and place these on poker chips of four colors. Deposit the chips in four small boxes of matching colors. A pupil starts the game by choosing a color and then gives a spinner a whirl. He picks as many chips from his color section as the spinner indicates. If he fails to say one of the words he is told what it is, but he must return the chip to the box and pass the spinner to the next player. The winner is the pupil who has acquired the most chips. (For use with two to four children.)

Q. *Picture Checkerboard*:* The teacher writes sixteen nouns on the board in numbered order. The children fold a sheet of drawing paper into sixteen squares and number them correspondingly. They then draw pictures of the nouns on the numbered squares. Later, papers can be exchanged and corrected. (For use with individual children or a group of children.)

R. *Picture Dictionary Match*: Paste pictures cut from a ten-cent store dictionary in a row on a 9 by 12 inch card. Under each picture draw a space box 1½ by ½ inches. Prepare small word cards and put these in an envelope which remains attached to the picture card. By numbering the pictures and the backs of the word cards, this activity can be made self-corrective. (For use with individual children, potentially self-directive.)

S. *Picture Riddle Matcho*:* Children cut pictures from old magazines and place them in envelopes — five to an envelope. The teacher writes a riddle about one of the pictures and places it in the envelope with the pictures. The child who chooses the envelope selects the pictures which answer the riddle. A marking scheme can be devised to make this activity self-corrective. (For use with individual children, potentially self-directive.)

---

†A game devised by Edward Fry, Rutgers University.

T. *Ring a Word:* ⁕ Utilize heavy plywood in constructing a board 2 by 3 feet in size. Space five nails on the board and paint numbers from one to five under the nails. Print words on small cards and hang them on the nails. (Easiest cards should be on Number One nail and hardest cards on Number Five nail.) Equip children with a box of Mason jar rubber rings. The directions for the game are "Ring a word and score the points if you can say it." (For use with two or more children.)

U. *Shoestring Matcho:* Two rows of mixed synonyms or an antonym and synonym row are written side by side. Shoestrings are attached to the right of the first row by knotting the ends on the reverse side. The child designates the correct answer by slipping the shoestring into the proper hole before words in the second column. A marking scheme can be devised on the reverse side to make this activity self-corrective. (For use with individual children, potentially self-directive.)

V. *Tachistoscope:* Let a child find a picture that interests him. Mount this picture on oak tag and cut two horizontal slits 1½ inches long and ⅜ of an inch apart. Words to be learned are printed or typed on strips of oak tag about 1½ inches wide. The strips are then inserted in the slits and pulled through so one word is exposed at a time. (For use with children working in pairs.)

W. *Word Basket Ball:* ⁕ Remove the top and one of the long sides of a packing carton. Use green and white paint to give what remains the appearance of a basketball court. Baskets can be simulated by pasting two small paper bags on the outside ends of the box. If a player can call correctly a word he has drawn from a word pile, he pushes the word card through a slot above his team's basket and his side gets two points. If he calls incorrectly, someone on the other team tries. A referee will determine if the word is said correctly or not. The score can be kept by counting the number of cards in each bag. (For use with two children or two groups of children under proper direction.)

X. *Word Authors:* ⁕ Words are printed on corners of cards — four cards to a set. A set can consist of four colors, four animals, four synonyms and the like. Each child is dealt four cards and one child begins the game by calling for a word. If he gets the word, he may continue to call for words. When his opponent indicates that he does not have the card called for, the child draws from the deck of cards that is face down on the table. The child who acquires the most sets wins. (For use with two to four children, potentially self-directive.)

Y. *Word File Pictures:* The name of an object is printed at the top of a card, and a picture or drawing is placed below to illustrate it. On the opposite side of the cards just the word is printed. The child tries to read the word and then checks his response by looking at the picture on the front side of the card. (For use with individual children, potentially self-directive.)

Z. *Wordo:* ⁕ The teacher with the help of her children prepares cardboard master cards 8 by 11 inches in size. These master cards are blocked off vertically and horizontally into twenty-five small squares. The middle space is marked *free*. Individual words that are troublesome are placed on the twenty-four squares that remain. Each cardboard master card must have the same words but in different positions. The twenty-four words are typed or printed on small cards and placed in an envelope. As individual words are drawn from the envelope and called aloud, the players find the words on their master cards and cover them with a marker of some sort. The marker may be a kernel of corn, a bean or a small piece of cardboard. The first child to cover a row of words in a straight line, vertically, horizontally or diagonally, calls out "wordo." If he has not erred, he is declared the winner. (For use with two or more children, potentially self-directive.)

## Utilizing Context Clues

As stated by Hildreth, "inferring the meaning of a word from what went before, and deliberately reading ahead for clues to meaning, is an essential technique for word recognition." (3)

Because of its importance to word recognition, practice in utilizing contextual clues should be provided for disabled readers. Pupils should be given sample sentences which are designed to show that the necessary context may come before, after, or both before and after a strange word. Examples should be given which show that the context may be a phrase, a sentence or a paragraph; it may be an appositive, a definition, an example or another sentence related to that in which the unknown word appears.

When a child encounters a strange word and is stymied by it, we are too prone to encourage an immediate "sound-it-out" approach. It is more judicious to encourage the pupil to skip the unknown word and read the entire sentence. At this point, the pupil might ask himself, for example, "What word starting with *ch* would make sense in this sentence?" A combination of approaches is likely to be more effective than putting all word-attack eggs in one basket.

## Instructional Materials for Correcting
## Deficiencies in Context Skills

When individual pupils or groups of pupils are deficient in their use of context clues, corrective practice can be individualized by using teacher-made materials such as the following:

A. Present sentences in which words are missing. The pupils are instructed to read the sentences and decide which words fit the blanks most appropriately. Examples:

1. They put the _____ in the bank.
   *paper, letter, money*
2. The day was bright and _____.
   *sunny, dark, cloudy*
3. Bill had to _____ if he should _____ the fort against attack.
   *defend, decide*

B. Present sentences in which a phonic clue is given to aid the pupil in providing missing words. Pupils are instructed to think of words which fit the blanks most appropriately. Examples:

1. Betty said she would r_____ the ball on the floor.
2. The cat dr_____ the milk.
3. He was going to _____ow his shoe at the barking dog.

C. Present sentences which contain unusual words whose meaning can be arrived at by using contextual clues. Pupils are instructed to read the sentences carefully before deciding on an answer. Examples:

1. John will *deflate* the tire by opening the valve.
   Deflate means (1) put air in (2) let air out (3) turn over (4) damage
2. The *edifice* was of brick and covered a city block.
   Edifice means (1) bicycle (2) locomotive (3) building (4) ship
3. The old trunk was *capacious* enough to hold all John's clothes.
   Capacious means (1) unclean (2) colorful (3) small (4) large

## Encouraging Dictionary Usage

Disabled readers in the middle and upper grades should be encouraged to have a dictionary on hand when reading a book. The dictionary is a valuable aid in word identification, pronunciation and meaning. Unfortunately, many disabled readers have a distinct aversion for the dictionary. This antipathy, undoubtedly, is an outgrowth of their lack of skill in using the volume. In any event, it is necessary for a teacher to exercise all of his ingenuity when trying to instruct students in dictionary usage.

Subskills which are essential to locating words and pronouncing them should be systematically evaluated when a student is unable to use the dictionary. To help teachers in their evaluation and instructional program involving use of the dictionary, the following outline is provided.

1. Location skills
   a. Knowing alphabetical sequence;
   b. Determining what letters precede and follow a given letter;
   c. Alphabetizing words according to their beginning letters;

    d. Alphabetizing words according to beginning two- and three-letter patterns;

    e. Using guide words intelligently;

    f. Knowing the value of thumb indexes;

    g. Learning to open the dictionary that lacks thumb indexes at a point near the word.

2. Pronunciation Skills

    a. Using key words to interpret diacritical markings;

    b. Recognizing syllables;

    c. Understanding and interpreting primary and secondary accent marks;

    d. Understanding and appreciating the "schwa" sound;

    e. Reading phonetic spelling.

3. Definition Skills

    a. Realizing that a word may have multiple meanings;

    b. Comprehending definitions provided;

    c. Choosing from several definitions given the one that gives the best explanation of the meaning of the unknown word.

## Utilizing Phonics*

There are those who attribute all reading failure to a lack of phonic training. By the same token, there are those who attribute reading failure to an overemphasis on phonics. To attribute all reading failure to too little or too much phonics is unrealistic. The reasons why children do poorly in reading are multiple. Lack of phonic skill could at best be only one of the factors contributing to a child's disability.

Most teachers are in a quandary when it comes to phonics. This is understandable. Research has shown that many experienced teachers lack knowledge in this area. (4) Many have had little or no preparation in the teaching of phonics. In addition, the controversies that have raged and continue to rage over how reading should be taught add to the confusion. If the experts can't agree, what should teachers do? What specific information do teachers need to identify a pupil's weakness or disability in the phonic area? (See Inventory on page 82.)

Opinions regarding phonics and phonic systems are diverse. Most authorities, however, would agree with the following generalizations:

1. *Auditory perception is basic to a phonic program.* Unless a pupil can hear similarities and differences between sounds, he cannot be expected to associate sounds with printed letters. For pupils who lack auditory discrimination, a sequential program in ear training is recom-

---

*For definitions of phonics and related terminology, see Appendix A1.

mended. It would include auditory perception of initial consonants, blends, rhymes, medial vowels and syllables.*

2. *Phonics instruction should proceed from simple to complex.* It is unwise for a teacher to spend time on difficult principles that are limited in applicability when simpler elements and generalizations could be employed. For example, a pupil should learn the sounds of initial consonants and digraphs before being introduced to diphthongs.

3. *Periods devoted to phonics should be brief and enjoyable.* There is nothing exciting about phonics. Exposing a child to too much work on sounds at any one time can be deadening. To minimize boredom many teachers employ a game approach to learning phonics.

4. *The phonics program for a given child should be individualized.* A teacher should determine what phonic knowledge a child does and does not possess and then tailor a program to meet these needs. She should not cry phonics and proceed to give a child the entire treatment.

5. *Pupils should be led to discover phonic principles rather than be taught rules.* When, for example, the silent *e* rule is involved, a teacher should write on the blackboard several words exemplifying the principle. After each word is pronounced and attention is directed to the change from a short to a long vowel because of the final *e*, the children should be asked if they can make up a rule that applies. The child who discovers for himself the silent *e* generalization is more likely to remember it. More important, he is likely to use it.

6. *To be most effective, phonics should not be used as an isolated word-attack skill.* Phonics proves far more valuable when used in collaboration with other word-attack skills such as contextual and structural analysis.

## Instructional Materials for Correcting Deficiencies in Initial Consonant Sounds

When individual pupils or groups of pupils are deficient in initial consonant sounds, corrective practice can be individualized by using available commercial material such as:

A. (*The*) *Alphabet*: Thirty-three 10 inch by 10 inch color transparencies for projection purposes. Each transparency carries a letter accom-

---

*For particulars, see L. Scott and J. Thompson, *Phonics in Listening, in Speaking, in Reading, in Writing* (Manchester, Mo.: Webster Publishing, 1962), ch. II.

panied by three illustrative words and their pictures. (For use with a group of children; $99.50 a set; Visualcraft.)

B. *ABC Game:** A game that aids in teaching letter, word and picture recognition. Twenty-six pairs of cards having capitals on one card and small letters on the matching card are involved. The object of the game is to find the mate for every card in each player's hand until all players except one are left with no cards in their hands. (For use with two to four children, potentially self-directive; $1.00; Kenworthy.)

C. *Bulletin Board of Basic Phonics*: A set of thirty-five 6 inch by 9 inch cards with large type and colored pictures introducing difficult consonants, vowel digraphs and vowel sounds. In addition to a key word, six additional words employing the sound appear on each card. At the bottom of the card a key-word sentence is provided. (For use with individual children or a group of children; $2.75 per set; Educational Aids.)

D. *Consonant Flipstrips*: Two complete sets of key-word pictures printed in two colors with their corresponding letter symbols in the form of 3⅝ inch by 6¼ inch strips are involved. One set of strips may be folded so pictures and their related sounds are back to back; the second set may be cut in two, backed with flannel and used on a flannel board. (For use with individual children, children working in pairs or a small group of children, potentially self-directive; $1.95; Cenco.)

E. *Consonant Lotto:** Consonant Lotto consists of eight lotto cards, each of which contains six pictures of familiar objects. Forty-eight picture cover cards have different pictures to be matched by the beginning sound of the word with the pictures on the lotto cards. (For use with a group of children, potentially self-directive; $1.98; Garrard.)

F. *Consonant Pictures for Pegboard*: These materials consist of one hundred seventy-nine pictures in color and twenty-nine symbols printed on 3¾ inch by 4 inch cards for use on pegboard, chalk tray or as flash cards. (For use with individual children, children working in pairs or with a group of children under proper direction; $3.25; Ideal.)

G. *Dog House Game:** A phonetic game consisting of thirty-five phonograms along with eighty-four assorted consonants and consonant blends with which to build words. (For use with two or more children, potentially self-directive; $1.25; Kenworthy.)

H. *Five First Steps and Pop Words*: This instructional material involves one hundred fifty common sight or pop words printed in large, clear type on 4 inch by 6 inch cards. Consonant and vowel sounds are printed on colored cards and include sixteen easy consonants, four consonant digraphs, the sounds of *y* and the hard and soft *c* and *g* sounds. (For use with individual children, children working in pairs or with a group of children under proper direction; $1.65; Kenworthy.)

I. *Giant Consonant Cards*: Thirty 11¼ inch by 14 inch cards with color illustrations of familiar objects. Each card shows a consonant or consonant blend with the name of an object illustrated plus additional words containing the consonant or consonant blend. (For use with individual children, children working in pairs or a group of children, potentially self-directive; $3.00; Milton Bradley.)

J. *Go Fish* (Set I):* This is a rummy-like game designed to teach the sounds of initial consonants. (For use with two to four children, potentially self-directive; $1.65; Remedial Education Center.)

K. *Group Sounding Game*:* This game is a complete phonics course beginning with the recognition of initial consonants, blends and vowels and ending with syllabication of three syllable words. (For use with two or more children, potentially self-directive; $2.10; Garrard.)

L. *Initial and Final Consonant Charts*: These instructional materials involve fifteen charts that are 23 by 36 inches in size. Each chart supplies a variety of consonant pictures headed by their consonant symbol and a key picture. A manual of directions is included. (For use with individual children or a group of children, potentially self-directive; $8.00; Ideal.)

M. *Linguistic Block Series*:* Rolling Phonics, Consonants consisting of a set of ten blocks and involving eleven one-syllable words beginning with vowels and twelve consonants or consonant blends. Over eighty-five words can be built. (For use with individual children, children working in pairs or a small group of children; $4.40; Scott, Foresman.)

N. *Magic Cards*: These instructional materials consist of forty exercises printed on six 8½ inch by 11 inch ply cards. They are designed to stimulate learning of initial and final consonants. A transparent pocket in which the cards are inserted and on which answers are written with crayon is included. The pocket can be wiped clean to make it ready for the next exercise. (For use with individual children or children working in pair; $2.10; Ideal.)

O. *Mnemonic Phonics*:* This game is designed to teach one hundred ninety-six words common to reading or spoken primary vocabulary, thirty-six phonograms, and sixteen initial consonants. It is boxed with corrector, spinner and twenty-four varnished playing pages stapled to form two units. (For use with two children only; $1.95; Primary Playhouse.)

P. *Phonetic Drill Cards*: This instructional material involves twenty-three cards for three hundred forty-five word combinations. The lettering is one-inch high and the cards are 8 inches by 11¼ inches in size. Consonants and letter combinations for complete words are hinged for the formation of fifteen words on each card. (For use with individual children, children working in pairs or with a group of children under proper direction; $2.00; Milton Bradley.)

Q. *Phonetic Quizmo*:* A lotto-type game consisting of thirty-eight Quizmo cards, teacher's word list, direction card and markers. The game is designed to teach consonant sounds and consonant blends. (For use with two or more children, potentially self-directive; $2.00; Milton Bradley.)

R. *Phonetic Word Drill Cards*: These instructional materials involve three sets of cards. Each set has ten chart cards showing a different word ending on each side. Thus, there are two families of words on each basic chart card, or twenty families per set. Initial sound cards are suspended by plastic rings from the top of each basic chart card and are in line with the word endings. As each card is flipped, a new word appears and then the chart can be reversed and the operation repeated. With these three sets eight hundred sixty-four words can be formed. Sixty common word endings are involved. (For use with individual children, children working in pairs or with a group of children under proper direction; three sets, $2.50 each; Kenworthy.)

S. *Phono-Word Wheels* (Set A): The fifteen wheels in this set have a simple vocabulary of one hundred twenty words selected from commonly used basal series of readers at the primary level. Fifteen initial consonants are used and the lettering involved is large. (For use with individual children, children working in pairs or with a group of children under proper direction; $3.00; Steck.)

T. *See and Say Consonant Game:* * This game is designed to develop recognition of sounds made by single consonants and consonant combinations. Children learn consonants by looking at the pictures, saying the name of each object and listening for the sounds which consonants make. (For use with two or more children, potentially self-directive; $1.00; Milton Bradley.)

U. *Speech-to-Print Phonics*: Although this kit of material was initially designed as a readiness program, it may also be used as supplementary material with any basal series. The kit contains a teacher's manual and specific lessons in relating phonemes to printed forms. It includes consonants and vowels and twenty-one consonant blends. Special response cards are used by pupils so the teacher can detect any children who are experiencing difficulty. (For use with a group of children or an entire class; $24.00; Harcourt, Brace & World.)

V. *Split Words:* * A game consisting of wooden blocks involving consonants, consonant blends and word endings. The latter are printed in red. A dictionary listing and defining some five hundred words that can be built by combining the blocks in various ways is included. (For use with individual children, children working in pairs or a small group of children, potentially self-directive; $2.00; Teachers' Supplies.)

W. *Tumble Words:* * A vocabulary building game consisting of lettered cubes and a shaker. (For use with individual children or a group of children, potentially self-directive; $1.00; Kohner Brothers.)

X. *Webster Word Analysis Charts*: These instructional materials consist of five charts (23 by 35 inches in size) which constitute a permanent, visual guide to consonant sounds, vowel sounds, speech blends, vowel digraphs, prefixes and the principles of syllabication. (For use with individual children or a group of children, potentially self-directive; $9.00; Webster.)

Y. *Webster Word Wheels*: These practice wheels consist of twenty-five beginning blend wheels, twenty prefix wheels and eighteen suffix wheels. (For use with individual children or children working in pairs; $15.75; Webster.)
Z. *What the Letters Say*:* This beginning phonics game is designed to teach letter names and letter sounds. (For use with individual children or a group of children, potentially self-directive; $1.98; Garrard.)

When individual pupils or groups of pupils are deficient in initial consonant sounds, individualized practice can be provided by using teacher- or pupil-made materials such as the following:

A. *Arrange-O*: Place in an envelope a large picture of an object starting with an initial consonant sound you are teaching. In another envelope, place small pictures of objects, some of which begin with the sound involved. The child arranges the appropriate pictures in a column under the master picture. By using an identification scheme on the back of the pictures, this activity can be made self-corrective. (For use with individual children, potentially self-directive.)
B. *Baseball*:* A baseball diamond is drawn on the blackboard or on cardboard. Two groups of children are chosen. The pitcher flashes a letter. If the batter calls a word beginning with the letter, he has made a hit and moves to first base. Should the next batter score a hit also, he moves to first base and the first batter advances to second. Soon the runs begin to come in. Teams change sides just as soon as three outs (wrong answers) have been given. The team with the most runs wins. (For use with groups of children.)
C. *Clothespin Wheel*: Cut out a circular piece of tagboard about 12 inches in diameter. Paste or draw pictures of common objects around the periphery of the oak tag. Equip the child with a box of clothespins on each of which is printed an initial consonant. The child then matches the clothespins with the proper pictures. For example, the *c* clothespin would be placed over the picture of a cat; the *p* clothespin over the picture of a pear. (For use with individual children, potentially self-directive.)
D. *Consonant Fishing*:* Consonant cards are cut in the shape of a fish. A paper clip is slipped over each card. Fishermen are equipped with a pole (short stick) a fish line (20 inches of store string) and a fish hook (small magnet). Each child gets a turn trying to catch fish. If he can call a word that begins with the consonant sound on the fish he has caught, he may keep the fish. If he is unable to think of a suitable word, he returns the fish, face down, to the fishpond. (For use with two children or a group of children, potentially self-directive.)
E. *Consonant Lotto*:* The teacher with the help of her children prepares cardboard master cards 8 by 11 inches in size. These master cards

are blocked off vertically and horizontally into twenty-five small squares. The middle space is marked *free*. Individual letters and digraphs are placed on the twenty-four spaces that remain. Each cardboard master card must have the same letters but in different positions. Twenty-four words known by the children on sight that begin with the individual letters or consonant digraphs involved are placed in an envelope. As individual words drawn from the envelope are called, the players find the beginning letter or digraph on their master cards and cover it with a marker. The marker may be a kernel of corn, a bean, or a small piece of cardboard. The first child to cover a row of letters in a straight line, vertically, horizontally or diagonally, calls out "Lotto." If he has not erred, he is declared the winner. (For use with two children or a group of children, potentially self-directive.)

F. *Matching Letters and Objects*: The teacher pastes a number of small pictures on a sheet of oak tag. (A flannel board, if available, might be used.) The pictures should be of things the children can recognize easily. An envelope containing a number of consonants is clipped to the sheet of oak tag. The child removes the consonant cards and places them on or below the appropriate pictures. By use of an identification scheme on the backs of the cards, this activity can be made self-corrective. (For use with individual children, potentially self-directive.)

G. *Pockets*: Cut apart some cheap envelopes and mount them on a chart as pockets for 3 by 5 inch cards. A consonant is printed on each envelope. The 3 by 5 inch cards have pictures or drawings on them which are to be placed in the pockets beginning with the appropriate consonant sound. By using an identification scheme on the backs of the cards, this activity can be made self-corrective. (For use with individual children, potentially self-directive.)

H. *Spin and Call*:* Divide a large oak-tag circle into eight sections. Place a consonant in each section. Attach a large pointer to the center of the circle so it spins freely. The player spins the pointer and calls a word beginning with the particular consonant to which it points when coming to a stop. If a correct word is called, he scores a point. A record should be kept of the words called so no repetitions take place. (For use with two children or a group of children.)

I. *Taxi*:* With the help of children build a little village of letters beside each of which is a small paper house. There can be several streets in Alphabet Village. Tall Street can consist of those letters which extend above the line (*b, d, f, h, k, l* and *t*); Naughty Street can consist of those letters which extend below the line (*j, p* and *g*); Coward Street of those letters that go together to make a sound (*ch, sh, th* and *wh*); Vowel Street of the vowels; Main Street of any letters left over.

One child acts as Taxi driver. The other children ask the driver to take them to any word they want. The driver has to "drive" them to the house whose letter starts the word. (For use with a group of children.)

J. *Toss Game*:* With the use of alphabet blocks or building blocks on which initial consonants have been painted, children can take turns rolling blocks and giving words beginning with the letters that come up. (For use with two or more children, potentially self-directive.)

K. *Word Authors:* * Words are printed on corners of cards — four cards to a set. A set consists of four words beginning with the same consonant. Each child is dealt four cards. One child begins the game by calling for a card beginning with a certain initial consonant sound. If he gets the word, he may continue to call for words. When his opponent indicates that he does not have the card called, the child draws from the deck of cards that is face down on the table. The child who acquires the most sets wins. (For use with two to four children, potentially self-directive.)

L. *What Am I?:* * On individual cards write riddles which give initial sounds as clues. For example, "I am a tree-climbing animal. I have a long tail and like to swing from branches with it. I begin with the *m* sound. What am I?" Each child in the group has a chance at a riddle card. If he guesses the answer he is given the card. The child with the largest number of cards is the winner. By placing the answers on the backs of the cards this activity can be made self-corrective. (For use with a group of children, potentially self-directive.)

## Instructional Materials for Correcting Deficiencies in Consonant Blends

When individual pupils or groups of pupils are deficient in their knowledge of consonant blends, corrective practice can be individualized by using available commercial material such as the following:

A. *Blend-o-grams:* * A word game designed to teach common blends and word endings by proper matching. (For use with two to four children; $1.25; Teachers' Supplies.)

B. *Blends and Digraph Pictures for Pegboard:* This instructional material contains eighty picture cards and twenty-six consonant blend and digraph cards in full color. These are printed on 3¾ by 4 inch white index cards for use on pegboard, chalk tray or as flash cards. (For use with individual children, children working in pairs or with a group of children under proper direction; $3.00; Ideal.

C. *Blends and Digraphs:* Twenty 10 inch by 10 inch color transparencies for projection purposes. Each transparency carries several consonant blends accompanied by illustrative words and their pictures. (For use with a group of children; $79.50 a set; Visualcraft.)

D. *Dog House:* * A phonetic game consisting of thirty-five phonograms along with eighty-four assorted consonants and consonant blends with which to build words (For use with a group of children; $1.25; Kenworthy.)

E. *Giant Consonant Cards:* Thirty 11¼ inch by 11 inch cards with color illustrations of familiar objects. Each card shows a consonant or consonant blend with the name of an object illustrated plus additional words that contain the consonant or consonant blend. (For use with individual children, children working in pairs or a group of children; $3.00; Milton Bradley.)

F. *Go Fish*\* (Set II): This is a rummy-like game designed to teach the sounds of consonant blends. (For use with two to four children, potentially self-directive; $1.65; Remedial Education Center.)

G. *Group Sounding Game:*\* This game is a complete phonics course beginning with the recognition of initial consonants, blends and vowels, and ending with syllabication of three syllable words. (For use with two or more children, potentially self-directive; $2.10; Garrard.)

H. *Hammond's Phonics Charts*: A set of twenty-eight charts 15 inches by 10 inches in size. These charts cover consonant and vowel sounds, consonant blends and digraphs, vowel blends and principles. In addition to a key word set forth in bold type and visible from a distance, each chart carries an illustration of a key word accompanied by five other words employing the sound. (For use with individual children or a group of children; $23.80 for all four sets; Hammond.)

I. *Linguistic Block Series:*\* Rolling Phonics, Consonants, consists of a set of ten blocks involving eleven one-syllable words beginning with vowels and twelve consonants or consonant blends. Over eighty-five words can be built. (For use with individual children, children working in pairs or a small group of children; $4.40; Scott, Foresman.)

J. *Magic Cards — Blends and Digraphs*: These instructional materials consist of eight exercises on six 8½ by 11 inch ply cards. They are designed to stimulate the learning of consonant blends and digraphs. The set includes a durable transparent pocket into which the cards are inserted and on which the answers can be marked with wax crayons. The pocket can be wiped clean easily to make it ready for the next exercise. (For use with individual children or a small group of children; $1.00; Ideal.)

K. *Make a Word Game:*\* This material consists of sixty cards having single or blended consonants which are matched with sixty cards containing phonograms to be used as endings of words. (For use with individual children or a group of children; $1.50; Beckley Cardy.)

L. *Phonetic Quizmo:*\* A lotto-type game consisting of thirty-eight phonetic Quizmo cards, teacher's word list, direction card and markers. The game is designed to teach consonant sounds and consonant blends. (For use with two or more children, potentially self-directive; $2.00; Milton Bradley.)

M. *Phonetic Word Drill Cards*: These instructional materials involve three sets of cards. Each set has twin chart cards, showing a different word ending on each side. Thus, there are two families of words on each basic chart card, or twenty families per set. Initial sound cards are suspended by plastic rings from the top of each basic chart card and are in line with the word endings. As each card is flipped, a new word appears and then the chart can be reversed and the operation repeated. With these three sets, eight hundred sixty-four words can be formed. Sixty common word endings are involved. (For use with individual children, children working in pairs or with a group of children under proper direction; three sets, $2.50 each; Kenworthy.)

N. *Phono-Word Wheels* (Set B and Set I). The fifteen wheels in set B involve a vocabulary of one hundred ten words and employ six initial consonant blends, four digraphs and five word endings. Set I involves seventeen wheels, each of which contains a common initial blend. A total of one hundred thirty-four words are included. (For use with individual children, children working in pairs or with a group of children under proper direction; $3.00; Steck.)

O. *Speech-To-Print Phonics*: Although this kit of material was initially designed as a readiness program, it may also be used as supplementary material with any basal series. The kit contains a teacher's manual and specific lessons in relating phonemes to printed forms. It includes consonants and vowels and twenty-one consonant blends. Special response cards are used by pupils so the teacher can detect any children who are experiencing difficulty. (For use with a group of children or an entire class; $24.00; Harcourt, Brace & World.)

P. *Split Words:* A game consisting of wooden blocks involving consonants, consonant blends and word endings. The latter are printed in red. A dictionary listing and defining some five hundred words that can be built by combining the blocks in various ways is included. (For use with individual children, children working in pairs or a small group of children, potentially self-directive; $2.00; Teachers' Supplies.)

Q. *Webster Word Wheels*: These practice wheels consist of twenty-five beginning blend wheels, twenty prefix wheels, eighteen suffix wheels and eight two-letter consonant wheels. The wheels are color-coded and numbered in order of difficulty. The set comes in a colorful cardboard file box. (For use with individual children or children working in pairs; $15.75; Webster.)

R. *Word Blends*: A set of subdivided, folding cards that highlight consonant blends and digraphs. A total of one hundred forty-four words are formed. (For use with individual children, children working in pairs or a small group of children; $.75; Kenworthy.)

When individual pupils or groups of pupils are deficient in their knowledge of consonant blends, individualized practice can be provided by using teacher- or pupil-made materials such as the following:

A. *Authors with Beginnings:* Words are printed on corners of cards — four words to a set. A set consists of four words that begin with the same consonant blend. This can be highlighted by underlining the first two letters or writing them in red. Each child is dealt four cards and one child begins the game by calling for a word beginning with a given blend. If he gets the word he may continue to call for words. When his opponent indicates that he does not have the blend called for, the child draws from the deck of cards that is face down on the table. The child who acquires the most sets wins. (For use with two to four children, potentially self-directive.)

B. *Baseball:*\* A baseball diamond is drawn on the blackboard or on cardboard. Two groups of children are chosen. The pitcher flashes a consonant blend. If the batter calls a word beginning with the blend, he has made a hit and moves to first base. Should the next batter score a hit also, he moves to first base and the previous batter advances to second. Soon the runs begin to come in. Teams change sides just as soon as three outs (wrong answers) have been given. The team with the most "runs" wins. (For use with groups of children.)

C. *Blend Fishing:*\* Consonant blend cards are cut in the shape of fish. A paper clip is slipped over each card. Fishermen are equipped with a pole (short stick) a fish line (20 inches of store string) and a fish hook (small magnet). Each child gets a turn trying to catch a fish. If he can call a word that begins with the consonant blend sound on the fish he has caught, he may keep the fish. If he is unable to think of a suitable word, he returns the fish, face down, to the fish pond. (For use with two children or a group of children, potentially self-directive.)

D. *Clothespin Wheel:* Cut out a circular piece of tagboard about 12 inches in diameter. Paste or draw pictures of common objects around the periphery of the oak tag. Equip the child with a box of clothespins on each of which is printed a consonant blend. He then matches the clothespins with the proper pictures. For example, the *fr* clothespin would be placed over the picture of a frog; the *pl* clothespin over the picture of a plum. (For use with individual children, potentially self-directive.)

E. *Deezio:*\* A set of twenty-five cards is constructed. Recommended card size is 2½ by 3 inches. An initial blend is written in two diagonal corners. A word beginning with this initial blend is written in the center of the card. It is necessary to have at least two cards with the same initial blend, but the word in the center should differ. The twenty-fifth card will have no duplicate. This card has a drawing of a funny face and is "Deezio."

All cards are dealt to the players and each player immediately looks for pairs of cards with the same blends. He places these pairs in front of him, saying the word on each card as he puts them down. If he cannot read the words, another player may tell him, but he must hold the pair until his next turn. Then the player to the left of the person with the most cards begins playing by drawing a card. He draws a card from the player holding the most cards. The drawer attempts to match the card with one in his hand. If he has a pair, he places it in front of him and reads the words. If no match is made, he retains the card in his hand. The playing continues clockwise around the table. The player who matches all his cards first wins. The rest continue to play until one person is left with "Deezio;" he is the "Deezio." (For use with three to five children, potentially self-directive.) This game and the games Happy Ending and Word Flight were devised by Hildegard Ziegler et al., teachers at the Madison, Wisconsin public schools.

F. *Finding Partners:* Two types of cards are placed in an envelope — some involving word endings and others consonant blends. The cards are distributed to a group of children. Those children receiving cards with blends move around among the other children to see if they can form a word by combining their cards. When a word has been formed, the child says, "We made — — with our cards." Since there is the possibility that other blends may fit the ending, the teacher asks if anyone else can help make a word. The process continues until all pairing is exhausted. (For use with a group of children.)

G. *Lotto Blends:* With the help of her children, the teacher prepares cardboard master cards 8 by 11 inches in size. These master cards are blocked off vertically and horizontally into twenty-five small squares. The middle space is marked *free.* Individual consonant blends are placed on the twenty-four spaces that remain. Each master card must have the same blends on it but in different positions. Twenty-four words known by the children on sight that begin with the consonant blends are placed in an envelope. As individual words are drawn from the envelope and called, the players find the consonant blends on their master cards and cover them with a marker. The marker may be a kernel of corn, a bean or a small piece of cardboard. The first child to cover a row of letters in a straight line, vertically, horizontally or diagonally, calls out "Lotto." If he has not erred, he is declared the winner. (For use with a group of children, potentially self-directive.)

H. *Pockets:* Cut apart some cheap envelopes and mount them on a chart as pockets for 3 by 5 inch cards. A consonant blend is printed on each envelope. The cards have pictures or drawings on them which are to be placed in the pockets beginning with the appropriate consonant blend. By using an identification scheme on the backs of the cards, this activity can be made self-corrective. (For use with individual children, potentially self-directive.)

I. *Sound Box:* Choose a cardboard box with subdivisions — one that has been used to package bottles is ideal. By using common pins, label each subdivision with a small card on which a blend has been written. Players draw picture cards from a pile and attempt to place them in the spaces labeled with letters that represent the beginning blend sounds of the words pictured. Points can be given for correct choices. This activity can be made self-corrective by printing the correct letters on the backs of the picture cards. (For use with one or more children, potentially self-directive.)

J. *Spin and Call:* Divide a large oak-tag circle into eight sections. Attach a large pointer to the center of the circle so it spins freely. The player spins the pointer and calls a word beginning with the particular consonant blend to which it points when coming to a stop. If a correct word is called, he scores one point. A record should be kept of words called so no repetitions take place. (For use with two children or a group of children.)

K. *What Am I?:* On individual cards write riddles which give initial consonant blends as clues. For example, "I grow in bunches on trees. I am good to eat. I begin with a *gr* sound. What am I?" Each child in the group has a chance at a riddle card. If he guesses the answer he is given the card. The child with the largest number of cards is the winner. By placing the answers on the backs of the cards, this activity can be made self-corrective. (For use with a group of children, potentially self-directive.)

L. *Authors with Blends:* Words are printed on corners of cards — four cards to a set. A set consists of four words beginning with the same consonant blend. Each child is dealt four cards and one begins the game by calling for a card beginning with a certain consonant blend. If he gets the word, he may continue to call for words. When his opponent indicates that he does not have the card called for, the child draws from the deck of cards that is face down on the table. The child who acquires the most sets wins. (For use with two to four children, potentially self-directive.)

## Instructional Materials for Correcting Deficiencies in Vowel Sounds, Letter Combinations and Principles

When individual pupils or groups of pupils are deficient in their knowledge of vowel sounds, letter combinations or principles, corrective practice can be individualized by using commercial material such as the following:

A. *Bulletin Board of Basic Phonics:* A set of thirty-five 6 inch by 9 inch cards with large type and colored pictures introducing difficult consonants, vowel digraphs and vowel sounds. In addition to a key word, six additional words employing the sound appear on each card. At the bottom of the card a key-word sentence is provided. (For use with individual children or a group of children; $2.75 per set; Educational Aids.)

B. *End-in-E-Game:* This game is designed to show how words change as *e* is added. There are fifteen word cards, each with a flap that turns in to add the letter *e*, changing the word. For example, *at* with an *e* added is *ate*. There is a story to be used with the cards that adds fun to the learning. The letters on the cards involved are quite large. (For use with individual children, children working in pairs or with a group of children under proper direction; $.80; Ideal.)

C. *Giant Vowel Cards:* Thirty 11¼ inch by 14 inch cards with color illustrations of familiar objects. Each card shows a vowel with the name of an object illustrated plus additional words that contain the vowel. (For use with individual children, children working in pairs or a group of children; $3.00; Milton Bradley.)

D. *Group-size Vowel Cards*: These instructional materials consist of two cards each for all short and long vowels, digraphs, diphthongs and other vowel combinations with consonants. Four phonetic rules are covered. (For use with individual children, children working in pairs or with a group of children under proper direction; $2.00; Garrard.)

E. *Group Sounding Game*:* This game is a complete phonics course beginning with the recognition of initial consonants, blends and vowels, and ending with syllabication of three syllable words. (For use with two or more children, potentially self-directive; $2.10; Garrard.)

F. *Hammond's Phonics Charts*: A set of twenty-eight charts 15 inches by 10 inches in size. These charts cover consonant and vowel sounds, consonant blends and digraphs, vowel blends and principles. In addition to a key word set forth in bold type and visible from a distance, each chart carries an illustration of a key word accompanied by five other words employing the sound. (For use with individual children or a group of children; $23.80 for all four sets; Hammond.)

G. *Junior Phonic Rummy*:* This game employs one hundred ten most frequently occuring short vowel words from the most widely used first-grade basic reading books. A key picture is provided for each of the short vowel sounds. (For use with two or more children, potentially self-directive; $1.50; Kenworthy.)

H. *Linguistic Block Series*:*Rolling Phonics, Vowels, consists of a set of thirty word blocks involving one hundred sixty different words representing short, long and other vowel sounds. (For use with individual children, children working in pairs or a small group of children; $10.00; Scott, Foresman.)

I. *Magic Cards—Vowels*: These instructional materials consist of twenty-four exercises on six 8½ by 11 inch ply cards. Exercises can be reworked again and again because of a transparent plastic pocket into which cards are inserted and on which answers are marked with any wax crayon. The pocket is then wiped clean to make it ready for the next exercise. (For use with individual children or a group of children; $1.50; Ideal.)

J. *Magic Vowel*: A set of cards which carry silent *e* words on one side and the same words without the silent *e* on the other side. (For use with individual children, children working in pairs or a group of children; $1.50 a set; Educational Aids.)

K. *Match the Vowel*: A two-deck matching game designed to teach vowels and vowel combinations: digraphs and diphthongs. (For use with individual children, children working in pairs or a group of children; $1:50; Educational Aids.)

L. *Phonetic Word Wheel*: The Phonetic Word Wheel is a device that gives a child varied practice in recognition of vowels, consonants and phonetic blends. Countless variations of this game are possible depending on the needs of the pupils. (For use with individual children or children working in pairs; $.75; Milton Bradley.)

M. *Phonic Rummy** (four sets): These games are designed to teach short vowels and vowel principles. Each set contains two packs of sixty cards presenting words suitable for the grades on each set. (For use with two to four children, potentially self-directive; $1.50 per set; Kenworthy.)

N. *Quiet Pal Game:* A game that builds words with silent letters in them. The word card has a flap that turns over to cover the end letter. The word is changed instantly to make a new word — one with a silent letter, as *ran* to *rain* with its silent *i*. The set includes fifteen story cards. (For use with individual children, children working in pairs or with a group of children under proper direction; $.80; Ideal.)

O. *Short Vowel Drill:* This drill involves categorizing pictures of objects containing a short vowel sound. Each vowel is represented by a number of picture words. (For use with individual children or children working in pairs; $.80; Remedial.)

P. *Short Vowel Game:* This is a rummy-like game designed to teach the sounds of the short vowels. (For use with an individual child or children working in pairs; $.50; Beckley-Cardy, Co.)

Q. *Vowel Charts:* This set of vowel charts is in brilliant color showing vowel pictures, symbols and rules. Each set contains ten 23 by 36 inch charts (nine vowel charts and one key chart) with metal eyelets to prevent tearing and a complete manual of directions. (For use with individual children or a group of children, potentially self-directive; $5.50; Ideal.)

R. *Vowel Dominoes:* This game teaches the short vowel sounds through a version of dominoes. (For use with two to four children, potentially self-directive; $1.65; Remedial.)

S. *Vowel Flipstrips:* Two complete sets of key-word pictures printed in two colors with their corresponding letter symbols in the form of 3⅝ inch by 6¼ inch strips are involved. One set of strips may be folded so pictures and their related sounds are back to back; the second set may be cut in two, backed with flannel and used on a flannel board. (For use with individual children, children working in pairs or a small group of children; $1.95; Cenco.)

T. *Vowel Lotto:* Vowel Lotto is a game that gives practice in hearing and learning short vowels, long vowels, vowel digraphs and diphthongs. Children match cover card pictures with those on the lotto cards having the same vowel sound. (For use with two or more children, potentially self-directive; $1.98; Garrard.)

U. *Vowel Pictures for Pegboard:* These instructional materials include one hundred two picture cards, two hundred twenty-eight word cards and twenty-one vowel symbols cards 4 by 3¾ inches in size. These cards can be used on pegboard, chalk tray or as flash cards. For use with individual children or a group of children; $4.30; Ideal.)

V. *Vowel Wall Chart:* This chart contains seventeen fundamental vowel sounds and twenty-one subspellings with corresponding key-word pictures. The text appears in two colors on a durable latex-impregnated stock. Size 26 inches by 40 inches. ($3.00; Cenco.)

When individual pupils or groups of pupils are deficient in their knowledge of vowel sounds, letter combinations and principles, individualized practice can be provided by using teacher- or pupil-made materials such as the following:

A. *Ask Me:** Prepare about forty to fifty word cards on each of which is a word containing a vowel sound. Some cards should have duplicate vowel sounds although the words themselves should differ. Four cards are dealt to each player and the remainder are put in a pile on the table. The player to the left of the dealer reads one of his words. Other players holding cards with a similar vowel sound give their cards to the caller. The latter places any sets he acquires on the table. If the caller does not call his word correctly, he discards it but must draw another word from the pile. After drawing he waits until his next turn before calling for another card. The winner is the player with the fewest cards. (For use with two to four children, potentially self-directive.)

B. *Baseball:** A baseball diamond is drawn on the blackboard or on cardboard. Two groups of children are chosen. The pitcher flashes a word. If the batter can designate the short vowel sound in the word, he has made a hit and moves to first base. Should the next batter score a hit also, he moves to first base and the first batter advances to second. Soon the runs begin to come in. Teams change sides just as soon as three outs (wrong answers) have been given. The team with the most "runs" wins. (For use with groups of children.)

C. *Matching Vowels and Objects*: The teacher pastes a number of small pictures on a sheet of oak tag. The pictures should be of things the children can recognize easily. An envelope containing a number of vowels (several of each kind) is clipped to the sheet of oak tag. The child removes the vowel cards and places them on or below the pictures whose names contain the vowel sounds. (For use with individual children.)

D. *Pockets*: Cut apart some cheap envelopes and mount them on a chart as pockets for 3 by 5 inch cards. A vowel is printed on each envelope. The cards have pictures or drawings on them which are to be placed in the pockets having the appropriate vowel sounds. By using an identification scheme on the backs of the cards, this activity can be made self-corrective. (For use with individual children, potentially self-directive.)

E. *Shoe-box Match*: Paste pictures or drawings of objects beginning with a short vowel sound on the front of shoe boxes. Players engaging in this activity attempt to sort small picture cards containing short vowel sounds. These are placed in the appropriate shoe boxes. The activity can be made self-corrective by numbering, correspondingly, the boxes and the backs of the small picture cards. (For use with individual children, potentially self-directive.)

F. *Spin and Call:** Divide a large oak-tag circle into eight sections. Place a vowel in each section. Attach a large pointer to the center of the circle so it spins freely. The player spins the pointer and calls a word containing the short vowel to which it points when coming to a stop. If a correct word is called, he scores one point. A record should be kept of words called so no repetitions take place. (For use with two children or a group of children.)

G. *Win-a-Row:* ° Cut cards 7½ inches square. Rule five or more cards into 1½ inch squares so there are twenty-five squares on the cards. Write or print selected words in the squares. Write the same word in a different position on all the cards so no two cards are identical; however, each row must have one word with each of the short vowel sounds. Twenty-five different words with the short vowel sounds will be written on a number of small cards. These will be numbered 1, 2, 3, 4 and 5. Numbers will represent rows on the playing card. Small paper circles can be made to be used as counters or markers to cover the words. The game is played very much like Bingo. The caller reads a row number and a word from the small cards. The players cover a word in the designated row which has the same vowel sound as the word read. The child who first covers five words vertically, diagonally or horizontally, reads his winning row. If he has not erred, he is declared the winner and may be the caller for the next game. (For use with more than two children, potentially self-directive.)

## Supplementary Instructional Activities for Correcting Deficiencies in Vowel Sounds, Letter Combinations and Principles

When individual pupils or groups of pupils are deficient in their knowledge of vowel sounds, letter combinations or principles, provide individualized practice by employing activities such as the following°

A. The child is given a list of words. He underlines all the words that have the same vowel sound as that appearing in the first word.
B. The child is given a list of words containing long and short vowel sounds. He classifies the words into long and short vowels.
C. The child is given a list of words containing vowel blends or diphthongs. He classifies the words according to their vowel blends.
D. The child is given a list of words that have vowel combinations missing. He chooses that vowel combination from several given which will complete each word.
E. A series of pictures of objects is given to the child. He names each picture and tells whether the vowel in the name is long or short.
F. A list of words is given to the child. He checks the words in the list that have the same vowel sound.
G. The rules governing vowel sounds are given to the child along with a list of words. The child indicates the rule that governs the vowel

---

° All these activities can be made self-directive by furnishing simple directions and accompanying answer keys.

sound of the words by writing the number of the rule before or after each word.

H. The child is given a list of words, containing both the long and the short sounds of a given vowel. He checks the words that contain the long sound of the given vowel.

I. The child is given a list of words containing different long and short vowels. He draws a line under each word that contains a long vowel.

J. Lists of words containing long and short vowels are given to the child. He underlines each word that contains a short vowel.

## Utilizing Structural Analysis

Structural analysis involves the discernment of larger more meaningful units (morphemes) than individual consonants or blends. Included are root words, prefixes, suffixes, inflected endings and syllables. By studying the structure of unknown words pupils may note the following:

1. Variant endings based on common roots
   look        looking        looked
   talk        talking        talked
   wash        washes        washed
2. Compound words consisting of two familiar words
   sunshine
   milkman
   sometimes
3. Root words to which prefixes have been added
   unhappy
   export
   recount
4. Root words to which suffixes haxe been added
   blackness
   dangerous
   sinful
5. Root words to which both prefixes and suffixes have been added
   unkindly
   distrustful
   repayable

As a student advances and begins to encounter polysyllabic words, the ability to break such words into their component parts becomes increasingly valuable. To most teachers, this means teaching rules. But the teaching of syllabication rules is questioned by many authorities. Spache questions their value and cites a number of studies to corroborate his opinion. (5) Deighton, for example, advocates teaching only three principles: (1) Each syllable has a vowel sound, (2) prefixes are separate syllables, (3) doubled consonants may be split. Too many of the other rules, he says, are of doubtful value because of exceptions. (6)

Teachers who are convinced that principles of syllabication have value, will be interested in Clymer's study. (8) After analyzing the phonic principles found in the manuals, workbooks and readers of four basal series, Clymer singled out forty-five for evaluative purposes. Each phonic generalization was checked against words found in a composite list of all the words introduced in the four basic series from which the generalizaiton was drawn, plus words from the Gates Reading Vocabulary for the Primary Grades. The eight principles which pertained to syllabication are as follows:

| Generalization | Number of Words Against Which Generalization Was Tested | Per Cent of Utility |
|---|---|---|
| 1. In most two-syllable words, the first syllable is accented. | 971 | 85 |
| 2. If *a, in, re, ex, de* or *be* is the first syllable in a word, it is usually unaccented. | 99 | 87 |
| 3. In most two-syllable words that end in a consonant followed by *y*, the first syllable is accented and the last is unaccented. | 105 | 96 |
| 4. If the first vowel sound in a word is followed by two consonants, the first syllable usually ends with the first of the two consonants. | 563 | 72 |
| 5. If the first vowel sound in a word is followed by a single consonant, that consonant usually begins the second syllable. | 427 | 44 |
| 6. If the last syllable of a word ends in *le*, the consonant preceding the *le* usually begins the last syllable. | 64 | 97 |
| 7. When the first vowel element in a word is followed by *th, ch* or *sh*, these symbols are not broken when the word is divided into syllables and may go with either the first or second syllable. | 30 | 100 |
| 8. In a word of more than one syllable, the letter *v* usually goes with the preceding vowel to form a syllable. | 73 | 73 |

Since Clymer sets his criterion of acceptance at a seventy-five per cent level of utility, generalizations 4, 5 and 8 would be eliminated. It should be noted, however, that rule 8 was tested against a small number of words when comparisons were made with the samples involved in the testing of the forth and fifth rules. Considerable credence can be given to the value of the first 3 rules (these deal with accenting of syllables) since a more recent study by Winkley corroborates Clymer's findings in connection with them. As a matter of fact, Winkley's thorough evaluation of eighteen accent generalizations placed the aforementioned rules among eight that were rated as most significant. (9)

## Instructional Materials for Correcting Deficiencies in Structural Analysis

When individual pupils or groups of pupils are deficient in their knowledge of structural analysis, corrective practice can be individualized by using available commercial material such as the following:

A. *Grab*\* (Set IV): A sight vocabulary game consisting of fifteen polysyllabic words which are subdivided into individual syllables. (For use with two to four children, potentially self-directive; two sets on any level, $1.75; Teachers' Supplies.)

B. *Phonetic Word Drill Cards*: These instructional materials involve three sets of cards. Each set has ten chart cards, showing a different word ending on each side. Thus there are two families of words on each basic chart card, or twenty families per set. Suspended by plastic rings from the top of each basic chart card and in line with the word endings are initial sound cards. As each card is flipped, a new word appears and then the chart can be reversed and the operation repeated, showing an entirely different family of words. With these three sets eight hundred sixty-four words can be formed. These cover sixty common word endings. (For use with individual children, children working in pairs or with a group of children under proper direction; three sets, $2.50 each; Kenworthy.)

C. *Phono Word Wheels* (Sets II and III): Set II has seventeen wheels designed to give practice on the most common prefixes. Set III has seventeen wheels designed to give practice on the most common suffixes. Both sets involve a vocabulary of one hundred thirty-six words which are drawn from commonly used basal readers in grades five through seven. (For use with individual children, children working in pairs or with a group of children under proper direction; $3.00; Steck.)

D. *Syllable Game:*\* The Syllable Game contains three decks of cards. The words in the first two decks are of two syllables and the player learns by sight the syllables in these words. The third deck has words up to four syllables in length. (For use with one student or two students playing solitaire, potentially self-directive; $2.10; Garrard.)

E. *Third Syllable Game:*\* A set of cards that provides practice in attacking polysyllabic words one syllable at a time. (For use with individual children, children working in pairs or a group of children, potentially self-directive; $1.50; Educational Aids.)

F. *Word Prefixes*: A set of subdivided, folding cards that highlight twenty-three prefixes that blend to form two hundred sixteen words. The meaning of each prefix is given and the words being shown are keyed on back of each card. (For use with individual children, children working in pairs or a group of children; $.75; Kenworthy.)

G. *Word Suffixes*: A set of subdivided, folding cards that highlight twenty-four word endings. A total of one hundred forty-four words are formed. The meaning of each suffix is given and words being shown are keyed in small type. (For use with individual children, children working in pairs or a small group of children; $.75; Kenworthy.)

H. *Webster Word Analysis Charts*: These instructional materials consist of five charts (34 by 35 inches in size) which constitute a permanent, visual guide to consonant sounds, vowel sounds, speech blends, vowel digraphs, prefixes and the principles of syllabication, potentially self-directive; $9.00; Webster.)

I. *Webster Word Wheels*: These practice wheels consist of twenty-five beginning blend wheels, twenty prefix wheels, eighteen suffix wheels and eight two-letter consonant wheels. The wheels are color coded and numbered in order of difficulty. The set comes in a colorful cardboard file box. (For use with individual children or children working in pairs; $15.75; Webster.)

When individual pupils or groups of pupils are deficient in their knowledge of structural analysis, individualized practice can be provided by using teacher- or pupil-made materials such as the following:

A. *Authors with Endings:** Words are printed on corners of cards — four cards to a set. A set consists of four words that have the same ending. This can be highlighted by underlining the endings in red. Each child is dealt four cards and one child begins the game by calling for a word with a given ending. If he gets the word, he may continue to call for words. When his opponent indicates that he does not have the ending called for, the child draws from the deck of cards that is face down on the table. The child who acquires the most sets wins. (For use with two to four children, potentially self-directive.)

B. *Baseball:** Two groups of children are chosen. The pitcher flashes a word. If the batter can tell the number of syllables in the word he has made a hit and moves to first base. Should the next batter also score a hit, he moves to first base and the previous batter advances to second. Soon the runs begin to come in. Teams change sides just as soon as three outs (wrong answers) have been given. The team with the most "runs" wins. (For use with groups of children.)

C. *Happy Ending:** This is a structural analysis game consisting of one hundred eight playing cards divided into eleven units of eight cards and one unit of twelve cards. The first unit (12 cards) is labeled *Perfect Fit*. The second unit (four cards) is labeled *Wait* and four cards are labeled *surprise*. The remaining eleven units make up the rest of the deck and each of these units will have eight different words with the same ending. The ending is printed in color.

The cards are shuffled and eleven cards are dealt to each player. The remaining cards are put into a pack in the center of the table. The top card is turned face up next to the deck and starts the discarded pile.

Anyone having a *surprise* card in his hand places it on the table face up in front of him and immediately draws another card from the pack. The player to the left of the dealer begins playing. He will draw the card turned up or draw from the top of the deck. If he draws the turned up card, he must be able to use it immediately either in a triangle or on a triangle. (A triangle is three or more cards with the same ending put down face up in front of the player.) A player may add to any triangle that he or she has on the table. A triangle of three cards may have one *Perfect Fit* in it. *It is important that each card played on the table is read.* If a player cannot read the triangle or an individual card, his partner can attempt to read them. If neither can read the card or cards, a monitor may tell the player, but he must keep it or them in his hand until his next turn.

A player terminates his play by putting a card on the discard pile and reading it. If a player needs assistance in reading this card he discards it. The playing continues clockwise around the table. One person in the partnership keeps the cards in front of him, and his partner plays on them or adds to the "lay down." As the playing continues, the player who wants the top card of the discard pile for playing on a triangle or in a triangle must take all the cards in the pile and read and play the top one immediately.

*Perfect Fit* can be called any card and help to make three or more of a kind. A *Wait* card on a discarded pile *Stops* the discard pile for the next player who then must draw from the unused pack. A *Happy Ending* is made when seven cards with the same ending have been played. This may include the *Perfect Fits;* however, only three *Perfect Fits* can be used in one *Happy Ending.*

The game is over when a player has a *Happy Ending* and is rid of all the cards in his hands. The player will try to get as many *Happy Endings* as he can.

Scoring is as follows: A *Happy Ending* counts 100; going out counts 50; *surprises* count 50; *perfect fits* count 10; every other card counts five. The score of all the cards left in the hands of the other players when a player goes out is subtracted from his score on the table. The remaining score for each couple is added and tallied. The couple who first attains a score of 1,000 is declared winner. (For use with two sets of partners.)

D. *Word Flight:** This is a structural analysis game consisting of fifty-two playing cards on each of which is a two, three or four syllable word. The difficulty of the game can be increased by having many multiple-syllable words.

The playing board is constructed by placing a mimeographed map of the United States on tagboard. A flight route should be drawn between major cities. Miniature airplanes of different colors should be made for use by each player.

To begin the playing, the deck of cards is placed in the center of the table near the playing board. Each player draws his first card from the center deck. The player who draws a word with the least number of syllables is the first to play. If he has a one syllable word, he may travel to the first city on the route. If he has a two syllable word, he travels to the second city and so forth. Each player in turn draws a card, says the word on the card, tells how many syllables are in the word and moves his airplane along the flight route. If he cannot say the word or determine the number of syllables in it, some one tells him, but he cannot move his airplane. The player who reaches the home field first wins the game. (For use with two to four children, potentially self-directive.)

## Supplementary Instructional Activities for Correcting Deficiencies in Structural Analysis

When individual pupils or groups of pupils are deficient in their knowledge of structural analysis, corrective practice can be individualized by employing activities such as the following:*

A. Syllabication
  1. The child is given a list of common words. He divides the words into syllables.
  2. The child is given a list of words. He underlines words ending in a certain syllable such as -*ight* and -*ing*.
  3. The child is given a series of pictures. He names each object pictured and writes the number of syllables in the name under the picture.
  4. A list of words is given to the child. He indicates the number of syllables in each word.
  5. The child is given the rules governing syllabication together with a list of words. He divides the words into syllables and indicates which rule he used.

B. Suffixes
  1. A list of words containing suffixes is given to the child. He identifies the root word in each word.
  2. The child is given a list of words containing suffixes. He uses the root word in a sentence.
  3. The child is given a list of unknown words. He separates the suffix from the word and pronounces both suffix and root word.

---

*Many of these activities can be made self-directive by furnishing simple directions and accompanying answer keys.

4. The child is given a list of words with definitions after each word. He adds one of a given group of suffixes to the words so the newly formed word complies with the definition after the word.
5. The child is given a list of words. He makes new words by adding a given suffix to the words on the list.

C. Prefixes
1. The child is given a list of words. He writes a given prefix before the words and gives the meaning of the new words.
2. A series of sentences with one word missing in each is given to the child. He fills in the words using the correct prefixes.
3. A group of prefixes and a list of words with definitions are given to the child. He adds one of the prefixes from the group to each word so it corresponds to the definition written after each word.
4. A list of words with prefixes is given to the child. He writes the words without the prefix and indicates how the meaning has been changed.
5. The child is given a list of unknown words with a known prefix. He finds the meaning of the new word.
6. The child is given a list of words with prefixes. He underlines the prefixes.
7. The child is given a list of words containing common prefixes. He underlines the root word.

D. Common Compound Words
1. A list of compound words is given to the child. He draws a line between the two words making up each compound word.
2. Two columns of words are given to the child. He makes compound words by matching the words in one column with the words in the other column.
3. The child is given a list of compound words. He writes the two short words that make up the compound beside each word.
4. The child is given two lists of words. He combines words from the two lists to form single compound words.

E. Endings of Words
1. A series of phrases are given to the child. If a phrase refers to more than one, the child adds the plural to the subject of the phrases.
2. The child is given a group of pictures. The child names the objects in the pictures and gives the plural of the name if there is more than one object involved.
3. The child is given a list of singular words. He forms the plurals of each word in the list.
4. The child is given a list of words. He forms new words by adding given endings to the words.

## Using Workbooks

In an effort to help pupils build their word-recognition and word-analysis skills, teachers should capitalize on the vast supply of practice material available in the form of workbooks* Some of these workbooks are designed to accompany basal series; others are supplemental skill-type workbooks. Both types can be used to advantage. Following is a representative sample of workbooks that are suitable.

*A World of Words* by I. F. FORST, G. GOLDBERG and A. L. BOCK, Philadelphia: Winston. This workbook has as its principle objective the building of vocabulary for junior high students. Its method is essentially the successful direct method used to teach foreign language.

*Adventures in Dictionary Land* by E. E. LEWIS et al., New York: American Book Company. A series of three workbooks for dictionary training. These workbooks are suitable for use with students at or above the fourth-grade level.

*Building Words* by E. SAVAGE, Chicago: Beckley-Cardy Co. A first-grade workbook which provides ear and eye training in beginning, middle and ending sounds of words with emphasis on vowel sounds. Suggestions are given for the teacher.

*Building Word Power* by D. D. DURRELL and H. B. SULLIVAN, New York: World Book. This workbook is accompanied by a teacher's manual and is devoted to exercises in auditory and visual discrimination on the primary level.

*Building Reading Skills* by L. ARMSTRONG and R. HARGRAVE, Wichita: McCormick-Mathers. These six workbooks are for elementary grade children and are designed to build essential reading skills. Practice material is included to train children in phonetic and structural analysis, sight vocabulary development, word meaning, phrase perception, paragraph comprehension and the like. These workbooks can be used with any series of readers.

*Eye and Ear Fun* by C. STONE, Manchester Mo.: Webster Publishing. A series of four books which can be used in connection with any basic series of readers. The workbooks are designed to provide a carefully organized course for developing fluency, accuracy and independence in word recognition.

*Fun with Words and Pictures* by G. L. GARSON, Chicago: Follett Publishing Company. A series of workbooks for the primary grades. Considerable space is devoted to coloring and pasting.

*Functional Phonetic Books* by A. D. CORDTS, Westchester: Benefic Press. A series of three phonics workbooks that employs whole word approach (words appear contextually, in sentences) that is compatible with the look-say method of teaching reading. A teacher's manual also is available.

*Happy Times with Sounds* by L. M. THOMPSON, Boston: Allyn & Bacon, Inc. A series of three workbooks which gives training in sounding for the primary grades. A teacher's handbook accompanies the series.

*Iroquois Phonics Program* by W. K. EATON and B. F. FAMES, Syracuse: Iroquois. These three workbooks with accompanying manuals stress letter phonics, combinations and syllabication. Advanced sections include contextual reading.

---

*See pages 137-138 for a more detailed discussion of workbooks and their proper use.

*Learning the Letters* by M. A. STANGER and E. K. DONOHUE, New York: Oxford University Press. A series of six workbooks for the primary grades which stress the sounds of consonants and vowels.

*Learning the Letter Sounds* by P. MCKEE and L. M. HARRISON, Boston: Houghton Mifflin, Company. A first-grade workbook for teaching initial consonant sounds.

*Primary Seatwork* by J. MCDADE, Chicago: Plymouth Press. Seatwork material designed to teach reading by the nonoral method.

*Puzzle Pages* by F. SHELTON and L. TATE, Wichita: McCormick-Mathers. These simple workbooks for primer and first-grade work involve pasting and cutting of words and sentences in connection with pictures.

*Phonic Fun* by G. N. EDWARDS *et al.*, Chicago: Beckley-Cardy Co. Two workbooks for grades one and two presenting phonic elements (initial sounds, vowels and endings) with word frequencies as contained in basic readers.

*Phonics* by S. HERR, Los Angeles: Educational Research Associates. A series of three phonic workbooks for the elementary grades designed to give a thorough understanding of basic phonic principles through the use of extensive materials. Liberal use is made of pictures and illustrations.

*Phonics Skilltexts* by M. MCCRORY and P. WATTS, Columbus, Ohio: Charles E. Merrill Books, Inc. A series of four workbooks (A, B, C, D) for the elementary grades that give training in word-recognition skills through visual, auditory and kinesthetic activities.

*Phonogram Books* by P. B. RADNER, Maplewood, N. J.: Hammond Incorporated. A series of four 6 by 8 inch workbooks that teaches simple phonograms, vowel digraphs and medial phonograms, initial digraphs and terminal digraphs, respectively. Words employed are drawn from the speaking vocabulary of the beginner.

*Remedial Reading Drills* by T. G. HEGGE, S. A. KIRK and W. A. KIRK, Ann Arbor: George Wahr. A booklet for primary or intermediate grades containing isolated words in list form. Teaching centers around letter-by-letter sounding with kinesthetic reinforcement.

*Words Are Important* by H. C. HARDWICKE, C. S. Hammond & Company, Maplewood, N. J. A series of meaning vocabulary workbooks for junior and senior high school. Graded words are based on frequency categories of *Thorndike and Lorge Teacher's Word Book of 30,000 Words*.

## Employing Reading Games

In seeking material that will strengthen individual weaknesses many teachers turn to reading games* since they are or can be made self-directive. Although teachers have experienced varying degrees of suc-

---

*A half-hour sound filmstrip of unique reading games is available through Bailey Films, Incorporated, 6509 DeLongpre, Los Angeles, California, *Teaching Reading Through Games* by Delwyn G. Schubert and Leslie W. Nelson, 1963. For a more definitive statement on the subject of reading games, the reader can request the following free booklet from Garrard Press, Champaign, Ill.; *Reading Games in the Reading Program* by Delwyn G. Schubert, 1961.

cess with reading games, they are in general agreement that the play technique does arouse interest and provides needed motivation.

Reading games have advantages as effective instructional devices, but they also have their limitations. Most reading games are designed to provide extra practice in word recognition, word analysis and word meaning, but the material is limited to practice on words in isolation. Unless the games are supplemented by recreational reading and developmental instruction on meaningful content, their effectiveness in most cases will be of doubtful value. Especially valuable in this regard are the Dolch *Basic Vocabulary Series,* published by Garrard Press, which are written almost entirely with the Dolch two hundred twenty basic sight words and ninety-five commonest nouns. Unfortunately, too many teachers use games as mere busy work with no followup to determine their effectiveness. These teachers fail to evaluate and reevaluate reading games by asking, "When and for whom is this game valuable and useful?"

Care must be taken that the reading game employed is not too juvenile and that it provides meaningful practice in terms of the individual's reading difficulty. Often, too, meaningful practice can be assured only if the teacher or an able child provides some surveillance during the playing of the game. Certainly there is no need to continue a game for an individual or group when progress in the skill the game purports to develop comes to a halt. Once children fail to enjoy a game they fail to profit from it and it should be withdrawn.

Reading games provide self-competition when the results are recorded by the pupil. Keeping a record of the number of successes per unit of playing time proves motivation for the child. It also enables the teacher to evaluate pupil progress and determine the effectiveness of the game for the learner.

In short, when reading games are selected carefully on the basis of appropriate content, difficulty and pupil interest, and when the results are charted by the pupil and evaluated by the teacher, they serve as a useful individualized and self-directed instructional activity.

The reader will find that many of the instructional aids presented in this chapter take the form of games. As indicated on page 86, all games are designated by an asterisk.

### SUPPLEMENTARY PROBLEMS FOR ORAL AND WRITTEN DISCUSSION

1. Why are the skills of word analysis important in reading?
2. What are the advantages and limitations of reading games?
3. Use an appropriate reading game with a group of pupils. Provide an objective method of recording results. Evaluate its effectiveness.

4. Construct an original reading game and have it evaluated by your colleagues.
5. Select three or more items from the list of corrective material appearing in this chapter. Describe the nature and functions of these materials; revise the directions for these materials in order to make them more self-directive.

REFERENCES

1. *A Place to Start: A Graded Bibliography for Children Reading Difficulties* (Syracuse: Syracuse University Press); GEORGE SPACHE, *Good Reading for Poor Readers* (Champaign, Ill.: Garrard Publishing Company, 1966).
2. For a more extensive treatment see JOHN DEBOER and MARTHA DALLMAN, *The Teaching of Reading* (New York: Holt, Rinehart & Winston, Inc., 1964), pp. 105-106.
3. GERTRUDE HILDRETH, *Teaching Reading* (New York: Henry Holt and Company, Inc., 1959), p. 155.
4. DELWYN SCHUBERT, "Teachers and Word Analysis Skills," *Journal of Developmental Reading* (Summer, 1959), pp. 62-64.
5. GEORGE SPACHE, *Reading in the Elementary School* (Boston: Allyn & Bacon, Inc., 1964), pp. 309-311.
6. LEE DEIGHTON, *Vocabulary Development in the Classroom* (Bureau of Publications, Teachers College, Columbia University, 1959).
7. C. WINKLEY, "Which Accent Generalizations Are Worth Teaching?" *The Reading Teacher* (December, 1966), pp. 219-224.
8. THEODORE CLYMER, "The Utility of Phonic Generalizations in the Primary Grades," *The Reading Teacher* (January, 1963), pp. 252-258.
9. WINKLEY, *op. cit.*

SELECTED READINGS

BOND, GUY and MILES TINKER, *Reading Problems: Their Diagnosis and Correction* 2nd ed., New York: Appleton-Century-Crofts, 1967, ch. 12.
DEBOER, JOHN and MARTHA DALLMAN, *The Teaching of Reading*, New York: Holt, Rinehart & Winston, Inc., 1964, ch. 6B.
DURKIN, DOLORES, "Phonics Materials: A Big Seller," *The Reading Teacher*, April, 1967, pp. 610-614.
GRAY, WILLIAM, *On Their Own in Reading* 2nd ed., Chicago: Scott, Foresman & Company, 1960.
HARRIS, ALBERT, *How to Increase Reading Ability*, 4th ed., New York: Longmans, Green and Company, 1961, chs. 12-14.
SPACHE, GEORGE, *Toward Better Reading*, Champaign, Ill.: Garrard Publishing Company, 1963, ch. 13.

# Analyzing Difficulties in Comprehension and Study Skills

Reading is more than "barking at the print." Reading is a meaningful process. Because this is true, the child who fails to bring proper meaning to printed symbols and fails to comprehend what the writer wishes to convey is not reading.

## Difficulties with Basic Reading Skills

While comprehension is the all-important goal at all grade levels, generally it is not a problem to the average primary grade child. The narrative material used by authors of basal readers at this level employs well-controlled vocabularies which carefully stay within the average child's background of experience. Consequently, understanding the printed page becomes little more than blending sight and sound. Once the primary grade child has learned to associate familiar sounds with the new and unfamiliar written symbols on the printed page, he is able to understand the story the author wishes to convey. It is obvious, then, that a mastery of the basic reading skills is the "open sesame" to comprehension for most children in the primary grades. Since, however, there is a natural tendency on the part of children to accept what appears in print as sacrosanct, there is always a need for teachers to stimulate children to react critically to what has been read. (See Chapter 7 for suggestions as to how reading can be made a thinking process.)

Any weakness in the basic reading skills evidences itself quickly in the fourth grade and beyond. Expository materials are encountered and vocabulary burdens increase with alarming rapidity at these levels. The child whose basic sight vocabulary and word analysis skills are below par soon is in over his head. Not only is he troubled by high-frequency words which he should have mastered long ago, but he is bewildered by technical words in arithmetic such as *minuend, subtrahend* and *quotient,* and technical words in geography such as *latitude, longitude* and *doldrums.* As the number of unknown words increases, comprehension is impossible and mastery of the unknown symbols proves an overwhelming task because of their prevalence.

Evaluating a child's competence in the basic reading skills is an important first step in dealing with comprehension problems in the intermediate and upper grades. Too often teachers expend time and energy on trying to develop high-level comprehension skills when attention should first be devoted to building a basic sight vocabulary and to teaching independence in basic word-attack skills.

Pupils who comprehend material read to them by the teacher but who fail to comprehend when reading silently often are handicapped by basic reading skill deficiencies. Formal and informal listening tests, therefore, prove valuable in diagnosis. (See Appendix C for a description of listening tests.) Further corroboration or verification of sight-vocabulary and word-attack deficiencies that are needed can be had by employing formal and informal oral reading tests. (See Chapter 4 for a more complete discussion of this.)

WORD MEANING

In intermediate and upper grades, word meaning becomes an important factor in comprehension since students encounter many aurally unfamiliar words at these levels. When a student lacks a good meaning vocabulary, sentence comprehension and paragraph comprehension become difficult because of the many gaps in the continuity of the reading process. It is essential, therefore, to measure the size of a student's meaning vocabulary and to evaluate his ability to use the dictionary when diagnosing comprehension problems. Fortunately, most silent reading tests, both survey and diagnostic, include sections that are devoted to meaning vocabulary.

When a pupil's meaning vocabulary is meager, a teacher will find it profitable to inventory his background of experience. It will be found that some children are products of environments that have provided little or no cultural stimulation. If this is true, the school has the responsibility of giving the kinds of direct and indirect experiences needed to compensate for such impoverishment.

## SENTENCE COMPREHENSION

When expressing complete thoughts, the shortest basic unit is the sentence. The disabled reader who learns to understand sentences can move directly into paragraph comprehension.

A great deal more than meaning vocabulary is involved in sentence comprehension. Many poor readers can call all the words in a sentence and, seemingly, know the meaning of each word, but the overall meaning or concept of the sentence escapes them. Such a difficulty may stem from an inability to group words into meaningful thought units. Consider, for example, how difficult it is to comprehend the following sentence.

(It was a long)   (time after the)   (big fight had)   (taken place by)  (the roadside.)

Words go together to make thought units. The child who has not sensed the inherent rhythm within the language structure struggles vainly for meaning. How much easier and more meaningful the sentence becomes when the words are grouped into logical phrases.

(It was)   (a long time)   (after the big fight)   (had taken place)  (by the roadside.)

The simplest way to check phrasing ability is to ask a pupil to read aloud. Does he group the words into intelligent phrases? Are there slight pauses in the right places?

Another impediment to sentence comprehension which can be detected by having a child read aloud, is his inattention to punctuation. Ignoring commas can result in immediate confusion of sentence sense. Consider, for example, the following:

Jim, too, saw two of them.

Bill said to him, "Today, we shall go to the movies."

## PARAGRAPH COMPREHENSION

"The whole is more than the sum of its parts." A disabled reader often is inclined to consider each sentence in isolation from the rest of the sentences in a paragraph. He fails to connect all sentences into a unified whole. He sees the trees but misses the forest.

In order to comprehend a paragraph as a unified whole, two skills are absolutely essential. First, it is necessary for the reader to spot the main or central idea of the paragraph. Once he knows what the general idea of the paragraph is, related details fall into place.

Fortunately, most silent reading tests devote sections to paragraph comprehension enabling teachers to determine if pupils have weaknesses in this regard.

As was true with difficulty in sentence comprehension, inattention to punctuation must be considered as a possible cause of poor paragraph comprehension. Ignoring periods, question marks, semicolons and colons will result in running together the thoughts of sentences. A pupil's tendency to ignore these landmarks, which an author employs to emphasize the ideas he has organized into a paragraph, can be readily detected by having a pupil read aloud.

CRITICAL READING

We live in a democracy where it is essential for pupils to discern truth from falsehood and good from evil. Pupils are too prone to accept anything and everything in print as infallible. The statement, "I know it is true because I read it," is a familiar refrain.

Two important factors which are associated with a pupil's ability to read critically are intelligence and experiential background.

Children of superior intelligence are more likely to react critically to what they read than children of average or below average intelligence. Although the relationship between intelligence and critical reading is positive, a high-intelligence quotient doesn't assure high performance in critical reading. Even the very bright may have weaknesses in this regard.

Children who have a reservoir of rich experiences are in a better position to evaluate what is read than are children whose background of experiences is meager. Critical thinking is difficult when one possesses an inadequate frame of reference.

When a pupil reads, understands and then sanctions material containing contradictions, questionable opinions or improbable situations which should be obvious, a need for instruction in critical reading exists. Chapter 7 will provide a number of practical suggestions for helping students develop critical reading ability.

CONCENTRATION

Some students suffer comprehension difficulties because of mind-wandering tendencies. They read words and lines of print but find on turning a page that although their eyes were going through the mechanical process of reading, their minds were playing hide-and-go-seek. This inability to concentrate makes comprehension difficult and efforts should be made to uncover causes of the problem.

Visual difficulties, poor general health and emotional disturbances (see Chapter 4) are frequently responsible for concentration problems. Other factors that should be investigated when causal factors are probed include difficulty of the material being read, reader interest, lighting and the presence of distracting influences in the study environment.

## RETENTION

Since many reading comprehension tests are tests of retention (1) a pupil's ability to remember what he has read has a direct bearing on his comprehension test score.

Although some disabled readers can remember material they do not understand, the opposite is often true. Problem readers show little retention for what has been read. Although infrequent, the authors have encountered children who could not tell in their own words the thought of simple sentences just read.

When a disabled reader is forced to read material that is too difficult, poor retention is understandable. But when the reading material is relatively simple, why should retention be poor? Some children become victims of an unfortunate kind of conditioning brought about by teachers who consistently ask factual questions immediately after silent reading takes place. When this occurs year after year, it isn't surprising to find that children expect and wait to be pumped for information. Means of correcting this situation will be treated in the next chapter.

## FOLLOWING DIRECTIONS

Standardized reading tests frequently have a section devoted to following directions. There is a very good reason for this. We live in a gadget-filled world. The ability to understand and follow directions is essential to our efficient use of the latest, modern conveniences. Manuals of all kinds containing printed directions are available to the housewife, auto mechanic, radio technician and numerous other specialists who are part of our modern-day world. The inability to follow printed directions leads to frustration and costly errors.

The results of an inability to follow directions may be amusing, and in some instances, tragic. Hovious provides us with two anecdotes to illustrate this point. She tells of a family that went on a two weeks' vacation. "While they were gone, they wanted their house painted white, with green trimmings. When they came back, they found that the workmen had painted the vacant house next door! Naturally, the workers had to come back and paint the right house. They lost money and the house owner was inconvenienced — all because the painters did not follow directions." Another example involved a woman who was cleaning some clothes on the back porch. "Suddenly a terrific blast shook the house. Flames leaped out. Splinters flew. Plaster fell. What had happened? Why the cleaning fluid had exploded. On the bottle of cleaner there was a big warning not to use the fluid near an open flame, but the woman hadn't read the directions." (2)

## Silent Reading Tests: Survey

Most silent reading survey tests provide a meaning vocabulary score and a comprehension score and are helpful in determining the level at which pupils can read. Although most of these tests have a working time of only thirty to forty-five minutes and enable a teacher to locate retarded readers quickly, they do have limitations.

A teacher must recognize that a child's reading level, as indicated by a silent reading survey test, is often an overestimate of his instructional level. Silent reading tests are usually of the recognition type. They encourage guessing which often results in grade scores, especially for retarded readers, that average one grade or more above their effective reading level. Furthermore, when silent reading tests of the survey type are employed, it must not be assumed that several pupils in a given grade share the same difficulties because they received the same low score on the test. While the difficulty of the corrective material may be appropriate, further study will show that these pupils usually do not suffer from the same reading handicaps. The reading grade score on a silent reading test is based on the total correct responses. Each pupil has his own constellation of strengths and weaknesses of which an effective corrective program must take cognizance and be designed to meet. For example, in the skills of word analysis some pupils may be weak in beginning sounds and blends while others need help with vowel sounds and the principles of syllabication. Seldom do pupils in a class have identical weaknesses in many of the basic reading skills.

Most survey tests provide grade norms which the teacher may use as a rough measure of a child's reading level. Other norms frequently found include age norms and percentile norms. When a comparison is made between intelligence and reading, it is advisable to use age rather than grade scores.

A descriptive list of silent reading tests appears in Appendix C.

## Silent Reading Tests: Diagnostic

While most silent reading tests of the survey type measure only comprehension and meaning vocabulary, diagnostic silent reading tests are more analytical since they provide measures of such silent reading abilities as noting important details, discovering central thoughts, following directions, using reference skills, summarizing, outlining, organizing and reading maps, graphs and charts. (See Appendix C.)

## READING RATE AND COMPREHENSION

Efficiency in reading comprehension is directly related to a pupil's rate of reading. As he progresses from grade to grade his reading speed becomes a very significant factor in his over-all efficiency. Usually, the rapid reader is the efficient reader because impressions are stronger when thought concepts are received in rapid sequence.

It is a mistake to assume, however, that speed per se automatically results in increased reading comprehension. The efficient reader is fluent and his speed grows out of this fluency. The inefficient reader is not fluent and his effort to cover the ground more quickly involves hurried reading rather than rapid reading. Hurried reading results in a quick loss of intellectual breath and comprehension suffers.

Many pupils read slowly because they are inept at phrasing and read one word at a time. Word-by-word reading may be an outgrowth of overanalysis of words or the result of a meager sight vocabulary. If the situation continues for a length of time, the word-by-word pattern crystallizes into a habit and continues to persist even though word perception difficulties cease to be a problem. It is important, therefore, for the teacher to determine whether the pupil's word-by-word reading pattern is an outgrowth of habituation or whether deficiencies in basic skills are involved. (3) Oral reading tests and word-recognition tests can be employed to make this diagnosis.

Although many silent reading tests include estimates of reading rate, teachers may wish to make informal appraisals of their own. This can be done by asking pupils to read a selection silently while the teacher records the passing time on the blackboard in ten-second intervals. The readers are asked to record the largest number on the board immediately on completion of the selection. Once this has been done, simple mathematical procedure (dividing the words read by the seconds involved and then multiplying the results by 60) will give a words-per-minute score.

While silent reading is taking place, the teacher should scrutinize each pupil for habits that are known to be detrimental to reading speed. These include finger pointing, head wagging and lip movements. The latter habit is manifest in many primary grade pupils because of the instructional emphasis on oral reading. At these early stages, it is not of great concern since the majority of children read no faster silently than they do orally. In the intermediate grades, however, when silent reading speeds begin to exceed oral reading speeds, pupils are admonished when subvocalization is detected. At these grade levels pupils should be able to read two or three times faster silently than orally. Any movement of the vocal mechanism during silent reading can do nothing but impede a pupil's speed.

FLEXIBILITY AND READING SPEED

Other things being equal, a child's speed of comprehension is dependent on the difficulty of the material read. Good readers are flexible readers who vary and adapt their rates to the nature of the content and the purposes for which they are reading. Poor readers are inept in this regard. A valuable index of efficiency on a silent reading test is the ratio of comprehension items answered correctly to those attempted. It is advisable for a teacher to express the results in fractional form. For example, a glance at the fraction 18/20 would indicate that twenty comprehension items were attempted and eighteen were answered correctly, resulting in an accuracy score of 90 per cent. (A score of 80 per cent is the usual minimum acceptable.) Such a procedure enables the teacher to categorize a child as a fast-accurate reader, a fast-inaccurate reader, an average-accurate reader, an average-inaccurate reader, a slow-accurate reader or a slow-inaccurate reader. This information is very important when making a diagnosis.

## Suggested Procedures in Diagnosing Comprehension Difficulties Through the Use of Standardized Silent Reading Tests

1. *Basic Reading Skills*: See Chapter 4.
2. *Comprehension*:* To locate independent readers who are deficient in one or more of the comprehension skills, administer a diagnostic silent reading test to pupils above the primary grades who are retarded in silent reading but are not deficient in word attack skill. Convert raw scores to grade scores in sentence meaning, paragraph comprehension, locating central thoughts and the like.
3. *Meaning Vocabulary*: To locate pupils who are deficient in meaning vocabulary, convert raw scores in meaning vocabulary to grade scores for pupils above the primary grades who are independent readers but who are retarded in comprehension. Record results on the Reading Inventory (Ch. 4).
4. *Work Study Skills*: To locate independent readers who are deficient in one or more of the study skills, convert work study skill's scores

---

*See item 3 on page 80 for procedures in locating retarded readers.

from a study skills test or a diagnostic reading test; study skill's sections, to grade scores.

5. *Rate of Comprehension*: To locate pupils who have a slow rate of comprehension, administer a rate of reading test to independent readers above the fifth grade. Convert raw scores to grade scores.

## Oral Reading Tests and Teacher Observation

1. *Oral Reading Tests*: To locate word-by-word readers whose inability to phrase and read in thought units is impeding their comprehension and rate of reading, administer formal or informal oral reading tests to pupils above the primary grades. Record results on the *Reading Inventory and Progress Record* (see end of Chapter 4) and the *Diagnostic Reading Summary* at the end of this chapter.

2. *Subvocalization*: To locate pupils who articulate words as they read, observe lip movements of pupils above the primary grades as they read silently. Record results on the reading inventory. If lip movements are not present, vibration of the vocal cords can be detected by the teacher by placing the tips of the fingers against both sides of the pupil's throat, just above the larynx, while he reads silently.

3. *Finger Pointing and Head Wagging*: Observe pupils above the primary grades as they read silently in order to locate those who use their fingers or other objects for pointing at a word. Record results on the reading inventory. Observe pupils above the primary grades as they read silently in order to locate those who move their heads in pendulum-like fashion. Record results on the Reading Inventory.

## Individual Diagnostic Reading Summary

After the diagnosis of reading difficulties in comprehension and study skills has been made, the significant data should be recorded on the *Reading Inventory and Progress Record* which appears near the end of Chapter 4. (This form provides space for recording changes in specific disabilities at the end of each instructional period — week, month, etc.)

The diagnosis now can be extended by assembling data from other sources: oral and silent reading tests, listening tests, personality tests, intelligence tests, school records, observations and interviews. The resulting analysis will help establish a pupil's reading potential, present reading level, specific reading difficulties and hazards to learning, and it will assist the teacher in prescribing appropriate corrective instruction. The *Individual Diagnostic Reading Summary* which follows is suggestive of a convenient method of recording these data. Chapters 5, 7 and 8 provide a comprehensive list of instructional material useful in individualized correction.

INDIVIDUAL DIAGNOSTIC READING SUMMARY

Pupil ........................................ School ........................ Grade ......... Age.........

Teacher ................................................................ Date ...........................

### Test Results

Oral Reading Test ........................ Silent Reading Test .......................

Oral Reading Scores: Accuracy ........... Comprehension .......... Rate ...........

Grade Equivalents: Accuracy .......... Comprehension .......... Rate ..........

Silent Reading Grade Scores:

    Comprehension ............... Meaning Vocabulary ............... Rate ...............

Group Intelligence Test:

    Date ............... M.A. (Total) ........... Lang. ........... Nonlang. ..........

Group Intelligence Test:

    Date ...................... I.Q. (Total) ........... Lang. ........... Nonlang. ..........

Oral Reading Retardation: From Grade ........... From Nonlang. M .A. ...........

Oral Reading Retardation: From Grade .............. From Auding Level ...........

Silent Reading Retardation: From Grade ........... From Nonlang. M. A. ...........

Silent Reading Retardation: From Grade .............. From Auding Level ...........

Scholarship ...............................................................................................

Onset of Reading Problem ...........................................................................

### Hazards to Learning

Health ......................................................................................................

Hearing ....................................................................................................

Vision ......................................................................................................

Personal Adjustment ....................................................................................

Out of School Environment ..........................................................................

Hazards to Learning in Need of Correction ....................................................

School Program Designed to Promote Improved Conditions for Learning

..........................................................................................................................................

..........................................................................................................................................

..........................................................................................................................................

..........................................................................................................................................

..........................................................................................................................................

..........................................................................................................................................

..........................................................................................................................................

..........................................................................................................................................

..........................................................................................................................................

..........................................................................................................................................

### *Specific Reading Difficulties*

Prevalent Errors from Oral Reading (Informal) .......................................................

..........................................................................................................................................

..........................................................................................................................................

Prevalent Errors in Oral Reading Test .......................................................................

..........................................................................................................................................

..........................................................................................................................................

..........................................................................................................................................

Difficulties in Silent Reading ....................................................................................

..........................................................................................................................................

..........................................................................................................................................

..........................................................................................................................................

Faulty Reading Habits ...............................................................................................

..........................................................................................................................................

..........................................................................................................................................

### *Recommended Improvement Program in Reading*

Child's Potential Reading Level ................................................................................
Reading Skills to Be Corrected and Mastered:
Word Perception ........................................................................................................

..........................................................................................................................................

Word Analysis .............................................................................................................

..........................................................................................................................................

..........................................................................................................................................

Meaning Vocabulary ..................................................................................................

..........................................................................................................................................

..........................................................................................................................................

Comprehension ............................................................................................................

..........................................................................................................................................

..........................................................................................................................................

Study Skills ....................................................................................................................

Rate of Comprehension ............................................................................................

..........................................................................................................................................

..........................................................................................................................................

Appropriate Instructional Difficulty Level ..... Independent Reading Level ......

Corrective Material Recommended ........................................................................

..........................................................................................................................................

..........................................................................................................................................

Difficulty of Material ................. Special Methods Recommended ..................

..........................................................................................................................................

..........................................................................................................................................

..........................................................................................................................................

..........................................................................................................................................

Fields of Interest for Recreational Reading .......................................................

..........................................................................................................................................

..........................................................................................................................................

..........................................................................................................................................

..........................................................................................................................................

### SUPPLEMENTARY PROBLEMS FOR ORAL AND WRITTEN DISCUSSION

1. What are the limitations in using a silent reading test to locate a pupil's difficulties in reading?
2. Obtain the following test results for a pupil in the intermediate or upper grades: verbal mental age, nonverbal mental age, oral reading grade score, silent reading grade score, listening score, vocabulary grade score and rate of reading grade score. Summarize and interpret the results.
3. Obtain test results for a poor reader, an average reader and an accelerated reader. Determine the reading potential of each pupil.
4. What are the uses of the dictionary in a reading program in the intermediate and upper grades?
5. What is subvocalization and how does it influence reading?
6. What are the study skills and why are they important?

### REFERENCES

1. WALTER BARBE, "Measuring Reading Comprehension," *The Clearing House* (February, 1958), p. 343.
2. CAROL HOVIOUS, *Flying the Printways* (Boston: D. C. Heath & Company, 1938), p. 355.

3. HELEN ROBINSON and HELEN SMITH, "Rate Problems in the Reading Clinic," *The Reading Teacher* (May, 1962), pp. 421-426.

## SELECTED READINGS

BOND, GUY and MILES TINKER, *Reading Problems: Their Diagnosis and Correction* 2nd ed., New York: Appleton-Century-Crofts, 1967, pp. 274-282.

DEBOER, JOHN and MARTHA DALLMAN, *The Teaching of Reading*, New York: Holt, Rinehart & Winston, Inc., 1964, ch. 7A.

OTTO, WAYNE and RICHARD McMENEMY, *Corrective and Remedial Teaching*, Boston: Houghton Mifflin Company, 1966, pp. 181-187.

SCHUBERT, DELWYN, *Readings in Reading: Practice-Theory-Research*, New York: Thomas Y. Crowell Company, 1968, selection 26 by Barke.

# Chapter

# 7

# Correcting and Improving Comprehension Difficulties

This chapter is devoted to specific games, techniques and materials that are of value in helping children overcome deficiencies in reading comprehension if properly used. The teacher who wishes to help pupils whose comprehension problems stem from limited sight and meaning vocabularies is referred to Chapters 5 and 6.

## Workbooks

Workbooks which are widely used in developmental and corrective reading programs are of two types: those that accompany basal readers and those that are independent of any series of readers. The former are designed for group instruction directed by the teacher. Their content usually is divided into units paralleling the basal reader and is designed to provide additional practice on those reading skills developed in the basal reader.

The content of independent workbooks does not parallel basal readers. Some independent workbooks emphasize a single group of skills such as word analysis or comprehension. Usually their difficulty is not expressed in grade levels and many of them provide simple directions written for the pupils. Because of this, the teacher is able to utilize books on several levels of difficulty in meeting class needs.

Independent workbooks are of particular value in meeting the needs of pupils above the third grade who are retarded one to three years in their reading skills. For these pupils, the regular basal reader and the accompanying workbooks are too difficult. In such cases, the teacher can turn to an independent series of workbooks for the purpose of selecting those of optimum difficulty for specific pupils. Such workbooks should have simple directions that have been written for the pupils so they can pursue the materials independently at their own rate.

An example of a particularly popular independent workbook series is the *Readers Digest Reading Skill Series.*\* This series contains short and highly motivating selections that have great appeal and are ideally suited to developmental and remedial work. Three booklets are now available on each grade level from two to eight. A variety of exercises for developing comprehension, rate and vocabulary are included. If used in conjunction with the teacher's manual (answers to questions are to be found therein), most of the exercises can be made self-corrective.

All pupils who are retarded in any reading skills should be assigned only the skills or units they have not mastered. If the workbook does not provide enough practice, a second book should be provided in which the desired units are indicated. Answer sheets on which responses are to be written should be furnished so the books are not consumed by one pupil but can be used over and over by many children.

Another method of providing flexibility with effectiveness in the use of workbooks is to secure two copies of two or three series of independent workbooks. Cut the pages apart and mount them on tagboard. Assemble and classify the material by units or skills according to the level of difficulty and then provide a file in which the pupil can readily locate the exercises he needs. Mounting paper of various colors can be employed to designate levels of difficulty, if desired. By combining materials from two or three workbooks an adequate supply of self-directed practice material on several levels of difficulty is assured. Having the pupils write their responses on separate answer sheets insures continued use of the workbook exercises.

When evolving an answer file, it is best to write the answers to single exercises on small cards. Exercises and cards must be marked to correspond. Letters or numbers can be used for this purpose.

Following is a representative list of workbooks that contains material suitable for developing pupils' comprehension and study skills.

*Better Reading* by J. C. GAINSBURG and S. I. SPECTOR, New York: Globe Book Company, Inc., 1962. A recently revised and modernized text for corrective work on the high-school level. Exercises are provided on skimming, main ideas, outlining and other reading areas.

*Cowboy Sam Workbooks* by E. W. CHANDLER, Chicago: Beckley-Cardy Co. A series of four workbooks which parallel the *Cowboy Sam Readers.*

---

\*Booklets covering grades 2 to 6 cost $.51 each; booklets for grades 6 to 8 cost $.60.

The workbooks range from primer to third-grade level and provide checks for reading vocabulary, understanding, following directions and so forth. Space is provided for coloring.

*Developmental Reading Text-workbook Series* by W. H. BURTON *et al.*, Indianapolis: The Bobbs-Merrill Co., Inc., 1961. This series provides a complete developmental program in reading. Each workbook is organized into units with each unit consisting of a story followed by exercises in comprehension and word-analysis skills. The series can be used in conjunction with or supplementary to basal reading materials to reinforce learning. It also can be used independently of basal reading materials, as in programs emphasizing individualized or independent reading.

*Diagnostic Reading Workbooks* by R. F. GREENWOOD and J. V. WILLIAM, Columbus, Ohio: Harrison. This series of workbooks is designed to give elementary children practice in four important skills. These include (1) ability to comprehend facts, (2) ability to do independent things and to evaluate, (3) development of vocabulary and word mastery, (4) ability to find the main ideas in a selection. Grade level is indicated by stars on the cover and title page.

*Diagnostic Tests and Exercises in Reading* by L. J. BRUECKNER and W. D. LEWIS, Philadelphia: Winston Co., 1935. A workbook for retarded readers having fourth-grade reading ability. It contains tests and exercises in word recognition, vocabulary, phrasing, central thoughts, related details and rate.

*Mastery of Reading* by M. BAILEY and U. LEAVELL, New York: American Book Company. These three workbooks are for junior high-school students and can be used independently of the three texts they parallel. Each chapter provides students with drills and exercises centered around a single reading skill.

*Mother Hubbard's Seatwork Cupboard* by D. E. KIBBE, Eau Claire, Wisc: E.M. Hale and Company. Two workbooks are involved. The first workbook is for first-grade children and concentrates on ninety-three words. Word-picture matching, coloring and pasting are the predominant activities. The second workbook introduces sentence and paragraph reading.

*My Work Book in Reading* by E. M. ALDREDGE and J. F. McKEE, Chicago: Beckley-Cardy Co. These workbooks in reading for the primary grades contain a variety of reading and numbers materials. Considerable space is devoted to coloring and pasting.

*Practice Readers* by C. R. STONE and C. C. GRAVER, Manchester, Mo.: Webster Publishing, 1961. A series of four workbooks consisting of short selections followed by exercises pertaining to direct details, implied details, meaning of the whole, correctness of a statement in relation to the selection, understanding the meaning of reference words and perception of the truth or falseness of a statement.

*Practice Exercises in Reading* by A. I. GATES and C. C. PEARDON, Bureau of of Publication, Teachers College, Columbia University, 1963. A series of four workbooks which train students in the four types of reading corresponding to the types of ability measured by the Gates Silent Reading Tests. These involve (1) reading to appreciate the general significance of a selection, (2) reading to predict the outcome of given events, (3) reading to understand precise directions, (4) reading to note details. These widely used booklets are provided for grades three to six.

*Reading Essential Series* by U. W. LEAVELL et al., Austin, Texas: Steck-Vaughn Company, 1953. This series of workbooks which covers grades one through eight can be used to fit different reading levels in the various grades. Exercises include the development of phonetic skills, structural analysis, dictionary skills and comprehension skills. The selections have high-interest appeal and are carefully graded.

*Reading for Meaning* by W. S. GUILER and J. H. COLEMAN, Philadelphia: J. B. Lippincott Co., 1935. A series of nine workbooks designed to improve the following basic reading skills: (1) word meanings, (2) total meaning, (3) central thought, (4) detailed meanings, (5) organization, (6) summarization.

*Reading Skilltext* by E. M. JOHNSON, Columbus, Ohio: Charles E. Merrill Books, Inc., 1956. A series of six workbooks that consist of illustrated stories followed by questions pertaining to comprehension, word meanings and word attack skills.

*Reading Workbooks* by A. L. McDONALD, Austin, Texas: Steck-Vaughn Company. Three workbooks for grades one and two which provide readiness material and purposeful activities to develop reading skills.

*SRA Better Reading Books* by E. A. SIMPSON, Chicago: Science Research Associates, 1962. A series of four workbooks for grades 5 to 6, 7 to 8, 9 to 10 and 11 to 12, respectively. The workbooks consist of timed-reading selections followed by multiple-choice questions.

*Standard Test Lessons in Reading* by W. A. McCALL and L. M. CRABBS, Bureau of Publications, Teachers College, Columbia University, 1961. These widely used workbooks cover grades two to twelve. Five workbooks are involved, each of which contains short selections followed by questions and grade scores.

*Think and Do* by W. S. GRAY, A. S. ARTLEY and M. MONROE, Chicago: Scott, Foresman & Company. A series of workbooks designed to accompany the Scott, Foresman basic readers. These workbooks cover grades 1 to 8 and can be used independently of the series by pupils who need carefully planned practice.

*Your Reading Guide* by N. F. RYAN, Chicago: Lyons & Carnahan, 1956. Two workbooks for junior high level that pertain to reading and study skills.

## Corrective Practice for Pupils
## Deficient in Word Meaning Vocabulary*

To acquire a large meaning vocabulary, one must read widely and must possess a curiosity about new words. Helpful, too, is a system whereby new words can be recorded and reviewed until mastered.

A number of years ago the reading specialist, Luella Cole, evolved a vocabulary-building system for children that was completely indi-

---

*Some of the materials and techniques described in Chapter 5 in connection with developing sight vocabulary can also be used for meaning vocabulary development.

vidualized and self-directive. It is ideally suited for corrective work. She described it as follows:

> There is only one really efficient way of individualizing training in word study, and that is to have each pupil keep track of the words he does not know. The procedures involved are simple. The teacher first supplies each child with twenty-five or thirty slips of paper. If she can obtain 3″ by 5″ library cards and cut them in half, these small cards are better than paper slips because they can be handled more easily. She then instructs the pupils to copy each unknown word out of the books they read, writing one word on each card. The cards should be in readiness whenever the pupil is reading anything, no matter what the subject matter of the book may be. Since almost all the words thus recorded will be within a child's understanding as soon as they are pronounced, the teacher should let the pupils get together from time to time in groups of three, in which each one shows the others the words he does not know. Most of the words that have been collected by all three will be recognized by one child or another. Any remaining words may be looked up in the dictionary if the children are old enough or handed to the teacher for her to explain. After the words are identified, each pupil goes through his own cards, saying each word he can remember over to himself. The cards containing those words he can now identify he puts in one pile; the words he cannot remember he puts in another. (1)

Cole suggests that the children continue quizzing each other until the pile of unknown words has disappeared. When pupils accumulate twenty to thirty cards, the reading period should be used for the drill described. Cards are to be kept and reviewed two or three times before they are discarded.

Facile use of the dictionary is a real asset to meaning vocabulary development. The various subskills involved in efficient dictionary usage should be catalogued and pupils in the upper grades who show weaknesses should be given proper remedial instruction. (See pages     for a discussion of dictionary skills.)

Teachers are often in a quandary regarding which words pupils should learn. In making a decision as to the importance of specific words, the teacher should consult the following:

Luella Cole. *The Teachers Handbook of Technical Vocabulary,* New York: Holt, Rinehart & Winston, Inc., 1938.

Harold Herber, *Success with Words,* New York: Scholastic Book Service, 1964.

Edward Thorndike and Irving Lorge. *The Teachers Word Book of 30,000 Words,* Bureau of Publications, Teachers College, Columbia University, 1944.

The book by Thorndike and Lorge deals with general vocabulary while the other two contain listings of words in various subject matter fields.

One of the most fascinating approaches to vocabulary enrichment involves a study of etymology, the origin or development of words. Pupils of all ages are intrigued by it. Since we have begged, borrowed and stolen words with compunction from everyone — the Spanish, French, American Indians and others — there is no dearth of words from which to choose.

Every teacher ought to have a book in his professional library such as Wilfred Funk's *Word Origins and Their Romantic Stories.** It's an open sesame to many hours of enjoyment and personal enrichment. In addition, it proves a valuable source of instructional material for stimulating the vocabulary development of readers of all ages.

Since a large number of words in the English language start with prefixes, a knowledge of them is helpful when unfamiliar words are encountered. Some of the most common prefixes are as follows: (2)

| | | |
|---|---|---|
| *ab* (from) | *dis* (apart) | *ob, op, ov* (against) |
| *ad, a, ap, at* (to) | *en* (in) | *pre* (before) |
| *be* (by) | *ex, e* (out of) | *pro* (in front of) |
| *com, con, col* (with) | *in, en, im, em* (into) | *re* (back, again) |
| *de* (from) | *in* (not) | *sub* (under) |
| | | *un* (not) |

Suffixes are more difficult for children to learn than prefixes. Fortunately, suffixes are less valuable as clues than prefixes since they are less consistent in their meanings. Some of the more common suffixes are *ment, tion, able, ous, ly, er, ful, less, ness, ing, age, ed, ance.*

Many words in the English language mean approximately the same thing. Children learn that such words are called synonyms. Words that are opposite in meaning are antonyms. Pupils enjoy and benefit from exercises dealing with synonyms and antonyms. An excellent source of synonyms and antonyms can be found in Fernald's *English Synonyms, Antonyms, and Prepositions.†* This book is far superior to other books of its kind because it not only lists synonyms and antonyms but employs them in sentences. In this way, fine differentiations between words are readily discernible. The words presented vary greatly in difficulty; therefore, teachers at all grade levels find it valuable for instructional purposes.

---

*New York: Grosset & Dunlap, Inc., 1950.
†New York: Funk & Wagnalls, 1954.

Additional kinds of corrective practice for pupils who are deficient in their meaning vocabulary can be individualized by using materials and techniques such as the following.

A. *Add On*: Numbered lists of three words belonging to a category are followed by blank spaces. Pupils are encouraged to think of other words that fit the same classification. Examples:

1. small, minute, little, ___, ___.
2. coat, hat, shoes, ___, ___.
3. dog, cat, horse, ___, ___.

Probable answers can appear on the back of the exercise. (For use with individual pupils, potentially self-directive.)

B. *Classifying Words*: Present lists of words which pupils must classify under three or more headings. Examples:

|  | *Vegetables* | *Fruits* | *Meats* |
|---|---|---|---|
| 1. carrots | 4. celery | | |
| 2. apples | 5. oranges | | |
| 3. pork | 6. lamb | | |

Correct answers can appear on the back of the exercise. (For use with individual pupils, potentially self-directive.)

C. *Cross It Out*: Numbered lists of words which belong to a specific classification are presented along with one word which is completely foreign to the group. Pupils are told to cross out the word which does not belong with the others. Examples:

1. run, jump, walk, sleep, crawl
2. cold, hot, windy, chilly, torrid
3. milk, turpentine, cocoa, coffee, tea

Correct answers can appear on the back of the exercise. (For use with individual pupils, potentially self-directive.)

D. *Label Me*: Paste a large picture of any scene relating to the unit being taught on a piece of tagboard. Provide small word cards and put these in an accompanying envelope. Pupils are directed to place the word cards on or near the proper items in the picture. Correct answers in the form of pictures can appear on the back of the individual word cards. (For use with individual pupils, potentially self-directive.)

E. *Matching*: Prepare parallel columns of synonyms or antonyms and direct pupils to match the two. Examples:

1. strong ___        a. gigantic
2. large ___        b. powerful
3. fast ___        c. rapid

Correct answers can appear on the back of the exercise. (For use with individual pupils, potentially self-directive.)

F. *Picture Dictionaries*: Pupils are instructed to build a dictionary of words they have encountered in their reading. Old books, magazines, workbooks and newspapers can be furnished to provide pictures for illustrating the words. Pictures can also be drawn by the children for illustrative purposes. A shoe box that has been painted with tempera colors is fine for housing the materials. Dividers can be cut from tagboard and labeled with letters of the alphabet. (For use with individual children, potentially self-directive.)

G. *Prefixes, Suffixes and Word Stems*: Devise exercises consisting of three prefixes, suffixes or word stems for which examples of usage are given. Pupils will think of additional words. Examples:

1. *pre* (before): preheat, preschool, _____, _____.
2. *re* (again, back): repay, refill, _____, _____.
3. *un* (not): unhappy, unhurt, _____, _____.

Probable answers may appear on the back of the exercise. (For use with individual pupils, potentially self-directive.)

H. *Puzzle Words*: Furnish pupils with space blanks designed to accommodate words which are defined. The definitions should be in mixed order. Examples:

1. The wife of an American Indian (squaw)
2. A weapon for shooting arrows (bow)
3. A raccoon (coon)

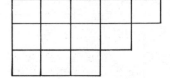

Correct answers can appear on the back of the exercise. (For use with individual pupils, potentially self-directive.)

I. *Riddles*: Riddles can be used to stimulate dictionary usage and interest in new words. Example:

1. There are many of us in Norway. We are frequently long and narrow. Steep, rocky banks come right down to the water of which we are made. We are called _____.

Correct answers can appear on the back of the exercise. (For use with individual pupils, potentially self-directive.)

J. *See, Hear or Smell?* List words which fall in one of these sensory categories. Pupils are expected to classify the words. Examples:

1. tulips
2. clocks
3. sunsets

Correct answers can appear on the back of the exercise. (For use with individual pupils, potentially self-directive.)

K. *Seeing Relationships*: Numbered lists of sample words having a certain relationship to each other are followed by several words in parentheses. The pupils must find and underline two words in the parentheses that have the same relationship as the sample words. Examples:

1. baker, bread (sailor, tailor, mason, teacher, clothes)
2. cup, coffee (bookcase, table, store, dresser, books)
3. dog, barks (cat, snake, horse, lion, roars)

Correct answers can appear on the back of the exercise. (For use with individual pupils, potentially self-directive.)

L. *Stick Me*: Paste pictures of objects on a suitably sized square of corkboard. Type words on small squares of oak tag and penetrate each with a common pin. When a pupil who engages in this activity finds a picture which matches a given word card, he labels it by pushing the pin through the picture into the corkboard beneath. (For use with individual children or children working in pairs.)

M. *Think of the Word*: Numbered sentences containing word groups for which an individual word can be substituted are presented. The pupil writes the word needed. He consults the dictionary if necessary. Examples:

1. The man was *being very careful* because the ice underfoot was thin. (cautious)
2. The general was afraid the enemy would *gain a victory over them.* (defeat)
3. The tiger was *going about slowly and secretly for something to eat or steal.* (prowling)

Correct answers can appear on the back of the exercise. (For use with individual pupils, potentially self-directive.)

N. *Which Is It?* Sentences are prepared with two inserted words in parentheses. The pupil chooses the one he considers correct. Examples:

1. The man was (right, write) about the distance.
2. The boy (road, rode) the horse home.
3. The (pail, pale) was filled with water.

Correct answers can appear on the back of the exercise. (For use with individual pupils, potentially self-directive.)

O. *Yes or No*: Numbered lists of words are followed by statements relating to the words. Pupils answer each statement "yes" or "no." Examples:

1. onion (This is something that makes your eyes water.)
2. cucumber (Your father drives this to work.)
3. bathe (You do this in a bathtub.)

Correct answers can appear on the back of the exercise. (For use with individual pupils, potentially self-directive.)

## Corrective Practice for Pupils
## Deficient in Sentence Comprehension

Pupils who experience sentence comprehension difficulties and an inability to group words into thought units, may profit from use of the Dolch Phrase Cards (Garrard Press). Helpful, too, is the tachistoscopic presentation of phrases using the Keystone Overhead Projector and Flashmeter (Keystone View Company) or the Tachist-O-Flasher with accompanying phrase filmstrips (Learning Through Seeing).

Reading aloud several sentences in which words are incorrectly grouped, dramatizes the need for proper phrasing in an entertaining manner. The following paragraph provides an example:

(For my) (breakfast I have) (jungle fruit, rice) (and coffee when) (I eat fresh) (fish from a) (stream or eggs) (from a little jungle) (town, things) (are not so) (very bad.)

Other kinds of corrective practice for pupils who are deficient in their ability to comprehend sentences can be individualized by using materials and techniques such as the following:

A. *Jumbled Sentences*: Disarrange sentences. Direct pupils to put the parts in proper order. Examples:

1. in an accident / Jane thought / were injured / that the boys.
2. is true / you read / don't believe / that everything.

Correctly arranged sentences can appear on the back of the exercise. (For use with individual pupils, potentially self-directive.)

B. *Missing Words*: Numbered sentences containing missing words are prepared. Pupils demonstrate comprehension of the sentences by choosing correct missing words. Examples:

1. Many people have _____ for family pets.
2. Children learn many interesting things in _____.
3. _____ are those times during the year when people should relax and enjoy themselves.
   a. dogs
   b. vacations
   c. schools

Correct answers can appear on the back of the exercise. (For use with individual pupils, potentially self-directive.)

C. *Omit Two*: Mount a picture on an individual card together with three sentences that tell something about the picture. Print two extra sentences that do not relate to the picture. Pupils are instructed to find the two irrelevant sentences. Correct answers can appear on the back of the exercise. (For use with individual pupils, potentially self-directive.)

D. *Pictures and Sentences*: Two or three pictures are mounted on individual cards together with fifteen or twenty sentences which have been printed on separate cards. Pupils are instructed to read each sentence and match it with the picture to which it refers. A marking scheme can be devised on the reverse side of the cards to make this activity self-corrective. (For use with individual pupils, potentially self-directive.)

E. *Punctuate Me*: Type paragraphs in which all periods and capital letters have been omitted. Pupils are directed to designate the beginnings and endings of sentences by employing proper punctuation and capitalization. The correctly written paragraphs can appear on the back of the exercise. (For use with individual pupils, potentially self-directive.)

F. *Sentence Detective*: Give directions which refer pupils to a picture appearing in a story previously read. Ask them to find all sentences on the page or pages that give more information than what is found in the picture. Correct sentences can appear on the back of the exercise. (For use with individual pupils, potentially self-directive.)

G. *Sentence Match*: Four sentences are prepared. Two of the four say approximately the same thing. Pupils are directed to find the synonymous sentences. Examples:

1. The man went on and on until he became very tired.
2. The man wandered about until he found what he was looking for.
3. The man entered the wilderness looking for a place to build a cabin.
4. The man continued walking for a great distance until he was exhausted.

Correct answers can appear on the back of the exercise. (For use with individual pupils, potentially self-directive.)

H. *Split Sentences*: Pupils are given two envelopes. One envelope contains cards with sentence beginnings and the other contains cards with sentence endings. Pupils are directed to match suitable parts to form sentences. Examples:

1. Jack and Jill went up the hill          a. lighter and warmer.
2. I ran and ran until I was               b. all out of breath.
3. As the sun began to rise it became      c. to fetch a pail of water.

Correct answers can appear on the back of the exercise. (For use with individual pupils, potentially self-directive.)

I. *True or False*: True and false statements that are related or unrelated to the reading lesson can be used to help develop sentence comprehension. Since many such statements are humorous, children enjoy these exercises immensely. Examples:

1. A 12-year-old boy can run 100 miles an hour.
2. This sentence has more than seven words in it.
3. A wild tiger would make a fine house pet.

Correct answers can appear on the back of the exercise. (For use with individual pupils, potentially self-directive.)

J. *When, What, Where?* Sentences which tell when, what or where are prepared. Pupils read each sentence and categorize it according to these designations. Examples:

1. The Jones family spent their summer in the country.
2. A slender piece of metal that is driven into two blocks of wood can hold them together.
3. He said the world would come to an end last week.

Correct answers can appear on the back of the exercise. (For use with individual pupils, potentially self-directive.)

K. *Where's the Joker?* Numbered sentences pertaining to a given subject are presented together with a sentence that does not belong. Pupils are directed to find the foreign sentence. Examples:

1. The car is a Ford. 2 The body is red and the wheels are black. 3. The sky became dark and cloudy. 4. The top speed is 100 miles an hour.

Correct answers can appear on the back of the exercise. (For use with individual pupils, potentially self-directive.)

## Corrective Practice Material for Deficiencies in Following Directions

When individual pupils or groups of pupils are deficient in their ability to follow directions, corrective practice can be individualized by using materials and techniques such as the following:

A. *Can You Eat Me?* Pupils are given a list of simple words with the directions, "Find things you can eat." Examples:

1. orange
2. window
3. door
4. crayon
5. butter
6. cookie

Correct answers can appear on the back of the exercise. (For use with individual pupils, potentially self-directive.)

B. *Do This:* Pupils are given a list of simple words with directions, "Draw a circle around all words you can make pictures of." Examples:

| 1. go | 4. chicken |
|-------|-----------|
| 2. dog | 5. see |
| 3. squirrel | 6. with |

Correct answers can appear on the back of the exercise. (For use with individual pupils, potentially self-directive.)

C. *Following Directions*: Provide pupils with a number of statements such as the following:

1. If the fifth letter in the alphabet is E write that letter in this space ___.
2. Draw a circle around all words in this sentence that have four letters.
3. If March comes after June write your last name backwards in this space _____.

Correct answers for most of the directions can appear on the back of the exercise. (For use with individual pupils, potentially self-directive.)

D. *Read and Do*: Pupils are given a number of directions to carry out:

1. Draw a house.
2. Put three windows in the house.
3. Put two panes of glass in each window.
4. Draw a chimney on the right-hand side of the roof.
5. Color the chimney brown.
6. Color the house red.
7. Draw a circle on the bottom right-hand side of your paper.
8. Now draw a square around the circle.

(For use with individual pupils, potentially self-directive.)

E. *What's Cooking?* Provide girls with directions for preparing different foods (French toast, pancakes, pies, etc.) and require them to identify the particular dish or food involved. Correct answers can appear on the back of the exercise. (For use with individual pupils, potentially self-directive.)

F. *What's Wrong?* Provide boys with directions for making or assembling model airplanes, mixing paint, repairing flat tires and so forth; provide girls with various cooking recipes. Reverse some of the directions. Pupils are expected to indicate what is wrong. Correct answers can appear on the back of the exercise. (For use with individual pupils, potentially self-directive.)

## Corrective Practice Material for Deficiencies in Locating Central Thoughts

When individual pupils or groups of pupils are deficient in their ability to find central thoughts of paragraphs, corrective practice can be individualized by using materials and techniques as those following:

A. *Best Central Thought*: Select short paragraphs and have them followed by several statements. Pupils are directed to read each paragraph and then choose the particular statement they feel is the most adequate expression of the central thought. Correct answers can appear on the back of the exercise. (For use with individual pupils, potentially self-directive.)

B. *Composing Topic Sentences*: Furnish pupils with paragraphs consisting of details (the key sentences must be removed) and direct them to write their own key sentences. Later they compare their efforts with the original key sentences found on the back of the exercise. (For use with individual pupils, potentially self-directive.)

C. *Decapitated Headings*: Cut headings from three or four short articles. Place the headings in one envelope and the articles in another. Pupils are directed to match the headings with the proper articles. A marking scheme appearing on the back of the headings and articles can be used to make the exercises self-corrective. (For use with individual pupils, potentially self-directive.)

   A more difficult version of exercises using the decapitated-heading technique involves having pupils compose their own headings. Later they compare their efforts with those of the journalists who wrote the articles.

D. *Find the Paragraph*: Designate a story or articles in a book to which pupils have access. Provide a series of key sentences. Pupils are instructed to find the paragraph from which each was taken. Key paragraphs can appear on the back of the exercise. (For use with individual pupils, potentially self-directive.)

E. *What's the Number?* Number the sentences in paragraphs and direct pupils to find the number of the key sentence. Correct answers can appear on the back of the exercise. (For use with individual pupils, potentially self-directive.)

## Corrective Practice Material for Deficiencies in Detecting and Remembering Details

When individual pupils or groups of pupils are deficient in their ability to read for details, corrective practice can be individualized by using materials and techniques such as the following:

A. *Answering Questions*: Provide pupils with paragraphs followed by questions (true-false or multiple-choice) which are designed to test understanding of the details in each paragraph. Correct answers can appear on the back of each exercise. (For use with individual pupils, potentially self-directive.)

B. *Finding Irrelevant Details*: Provide pupils with paragraphs in which the sentences have been numbered. One of the sentences carries an irrelevant detail. Pupils are directed to read each paragraph carefully and detect the irrelevant sentence. Correct answers can appear on the back of the exercise. (For use with individual pupils, potentially self-directive.)

C. *Finding Nonsense Phrases*: Provide pupils with a series of paragraphs in each of which a nonsensical phrase has been inserted. Pupils are directed to read each paragraph carefully and detect the absurd phrase. Correct answers can appear on the back of the exercise. (For use with individual pupils, potentially self-directive.)

D. *Skeletal Outlines*: Provide pupils with an outline of a selection which presents main ideas but no details. Pupils are instructed to read the selection and complete the outline. The complete outline can appear on the back of the exercise. (For use with individual pupils, potentially self-directive.)

E. *Which Paragraph Is Best?* Mount a detailed picture on a piece of cardboard. In an accompanying envelope, provide pupils with three by five inch cards on which individual paragraphs about the picture have been typed and numbered. Pupils are directed to find the paragraph which gives the most accurate details about the picture. Correct answers can appear on the back of the exercise. (For use with individual pupils, potentially self-directive.)

F. *Writing Details*: Provide pupils with a main idea and direct them to compose a paragraph by adding related details. (For use with individual pupils.)

## Corrective Practice Material for Deficiencies in Following a Sequence of Events

When individual pupils or groups of pupils are deficient in their ability to follow a sequence of events, corrective practice can be individualized by using materials and techniques such as the following:

A. *Drawing Endings*: Mount a series of pictures that tell a sequential story on cardboard. Omit the last picture and place it in an accompanying envelope. Pupils are directed to draw the last picture. After the drawing, pupils may compare their efforts with the picture in the envelope. (For use with individual children, potentially self-directive.)

B. *How Does It End?* Present unfinished stories which stop at a critical point. Pupils are directed to make up suitable endings. The story ending can appear on the back of the exercise. (For use with individual pupils, potentially self-directive.)

C. *Paragraph Shuffle*: Prepare stories in which the numbered paragraphs are out of order. Pupils are directed to rearrange the paragraphs so the sequence is proper. Correct answers can appear on the back of the exercise. (For use with individual pupils, potentially self-directive.)

D. *Sentence Shuffle*: Prepare short stories in which the numbered sentences are out of order. Pupils are directed to rearrange the sentences so the sequence is proper. Example:

1. The strange man walked to the door and rapped.
2. The man was invited into the house.
3. The dog barked when he heard the sound.
4. The lady of the house went to the door and opened it.

Correct answers can appear on the back of the exercise. (For use with individual pupils, potentially self-directive.)

## Corrective Practice for Pupils Deficient in Critical Reading Ability

Teachers will find the following suggestions helpful in working with pupils who do not critically evaluate the material they read:

1. *Encourage students to talk back to the book.* Have them evaluate statements in the light of their previous knowledge and beliefs. The good reader is always on his guard. He asks himself questions such as, "Does that make good sense?" "Is that possible?"

2. *Encourage pupils to check copyright dates.* Indicate the rapid advance that has taken place in many fields during the last few years. What may have been true a few years ago does not always hold today. The following serve as examples:

a. "The top speed for all fighter craft does not exceed 500 miles per hour." Copyright 1941.
b. "The population of the United States totals 130,000,000." Copyright 1947.

3. *Give pupils training in distinguishing between statements of fact and opinion.* Show that opinions are merely beliefs which cannot be supported by objective evidence and that facts, on the contrary, are capable of being proved through objective evidence. Use statements such as the four listed:

a. Men make better legislators than women. (Opinion)
b. The majority of legislators are men. (Fact)
c. California oranges are better than Florida oranges. (Opinion)
d. Oranges contain vitamin C. (Fact)

4. *Have pupils compare several sources of information.* Select from a given field different authorities who contradict each other, or bring to class two newspapers or magazines of opposed political complexions and compare them. Strike up a discussion as to why discrepancies exist.

Exercises such as these will indicate to pupils that a critical reader does not accept as final the viewpoint of any one author.

5. *Have pupils investigate an author's competence and possible prejudice.* Students should learn to look at the title page or book cover for information pertaining to an author's background and experience. Checking the appropriate *Who's Who* and sampling the opinions of other authorities are also helpful in determining the reliability of an author. Frequently, the preface is of value in giving a clue as to an author's purpose in writing. Bringing to class for study a number of advertisements or political speeches is an excellent way to train students to recognize prejudiced writings.

6. *Encourage students to test statements for possible exceptions.* Many authors make dogmatic and sweeping statements which do not hold under all circumstances. The following are suggestive of suitable drill:

a. An apple a day keeps the doctor away.
b. You can't teach an old dog new tricks.
c. He who hesitates is lost.

7. *Train students to identify and be on the alert for various advertising and propaganda devices that are commonly used to influence people.* Students should be made aware of the needs to which writers of this kind appeal. Some of the most common are (a) the social need: the desire to be accepted by the group by doing what it does; (b) the ego need: the desire to feel important; (c) the physical need: comfort, food, rest; (d) the desire for social and economic security; (e) the desire for excitement. Paragraphs like the following might be used to sensitize students to how advertisers capitalize on these needs:

> Rideway is the car of tomorrow. It's faster, it's smoother, and more economical than any car manufactured. Sales are mounting by leaps and bounds. People from all walks of life are choosing this upper class car. Be smart. Stay out in front. Buy the beautiful and economical adventure car of the future. Rideway.

## Corrective Practice for Pupils Deficient in the Ability to Remember What They Have Read

A pupil's ability to remember what he has read has little value unless understanding accompanies it. On the other hand, understanding what one has read is of questionable value if nothing can be retained.

Usually, as pupils improve in their ability to sustain attention and become more adept at spotting main ideas and related details, retention is enhanced. For the pupil who is chronically inattentive to the meaning of what he reads, the following procedure is suggested.

Start with a short sentence and direct the pupil to read it to himself. When he finishes, cover the sentence with a small card or close the book and ask, "What did it say?" If the pupil is unable to respond satisfactorily, allow him to reread the sentence and then query him again. Continue this on various occasions until he is able to tell, after a single reading, what a short sentence says. At this point, move on to more complex sentences.

The foregoing method is effective for the following reason. When a pupil realizes that as inevitably as death and taxes he has to tell you what he has read, he begins to pay closer attention. Greater concentration spells better retention.

### Corrective Practice for Pupils Who Have Difficulty in Concentrating

Concentration difficulties often are associated with emotional disturbances. The teacher, therefore, should do what she can to uncover any causes of emotional disturbances. If the services of a school psychologist are available, his help should be enlisted.

Practical suggestions which a teacher can give to pupils who have difficulty concentrating are as follows:

1. *Assume a questioning attitude.* Instruct pupils to immediately turn all headings into questions so they are seeking something when reading takes place. The words *how, what, when, where* and *why* are helpful in this regard. For example, the section heading "Causes of Tooth Decay" should become "What are the causes of tooth decay?" By assuming a questioning attitude children become active readers rather than passive readers. Active readers have little trouble concentrating.

2. *Reduce distracting influences.* Pupils would not think of playing tennis while trying to memorize a poem. Yet at home they frequently read while listening to the radio. No wonder concentration is difficult!

For maximum concentration at home, pupils should study by themselves, away from the family and all distracting influences. Pictures, banners and souvenirs should be removed from view. If possible, their desks should face a blank wall. Blank walls offer books little competition.

When studying in a library, pupils should seat themselves in a place where they will not be disturbed. Sitting near friends who will tempt them to visit is not recommended. It is also advisable for pupils to sit with their backs toward the library entrance. This will discourage their looking up to check on the identity of newcomers.

3. *Sit in a straight-backed chair.* Soft chairs and reclining davenports are not conducive to maximum concentration. Through the years of conditioning they have become associated with rest and relaxation. The slight muscular tension that accompanies sitting up in a straight chair keeps students alert and makes concentration easier.

4. *Work rapidly.* The auto racer driving to win has to attain a maximum speed and hold it. The greater his speed the greater his need to concentrate on steering. To divert any part of his full attention from the task at hand would be to lose the race. Similarly, readers who force themselves to work as fast as they can to accomplish their purpose have no time for mind wandering.

5. *Adopt a study schedule.* Pupils should plan and adhere to a schedule which will require them to study the same subject in the same place at the same time each day. It is easier to get down to business and concentrate on those things which have become routine and habitual.

6. *Provide proper lighting.* Reading makes heavy demands on the eyes. Frequently, improper lighting in the home causes visual fatigue which quickly hinders concentration. To reduce eye strain, pupils should read under lights that are sufficiently strong. Desk lamps should be equipped with a minimum wattage of 75 and floor lamps should have 150 watts. In addition to direct lighting on their book, the entire room in which pupils read should be dimly lighted. This reduces extreme contrasts which the eyes cannot tolerate. Glare should be guarded against by covering shiny surfaces or shifting lamps slightly to avoid reflections. Finally, students should be told not to read on and on without respite. Occasionally, they should rest their eyes by closing them or by looking at a distant object across the room or through a window.

A method of study that can aid concentration and boost retention tremendously was evolved by Francis Robinson more than two decades ago. It is particularly effective with content field material and could be introduced most profitably as early as the fourth-grade level. A simplified version of Robinson's survey Q3R method of study follows:

*Survey:* Have the pupil read quickly all the headings in the chapter or article to see the big points that are to be developed. This survey should not take more than two or three minutes. Darkened paragraph headings, italicized headings, pictures, graphs and summary statements should receive attention. This orientation will help the pupil organize ideas as he reads them later.

*Question*: Now have the pupil begin to work. Tell him to turn the first heading into a question. This can be done by using "what," "why," "where," "when" or "how." The question will arouse his curiosity and increase his comprehension. It will bring to his mind information already known and will help him understand the section more quickly. Most important, the question will make important points stand out while explanatory details will be recognized as such. Turning a heading into a question should be done immediately when reading the heading.

*Read*: The pupil now reads to find the answer or answers to the question. This is not a passive plowing along but an *active search* for answers.

*Recite*: (This is the most important step in the Survey Q3R Method.) The pupil now looks away from the book and briefly recites the answer in his own words. If he can't do this he glances at the book again. A second attempt is made to recite. He continues to read and recite as long as necessary. An excellent way to do this reciting from memory is to have the pupil jot down under the question he writes out, cue phrases in outline form.

When he is satisfied he knows what he has read, he repeats steps 2, 3, 4 on each succeeding headed section. That is, he turns the next heading into a question, reads to answer that question and then recites the answer by jotting down cue phrases in outline form. He reads in this way until the lesson is completed.

*Review*: When the lesson has thus been read through, the pupil looks over his notes to get a bird's-eye view of the lesson and checks his memory again by quickly reciting the subpoints under each heading. He can do this by covering up his notes and trying to recall the main points and by covering the main points while he tries to recall the subpoints under them. (3)

## Mechanical Devices for Improving
## Rate of Comprehension

Manufacturers wish to convince us that mechanical devices have great value in helping pupils overcome reading difficulties. Magazines have popularized mechanical gadgets and often give the impression that they constitute a panacea for ills. Much of this, of course, is an outgrowth of a tremendous emphasis on "speed reading."

Controlled readers, tachistoscopes and pacers of many types are found in schools throughout the country. How valuable are these machines?

Spache, in his discussion of the machine approach to reading rate, indicates the following concerns:

1. Does a pupil's accomplishment achieved while using machines transfer to the act of book reading?
2. What dangers to vision does the machine approach pose?
3. What are the effects of after-image on recall following tachistoscopic presentation?
4. Do machines that expose material in a constant fixed span introduce an element of artificiality that should be given consideration? (4)

In his review of research relevant to the use of mechanical devices in the teaching of reading, Karlin concludes:

> From some of these studies it appears that gains in rate of reading can be achieved through the use of a mechanical device. To what extent credit may be given to such a device for such achievement is unknown. Few, if any, of these studies were sufficiently tight to minimize the influences of extraneous variables upon the outcomes.

> A second conclusion may be reached: In eleven of the twelve investigations which measured natural reading against machine reading, the groups that received training in the former either equaled or surpassed the machine groups in rate of reading. From these data it can be said that outcomes in speed of reading similar to those achieved through the use of special instruments may be expected from suitable reading instruction which does not include these same instruments. (5)

Although studies of the future may prove to the contrary, available data seem to indicate that unless money is plentiful, a school would be wiser to invest in good books and efficient teachers than in machines.

A descriptive list of some of the mechanical devices available for improving rate of comprehension are as follows:

A. Tachistoscopes
  1. *AVR Flash Tachment*: A tachistoscope usable with both slide and filmstrip projectors. (Audio-Visual Research; $5.95.)
  2. *Craig Reader*: A combination tachistoscope and controlled reader using filmstrips mounted on plastic. One to three individuals can use the device simultaneously. (Craig Research, Incorporated; $229.50.)
  3. *Electronic T-Matic 150*: A tachistoscopic filmstrip projector designed for use at both far point and near point. Interval of exposure ranges from 1/100th to four seconds. (Psychotechnics, Incorporated. $99.50; Filmstrip Unit, $42.50.)
  4. *Electro-Tach*: A tachistoscope for individual use. It employs an electronic flash unit and has shutter speeds of 1/100, 1/50, 1/25, 1/10 and 1 second. Five-hundred targets accompany purchase of the machine. (Lafayette; $98.00.)
  5. *E-S-T 10 Eye Span Trainer*: A simple hand-operated shutter for individual training in flash recognition of numbers, phrases and other training material. Slides of various material are included. (Audio-Visual Research; $8.95.)

6. *Flash-Meter*: A tachistoscopic attachment for the Keystone Over-head Projector which permits varying the interval of exposure from "time" to 1/100th of a second. (Keystone View Company; $101.00.)

7. *Flash-X*: A hand-tachistoscope attachment for individual training using 4¾ inch discs. (Educational Developmental Laboratories; $7.20.)

8. *Perceptoscope*: A combination tachistoscope and controlled reader employing two filmstrips, one of which takes the place of a shutter. (Perceptual Development Laboratories; $1,275.)

9. *Rheem-T-Scope*: A light, portable, tachistoscope which employs circular reels with forty-two exposures per reel. The interval of exposure varies from 1/10 to 1/100th of a second. (Rheem Cali-fone; $132.00.)

10. *Speed-i-o-Scope*: A tachistoscopic attachment for slide or film-strip projectors having a front lens diameter of 2 1/16 inches. It permits varying the interval of exposure from "time" to 1/100th of a second. (Society for Visual Education; $93.00.)

11. *SVE Tach-adapter*: A one-speed tachistoscope usable with slides or filmstrip projectors. (Society for Visual Education; $7.50.)

12. *Tachist-O-Flasher*: A tachistoscope that projects single frame filmstrips for individual or group training. (Learning Through Seeing; $10.00.)

13. *Tachist-O-Viewer*: A simply operated four-speed tachistoscopic device for individual student use. It also can be used as a regular filmstrip previewer. (Learning Through Seeing; $89.50.)

14. *Tach-X*: A tachistoscope using filmstrips which permits varying the interval of exposure from 1½ seconds to 1/100th of a second. (Educational Developmental Laboratories; $185; case, $15.00.)

15. *T-AP All-Purpose Tachistoscope Attachment*: A tachistoscopic attachment usable with any make of projector. It is adjustable in height. Speeds are 1/100, 1/50, 1/25, 1/10, 1/5, 1/2 and 1 second. (Lafayette; $98.00.)

16. *T-AP Electric*: An improvement of the T-AP Tachistoscope. It is designed for use with a remote-controlled projector. (Lafay-ette; $157.00.)

17. *VS-1 Tachistoscope*: A tachistoscope adaptable to any projector which has a lens barrel diameter between 1⅞ inches to 2¼ inches O.D. Shutter speeds are 1/100, 1/50, 1/25, 1/10, 1/5, 1/2 and 1 second. (Lafayette; $88.00.)

B. Controlled Readers and Pacers

1. *AVR Reading Rateometer*: An inexpensive device designed for individual use. It consists of an electrically driven plastic bar which descends over the page at a speed determined by the user. (Audio-Visual Research; $39.95.)

2. *Controlled Reader*: A device designed for group work (individual pupils can use it, however). It employs a filmstrip projector which exposes printed material on a screen at varying rates of speed as determined by the operator. The material can be exposed one line

at a time in a left to right manner by employing a moving slot. (Educational Developmental Laboratories, Incorporated; $260; a smaller model, the Controlled Reader Junior, is available for $190.)

3. *EDL Skimmer*: A device designed for individual use. It employs a beam of light to guide and pace the user in developing skimming and scanning techniques. (Educational Developmental Laboratories, Incorporated; $49.00.)

4. *Perceptoscope*: A versatile device designed for group work (individual pupils can use it, however). It employs two synchronized filmstrips. One filmstrip projects a page on the screen; the other filmstrip illumines the material one phrase at a time to pace the reader. The device can perform the functions of a slide or strip film projector, a motion picture projector, a tachistoscope and a special kind of projector for paced material. (Perceptual Development Laboratories; $1,275.)

5. *Shadowscope Reading Pacer*: A device designed for individual use. It employs an inch-wide beam of light to pace the user's reading speed. The horizontal beam gradually descends over the page at a speed controlled by the user. (Psychotechnics, Incorporated; $94.00; case, $27.50.)

6. *SRA Reading Accelerator, Model III*: A device designed for individual use. It is constructed of metal and employs a mechanically operated shutter which descends over the page of a book at a speed determined by the user. (Science Research Associates; $71.34.)

7. *SRA Reading Accelerator, Model IV*: A lightweight plastic version of the foregoing device. It weighs one and a half pounds. (Science Research Associates; $50.00.)

8. *Tachomatic 500*: A device designed for group work (individual pupils can use it, however). It is specifically designed for the presentation of Tachomatic film essays, in single line, two or three fixations per line, at rates from 100 to 1200 words per minute. (Psychotechnics, Incorporated; $295.)

9. *TDC Reading Rate Controller*: A device designed for individual use. It employs an electrically driven opaque shutter which descends over the page at a speed determined by the user. (Three Dimension Company; $255; case, $15.00.)

## Corrective Practice Materials for Improving Rate of Comprehension

When individual pupils or groups of pupils are deficient in rate of comprehension, corrective practices can be individualized by using teacher-made material such as follows:

A. Magazine articles that are fairly easy and interesting for the grade being taught are ideally suited for practice in improving rate of comprehension. It is suggested that expository articles, 500 to 1,000 words in length, be mounted on cardboard. On the back side of the cardboard, ten questions pertaining to the article should appear. A library-card pocket can be used to conceal a slip of paper on which the answers to the questions are written. A file of similar articles should be evolved so pupils can be given periodic practice in improving their comprehension rate. Each pupil is encouraged to keep his own progress chart and to enter into vigorous competition with himself. (See page 130 for information on giving informal speed tests.)

B. Provide pupils with 3 by 5 inch cards. Show them how to expose a line of print very briefly by means of a quick pull-push movement with the fingers. Encourage pupils to practice in this manner so they broaden their recognition span. (For use with individual pupils, potentially self-directive.)

C. Provide pupils with paragraphs in which they are instructed to underline key words. The selection with key words underlined can appear on the back of the exercise. (For use with individual pupils, potentially self-directive.)

D. Provide pupils with selections in which they are instructed to insert vertical lines between words to highlight the phrasing. The selection with lines inserted to show proper phrasing can appear on the back of the exercise. (For use with individual pupils, potentially self-directive.)

## Corrective Practice Material for Improving Deficiencies in Locating Information

When individual pupils or groups of pupils are deficient in their ability to locate information, corrective practice can be individualized by using materials and techniques such as the following:

A. Provide pupils with a pack of cards on each of which a topic appears. Pupils are directed to place the cards in alphabetical order. Numbers can be written on the backs of the cards to indicate correct sequence. (For use with individual pupils, potentially self-directive.)

B. Provide pupils with a list of words and instruct them to place these in alphabetical order. The correct sequence can appear on the back of the exercise. (For use with individual pupils, potentially self-directive.)

C. Remove a page from the table of contents of a discarded book and mount it on cardboard. Follow the selection by specific questions such as, "How many topics are listed?" "On what page would you first find information about ___?" "What kind of book do you think this was?" Correct answers can appear on the back of the exercise. (For use with individual pupils, potentially self-directive.)

D. The index of the want ads from a daily paper can be cut out and mounted on a piece of cardboard. Pupils are asked questions such as, "In what section would you look if you wished to buy a violin?"

"Where would you look if you were interested in used furniture?"
Correct answer can appear on the back of the exercise. (For use
with individual pupils, potentially self-directive.)

E. The index of the features from the Sunday paper can be cut out and
mounted on a piece of cardboard. Pupils are asked questions such
as, "On what page would you find an article about space travel?"
"If you wish to go to the movies, where would you find the theaters
listed?" Correct answers can appear on the back of the exercise. (For
use with individual pupils, potentially self-directive.)

F. Provide pupils with a series of questions based on an indexed book
to which they have access. Pupils are directed to indicate the key
word in the question which appears in the index. For example, "How
much *iron ore* is mined yearly in the United States?" Correct answers
can appear on the back of the exercise. (For use with individual
pupils, potentially self-directive.)

G. Ask pupils which of four-numbered words or phrases, if looked up
in an index, would *not* be likely to lead to the answer of a given
question. For example, "What water routes in America are considered
important? 1. rivers 2. lakes 3. canals 4. rainstorms." Correct answers
can appear on the back of the exercise. (For use with individual
pupils, potentially self-directive.)

H. Provide pupils with a question and instruct them to think of headings under which the information might be found if an index were
consulted. Possible correct answers can appear on the back of the
exercise. (For use with individual pupils, potentially self-directive.)

I. Provide pupils with a list of reference books to which they have had
access. Follow this by a series of questions. Pupils are instructed to
indicate which reference books would be consulted to answer the
questions involved. Correct answers can appear on the back of the
exercise. (For use with individual pupils, potentially self-directive.)

## Corrective Practice Material for Improving
## Deficiencies in Reading Maps,
## Charts, Tables and Graphs

When individual pupils or groups of pupils are deficient in their
ability to read maps, charts, tables and graphs, corrective practice can
be individualized by using materials and techniques such as the following:

A. Provide pupils with exercises consisting of mounted maps, charts,
tables and graphs that have been taken from discarded books or
magazines. Write a series of questions which pertain to the interpretation and use of each. For example, a bar graph pertaining to
the annual oil production of Texas, California, Louisiana, Oklahoma
and Kansas might be followed by true and false questions such as,

"Oklahoma produces more oil than California." "The state that produces the most oil is Texas." A map of Sweden might be followed by questions such as, "What is the name of the river passing through Goteburg?" "What city is located farthest south in Sweden?" Correct answers to questions can appear on the back of the exercises. (For use with individual pupils, potentially self-directive.)

B. Provide pupils with data of various kinds. Direct them to prepare their own charts, graphs and tables to represent these data. Correct representations can appear on the back of the exercises. (For use with individual pupils, potentially self-directive.)

## Corrective Practice Material for Improving Deficiencies in Outlining Skill

When individual pupils or groups of pupils are deficient in their ability to outline,* corrective practice can be individualized by using the following materials and techniques:

A. Provide pupils with paragraphs followed by a simplified outline of the main ideas and related details. Follow this by comparable paragraphs and a skeletal outline. Pupils are instructed to complete the skeletal outline. The correct outline can appear on the back of the exercise. (For use with individual pupils, potentially self-directive.)

B. List main ideas and related details in sequential order but do not indicate any degree of subordination. Pupils are directed to show subordination by numbering, lettering and indenting properly. The correct form can appear on the back of the exercise. (For use with individual pupils, potentially self-directive.)

C. Provide pupils with a number of main ideas and related details in mixed order. Pupils are directed to straighten out the sequence and show subordination by numbering, lettering and indenting properly. The correct outline can appear on the back of the exercise. (For use with individual pupils, potentially self-directive.)

D. Provide pupils with a number of paragraphs. Pupils are directed to discern the main ideas and related details and put them into proper outline form. The correct outline can appear on the back of the exercise. (For use with individual pupils, potentially self-directive.)

## Corrective Practice Material for Improving Deficiencies in Summarizing

When individual pupils or groups of pupils are deficient in their ability to summarize what they have read, corrective practice can be individualized by using the following materials and techniques:

---

*Since outlining skill is dependent on the ability to detect main ideas and related details, exercises designed to develop these sub-skills should be reviewed.

A. Refer pupils to a story in a book to which they have access. Place pictures which depict the story in an envelope together with some which are unrelated to the story. Instruct pupils to find the pictures that depict the story and to place these in proper sequence. A numbering scheme on the backs of the proper pictures can make this exercise self-corrective. (For use with individual pupils, potentially self-directive.)

B. Refer pupils to a story in a book to which they have access. Pupils are instructed to read the selection and then draw a series of pictures which tell the story. (For use with individual pupils, potentially self-directive.)

C. Provide pupils with a selection consisting of several paragraphs which is followed by a summary. Pupils are instructed to read the selection and then evaluate the summary in light of the following questions.

1. Does the summary include all main ideas?
   a. List any omitted.
2. Does the summary include all related details?
   a. List any omitted.
3. Does the summary include any unnecessary details?
   a. List these.
4. Does the summary keep ideas in proper order?
5. Does the summary use complete sentences?

Correct answers can appear on the back of the exercise. (For use with individual pupils, potentially self-directive.)

D. Provide pupils with a selection consisting of several paragraphs which is followed by several summaries. Pupils are instructed to read the selection and then decide which summary is best. The correct answer can appear on the back of the exercise. (For use with individual pupils, potentially self-directive.)

## Books for Wide Reading

A good classroom library and daily reading for fun are boons to an individualized program stressing instructional material of a self-directive nature. A word of warning, however; children will not find wide reading self-instructive if books and other materials are too difficult. If a child is going to grow in his reading skills — comprehension, speed, sight vocabulary, word analysis — books must be of optimum difficulty. Books of optimum difficulty, in this situation, are those which coincide with each child's *independent reading level*.

Silent reading test results provide a useful index of a pupil's frustration level in reading. The teacher should bear in mind that the grade placement score attained on a silent reading test usually represents a child's very best effort. Consequently, the independent reading level would be considerably below the level of the test score. For retarded readers and for those whose silent and oral reading test results have not been obtained, an informal method of arriving at a pupil's free reading level is recommended. (See page 15.)

SUPPLEMENTARY PROBLEMS FOR ORAL AND WRITTEN DISCUSSION

1. Select five principles of corrective instruction from the following list and discuss how they could be implemented in a school reading program.

   a. Correction must be based on a diagnosis of reading difficulties.
   b. A variety of materials should be provided.
   c. Materials used should be self-directive.
   d. Materials must be of optimum difficulty.
   e. Materials must be ample for each type of difficulty.
   f. Materials must sustain the child's interest.
   g. Materials must not carry a grade level and should have an appealing format.
   h. The teacher should be enthusiastic and reassuring.
   i. The teacher should be alert to manifestations of sensory defects.
   j. The teacher should be acquainted with the child's home environment.
   k. The teacher's relationship with the child should be wholesome.
   l. Hazards to the child's learning should be ameliorated whenever possible.
   m. The teacher must employ a variety of techniques.
   n. The child should be made aware of his reading difficulties.
   o. The child should be made aware of his progress and keep a record of it.
   p. The child should progress at his own rate.
   q. The program must not interfere with other enjoyable school activities.
   r. The program must foster a child's self-confidence.
   s. Recreational reading under supervision must become an integral part of the program.
   t. The program should engender in the child a love of reading.

2. Evaluate the place of workbooks as self-corrective materials.
3. Obtain a workbook in reading. Set up criteria for its evaluation and apply the criteria.
4. Procure several workbooks in reading on two or more levels of difficulty. Dissect, combine and assemble the workbooks to form a ready file of corrective reading material as described in Chapter 7.
5. Obtain a completed cumulative record for a pupil with a reading problem and record all pertinent data on the Diagnostic Reading Summary appearing in Chapter 6. What additional data are needed in order to provide a more complete diagnosis?
6. Select a pupil with a reading problem. Apply and consult all available and appropriate diagnostic techniques needed to analyze his problem. Utilize the Reading Inventory (Chapter 4) and the Reading Summary

(Chapter 6). From the data collected prepare a corrective program and record it on the Reading Summary (Chapter 6, Section C).

## REFERENCES

1. LUELLA COLE, *The Improvement of Reading*, copyright 1938 by Holt, Rinehart and Winston, Inc., copyright 1966 by Luella Cole, pp. 142-143.
2. RUSSELL STAUFFER, "A Study of Prefixes in the Thorndike List to Establish a List of Prefixes That Should Be Taught in the Elementary School," *Journal of Educational Research* (1942), pp. 453-458.
3. FRANCIS ROBINSON, *Effective Study* (New York: Harper, 1946), p. 28.
4. GEORGE SPACHE, *Toward Better Reading* (Champaign, Ill.: Garrard Publishing Co., 1962), pp. 260-264.
5. ROBERT KARLIN, "Machines and Reading: A Review of Research," *Clearing House* (February, 1958), p. 352.

## SELECTED READINGS

DEBOER, JOHN and MARTHA DALLMAN, *The Teaching of Reading* rev. ed., New York: Holt, Rinehart & Winston, Inc., 1964, chs. 7B, 8A, 8B, 9A, 9B.

DECHANT, EMERALD, *Improving the Teaching of Reading*, Englewood Cliffs, N. J.: Prentice-Hall, Inc., 1964, ch. 13.

HARRIS, ALBERT, *How to Increase Reading Ability* 4th ed., New York: Longmans, Green and Company, 1961, chs. 15, 16.

HEILMAN, ARTHUR, *Principles and Practices of Teaching Reading*, Columbus, Ohio: Charles E. Merrill Books, Incorporated, 1961.

SCHUBERT, DELWYN, *Readings in Reading: Practice-Theory-Research*, New York: Thomas Y. Crowell Company, 1968, selections 31, 32.

SPACHE, GEORGE, *Toward Better Reading*, Champaign, Ill.: Garrard Publishing Company, 1963, chs. 4, 14, 15.

TINKER, MILES, "Devices to Improve Speed of Reading," *The Reading Teacher*, April, 1967, pp. 605-609.

Chapter

# 8

# Multi-Level Materials and Devices for Improving Reading Skills Through Individualization

Chapters 5 and 7 were devoted to descriptions of materials, methods and devices* that were designed rather specifically to meet deficiencies in word perception, word analysis, comprehension and study skills. The content of this chapter is devoted to descriptions of commercial and teacher-made materials and devices applicable to several kinds of reading and/or study skills on various levels of difficulty.

## Magic Slates

Some heavy cardboard and a sheet of acetate can be turned into a magic slate. After the acetate is placed over the cardboard, the sides are taped, leaving the top and bottom open. With a magic slate of the proper size (9 inches by 12 inches is recommended) individual exercises can be slipped between the cardboard and the sheet of acetate and marked with crayon. Crayon marks will rub off very easily with a dry cloth or cleansing tissue. With five or six magic slates on hand, it isn't difficult to keep a sizable number of children working independently with a variety of materials of an individualized nature.

Many teachers provide children with answer files so they can carry on independently with a minimum amount of supervision. There is, however, an ingenious way of making an acetate-covered exercise of alternate choice items immediately self-corrective. To do this, the teacher

---

*Machines and other devices for improving rate of comprehension appear in chapter 7, pages 157-159.

should encircle the correct answers on the surface of a second sheet of transparent acetate which is hinged to the one on which the pupil will record his responses. The acetate sheet carrying the answers is then folded under the cardboard. When a pupil completes the exercise, he swings the hinged sheet of acetate over the one on which he has written his answers. If the superimposed key does not coincide with his answers, the pupil knows he has erred.

## Tachist-O-Filmstrips*

These filmstrips are organized into four kits: elementary, junior high, senior high and college adults. They are designed to help increase attention span, speed of perception, speed of recognition and accuracy of recognition. A more detailed listing of filmstrips on the elementary and junior high levels is as follows:

### Elementary Tachist-O-Film Program

| | |
|---|---|
| Phonics Practice I | Seeing Skills B |
| Phonics Practice II | Prefix Mastery |
| Instant Words I | Suffix Mastery |
| Instant Words II | Teacher's Manual |
| Instant Word Phrases I | Tachist-O-Flasher |
| Instant Word Phrases II | Reading Mastery C |

### Junior High Tachist-O-Film Program

| | |
|---|---|
| Instant Word Phrases I | Seeing Skills G |
| Instant Word Phrases II | Number Recognition C |
| Reading Mastery C | Phrase Mastery B |
| Reading Mastery D | Teacher's Manual |
| Prefix Mastery | Tachist-O-Flasher |
| Suffix Mastery | Word Mastery B |

(For use with individual pupils or a group of pupils; $349.50 per kit.)

## Language Master†

The Language Master is an instructional device that provides simultaneous auditory and visual stimulation. It is based on the principle of the tape recorder in that the cards employed with the device have lengths

---

*Available through Learning Through Seeing, Inc., Sunland, California.
†Available through Bell & Howell Company, 7100 McCormick Road, Chicago, Ill.

of magnetic tape adhered parallel to their bottom edges. This feature allows the Language Master unit to function as a dual-channel audio recorder and playback device with the following functions: The positioning of a concealed switch enables the instructor to record words, phrases and sentences on the master track. After such recordings have been completed and the switch returned to its normal position, the master track cannot be accidentally erased by the learner. The student may listen to the master-track recording as a model when he views the material in printed form. He may then record his own version on the student track. At this time, the student listens to his responses and checks them with master-track recording. The student can re-record his own efforts until he is satisfied that he has approximated the model recording. A detailed listing of the basic equipment and accessory cards follows:

Language Master, $250.00

Headphones, $28.00

Multi-Phone Panel (when used with headphones, allows six students to simultaneously listen to sound tracks, $26.00)

Interconnecting Cable (required for each multi-phone panel to be used, $2.00)

Dual Headphone Adapter (when used with headphones, teacher and student may listen to sound track, $3.75)

Language Master Pre-Recorded Card Sets, $35.00 each
    Vocabulary Builder Program
        Set I    Basic
        Set II   Intermediate
        Set III  Advanced
    Word-Picture Program
        Set I    Nouns: Everyday Things
        Set II   Verbs: Action Words
        Set III  Basic Concepts
    Language Stimulation Program
        Set I    Phrases
        Set II   Sentences
        Set III  Language Reinforcement and Auditory Retention Span
    English Development Program
        Set I    Practical Vocabulary and Expressions
        Set II   Everyday Expressions
    The Sounds of English Program
        Set I    Basic English Phonetics
    The Phonics Program
        Set I    Sound Blending and Beginning Phonetic Skills
        Set II   Consonant Blends and Irregular Phonetic Elements
        Set III  Word Building and Word Analysis Technique

## EFI Audio Flashcard System*

This self-learning system employs cards which are used in conjunction with a three push-button machine. The lesson cards employ color in depicting situations or objects. When used with the Model 101 Machine they remain stationary and provide six seconds audio and another six seconds for recording. Children can read descriptions and simultaneously hear the correct sounds. Also, they can record and compare their responses with the programmed lesson. The system is powered by AC or rechargeable batteries and has a built-in loudspeaker and microphone. A headset may be used if desired. Available card sets include familiar sounds in the home neighborhood and city; animal sounds on the farm and in the zoo; familiar rhymes and rhyming words; checking and evaluation — missing parts of animals, things and people; checking and evaluation — information, clothes, food, toys, and people, locational and directional words; likenesses and differences — circles, squares and triangles; likenesses and differences — shapes internal detail and direction; likenesses and differences — alike and different colors, likenesses and differences — matching visual forms (two and three letters). (For use with individual children, potentially self-directive; Model 101 Machine, $270.00; blank cards, $13.50 per 100; commercial card sets, $19.00 to $78.00.)

## Study-Scope†

The Study-Scope uses basic principles of programmed instruction and provides students with a method of self-instruction. It employs two plastic cylinders that fit together like a telescope. The outside one is opaque, with a question window and an answer window which is revealed when the pupil twists the Scope a quarter turn. The information, which has been printed commercially or by the teacher or student on a sheet, is inserted into the clear inner cylinder.

Fourteen units, each with eight program headings, are available. They include relationships; visual discrimination, readiness level; visual discrimination, advanced level; initial consonants; consonants; initial consonants, blends I; initial consonants, blends II; rhyming words; long and short vowels; vowel combinations; word structure and meaning, I; word structure and meaning, II; syllabication; possessives and plurals. (For use with individual pupils, potentially self-directive; one Study-Scope,

---

*Available through Electronic Futures, Inc., 57 Dodge Ave., North Haven, Conn.
†Available through Study-Scope Co., P.O. Box 689, Tyler, Texas.

one Study-Scribe, one Complete Teacher's Guide, one each of all Reading Programs, $15.00.)

## The Electric Board

A relatively inexpensive and versatile teaching device which intrigues pupils of all ages is the electric board. It is entirely self-instructive and can be used to teach many things. Through its use pupils can learn to match synonyms, antonyms and blends, as well as questions and answers of all sorts.

In constructing an electric board the first item needed is a wooden board. Pegboard is highly recommended because of the ready-made holes. The board may be of any desired dimensions but 24 by 30 inches seems to be an optimum size.

In addition to the board, the following materials are needed: stove bolts (about ½ inch in length), small pegboard hooks, No. 25 copper wire, a radio battery (about 4½ volts), a flashlight bulb, some 3 by 5 inch cards. The entire set of equipment needed should not cost more than $5.00.

Two-thirds of the board (from left to right) can be devoted to spaced stove bolts that are placed so sufficient room remains directly under each for a hook on which will hang a 3 by 5 inch card. Questions for which an answer must be found are written on these cards.

The answer column is set up at the right of the board. It consists of a series of bolts placed in a single, vertical row. Sufficient space between the bolts or to the right of the bolts is provided for small hooks on which answer cards will hang.

On the reverse side of the board, pieces of insulated wire are used to connect a bolt at the left of the board with one of the bolts in the answer column to the right. The battery is fastened to the base of the board on the back. A small hole is made in the board for inserting the bulb.

One of the battery terminals is now connected with one of the lamp-socket terminals. On the other battery terminal, a piece of free wire is connected. This wire should be long enough to reach completely around the board to the bolts in the answer column at the right. Another free wire is connected to the remaining lamp-socket terminal. This wire should be long enough to reach the remaining bolts (questions are under these) on the front of the board.

When the ends of both of the free wires are in contact with two bolts that have been connected behind the board, the light goes on. The pupil knows he has made a correct association.

## Tape Recorders

Children needing help with a basic sight vocabulary or word analysis skills can listen to a recorded voice while they read the same materials silently. Questions pertaining to the comprehension or evaluation of a selection also can be recorded. If an individual pupil is involved rather than a group, headphones can be provided to minimize any disturbance.

A typical recording by a teacher that is designed to give a pupil practice in recognition of initial consonants might be as follows:* "This is a test to see if you can hear the first letter in a word and the letter it stands for. I shall pronounce two words which begin with the same letter. You are to find the letter sound and circle it. Now look at row one. My words are wagon and window. Think of the letter wagon and window begin with. Find that letter in row one and circle it. You should have circled *w*." The teacher continues with other word pairs:

2. girl    gate
3. lion    leaf
4. etc.

"You will correct your own paper to see how well you have done. If you do not have the correct letter circled, place an X on the wrong answer and circle the correct letter.

1. wagon and window begin with a *w*
2. girl and gate begin with a *g*
3. etc.

"Place the number of correct answers in the upper right-hand corner of your paper. This is the end of your lesson."

Tape recordings have another value. Pupils who are given the opportunity of listening to a recording of their oral reading become aware of their errors. As they concentrate on improving their reading, subsequent recordings provide dramatic evidence of their achievement.

## Commercially-Made Tape Recordings

The EDL Listen and Read Program for junior and senior high school students† is ideally suited to an individualized and multilevel approach to the improvement of comprehension, rate of comprehension and study skill. The program consists of thirty tapes with the following titles:

---

*Creative Teaching with Tape*, St. Paul, Minn.: Revere-Mincom Division, 3M Company, pp. 14-15.
†Available through Educational Developmental Laboratories, 75 Prospect, Huntington, N.Y.

1. How Well Do You Listen?
2. Listening and Reading
3. Words and Your Senses
4. Meeting New Words
5. Unlocking Sentence Meaning
6. Sentences — from Simple to Complex
7. Using Signs and Signals in Reading
8. Spotting Topics in Paragraphs
9. Paragraph Keys
10. Following the Author's Organization
11. Check Your Study Habits
12. How to Study with SQ3R
13. Underlining with a Purpose
14. The Art of Note Taking
15. Outlining — Finding the Skeleton in Listening and Reading
16. The Language of Charts, Graphs, Maps and Diagrams
17. Compressing Ideas by Abbreviating and Summarizing
18. Shifting Gears in Reading
19. Skimming and Scanning
20. The Reading Habit
21. Reading Between the Lines
22. The Power of Persuasion
23. News of the Day
24. Figurative Language
25. Finding Viewpoints in Essays
26. The Magic of Storytelling
27. Looking into the Lives of Others — the Novel
28. Biography — the Story of People
29. The play's the Thing
30. The Sound of Poetry

The foregoing tapes can be used with any tape recorder. With the addition of a connecting jackbox for eight headphones, a number of students can work independently. An accompanying workbook, *Listen and Read,* contains exercises and response pages for each tape. Included in the workbook are comprehension checks, correlated reading material and comprehension charts. (For use with individual students or a group of students, potentially self-directive; set of thirty *Listen and Read Tapes,* $99.00; set of headphones, each set, $38.00; connecting jackbox for eight headphones, $9.95; *Listen and Read Workbook,* $1.80; *Teacher's Guide,* $.30.)

## Listen and Think*

The EDL *Listen and Think Program* for grades three to six is designed to improve listening comprehension and develop the specific thinking skills necessary for good listening and good reading. The program consists of fifteen tapes for each level — third grade, fourth grade, fifth grade, and sixth grade — or a total of sixty tapes.

The tapes can be used with any tape recorder. With the addition of a connecting jackbox for eight headphones, a number of students can work independently. An accompanying workbook, *Listen and Think Les-*

---

*Available through Educational Developmental Laboratories, 75 Prospect, Huntington, N.Y.

*son Book,* contains exercises requiring application of the thinking skill to be learned. (For use with individual students or a group of students, potentially self-directive; set of fifteen *Listen and Think* tapes at any grade level, $75.00; set of headphones, each set, $38.00; connecting jackbox for eight headphones, $9.95; *Listen and Think Lesson Book,* $.85.)

## Merrill Skilltapes/Skilltext Program*

The Charles E. Merrill Skilltapes/Skilltext Program provides forty to fifty hours per reading level of testing, teaching, practice, self-checking and final achievement testing, or about three hundred hours of remedial instruction on six levels. Skills that are developed include getting information, understanding ideas, organizing ideas, making judgments and studying words. The title of the Skilltapes that accompany the company's Skilltexts include the following:

Uncle Funny Bunny (grade three level)
Uncle Ben (grade four level)
Tom Trott (grade five level)
Pat, The Pilot (grade six level)
Modern Reading, Book 1 (junior-senior high level)
Modern Reading, Book 2 (junior-senior high level)

The purchaser has a choice of either sixteen replayable tapes recorded at 1⅞ ips, single track, or six replayable tapes recorded at 3¾ ips, dual track. Either series of tapes represents nine hours playing time. The publishers recommend purchase of the proper accompanying Skilltexts which sell for $.96. (For use with individual students or a group of students, potentially self-directive; Skilltapes, levels 3-6, $80.00; Skilltapes for Modern Reading, Books 1 and 2, $90.00.)

## Imperial Tapes†

The forty prerecorded tapes and thirty booklets of the Imperial Primary Reading Program make it possible for pupils to carry on independently. Each tape acts as the pupil's talking companion and guide for the wide range of reading activities provided. The materials are well suited for individuals or small groups of pupils with special needs. Reading categories covered by the tapes and booklets include the following:

---

*Available through Bobbs-Merrill Co., 4300 West 62nd St., Indianapolis, Indiana.
†Available through Imperial Productions, Inc., 247 W. Court St., Kankakee, Ill. 60901.

Readiness
  Developing proper attitude
  Following direction and left-to-right progression
  Associating meaning with recognition and categorizing of words and
    phrases
  Opposites
Study Skills
  Punctuation
  Locating information by choosing proper references
  Skimming, grasping relevant facts
  Locating the main idea
  Using table of contents and index
  Dictionary skills
  Using pictures, graphs and maps
Comprehension Skills
  Fourteen lessons at the preprimer, primer, first grade, second grade
    and third grade levels of comprehension
Word-attack Skills
  Initial consonants
  Word discrimination
  Final and medial consonants
  Consonant blends
  Long and short vowels
  Digraphs and dipthongs
  Closed and open syllables
  Prefixes and suffixes
  Context clues and discrimination of word meanings
  Accents

(For use with individual students or a group of students, potentially self-directive; set of 40 tapes and 30 pupil booklets for each tape, $279.00.)

## Rheem Califone Tapes*

The Rheem Califone Audio Reader is a self-instructive program using tapes (twenty on each level covering grades one through six) that are designed to develop vocabulary, spelling and comprehension skills. (For use with individual children or a group of children; $135.00 for tapes at each grade level; listening-post equipment is available at additional cost.)

---

*Available through Rheem Califone, 5922 Bowcroft Street, Los Angeles, California.

## Teacher-Made Filed Material

Teachers can evolve their own files of material by cutting up old copies of children's magazines or newspapers. Typewritten copies of children's own stories can be kept in notebooks for easy, interesting reading. Sometimes, too, copies of discarded readers can be obtained, dissected and accompanied by comprehension, vocabulary and word attack exercises of a self-directive nature. Workbooks of different types can be cut up and incorporated into a valuable file of self-corrective exercises.

Stiff-paper folders of different colors can be used to house separate numbers of *My Weekly Reader*. Upper grades can be provided with articles drawn from back issues of the *Reader's Digest*. These can be mounted in stiff-paper covers and placed in a subject file.

Children can be encouraged to assist in the cutting, pasting and mounting of materials. They can make attractive illustrated covers for certain stories and can classify them under headings like "Rocket Travel," "Airplanes," "The Wild West."

## Commercially Made Filed Material

Files of commercially made material such as the SRA Reading Laboratories and the EDL Study Skills-Library* have self-directive exercises accompanying them which pertain to practically all areas of reading improvement and study skills. These are extremely valuable in any program that stresses individualization. Following is a description of these materials.

### SRA READING LABORATORY 1A

These self-corrective materials are written on seven carefully graded reading levels — 1.2, 1.4, 1.7, 2.0, 2.3, 2.6 and 3.0 — and are designed to accommodate the range of individual differences found in first-grade classrooms. Skills provided for include basic sight vocabulary, word attack, vocabulary development, reading comprehension and listening comprehension. A color scheme is employed to designate grade levels. Additional materials for the individual pupil, class and teacher also are included. Replacement materials can be purchased. (For use with individual pupils or an entire classroom, potentially self-directive; $75.34.)

---

*Available through Science Research Associates, Inc. and Educational Developmental Laboratories, respectively. See Appendix E for complete addresses.

## SRA READING LABORATORY 1B

These self-corrective materials are written on eight carefully graded reading levels — 1.4, 1.7, 2.0, 2.3, 2.6, 3.0, 3.5 and 4.0 — and are designed to accommodate the range of individual differences found in second-grade classrooms. Skills provided for include basic sight vocabulary, word attack, vocabulary development, reading comprehension and listening comprehension. A color scheme is employed to designate difficulty levels. Additional materials for the individual pupil, class and teacher also are included. Replacement materials can be purchased. (For use with individual children or an entire classroom, potentially self-directive; $75.34.)

## SRA READING LABORATORY 1C

These self-corrective materials are written on ten carefully graded reading levels varying from 1.4 to 5.0. They are designed to accommodate the range of individual differences found in third-grade classrooms. Skills provided for include basic sight vocabulary, word attack, vocabulary development, reading comprehension and listening comprehension. A color scheme is employed to designate difficulty levels. Additional materials for the individual pupil, class and teacher also are included. Replacement materials can be purchased. (For use with individual pupils or an entire classroom, potentially self-directive; $75.34.)

## SRA READING LABORATORY 1—WORD GAMES

This box contains the phonics portion of the reading laboratory program. It is a separate laboratory designed to supplement laboratories 1a, 1b and 1c in grades 1, 2 and 3. It can also be used successfully in grades 4, 5 and 6. It consists of forty-four, color-coded, word-building games that help students develop their reading vocabulary to match their listening vocabulary. (Potentially self-directive; $116.67.)

## SRA READING LABORATORY 2A

These self-corrective materials are written on twelve carefully graded reading levels — 2.0, 2.3, 2.6, 3.0, 3.5, 4.0, 4.5, 5.0, 5.5, 6.0, 6.5 and 7.0 — and are designed to accommodate the range of individual differences found in fourth-grade classrooms. They also can be used in advanced third grades or slower fifth grades. Skills provided for include comprehension, retention, vocabulary, word attack and reading rate. A color scheme is used to designate difficulty levels. One student record book and one teacher's handbook are included. Replacement materials can be purchased. (For use with individual pupils or an entire classroom, potentially self-directive; $75.34.)

## SRA READING LABORATORY 2B

These self-corrective materials are written on twelve carefully graded reading levels — 3.0, 3.3, 3.6, 4.0, 4.5, 5.0, 5.5, 6.0, 6.5, 7.0, 7.5 and 8.0 — and are designed to accommodate the range of individual differences found in fifth-grade classrooms. They also can be used in advanced fourth grades or slower sixth grades. Skills provided for include comprehension, retention, vocabulary, word attack and reading rate. A color scheme is used to designate difficulty levels. One student record book and one teacher's handbook are included. Replacement materials can be purchased. (For use with individual pupils or an entire classroom, potentially self-directive; $75.34.)

## SRA READING LABORATORY 2C

These self-corrective materials are written on twelve carefully graded reading levels — 4.0, 4.3, 4.6, 5.0, 5.5, 6.0, 6.5, 7.0, 7.5, 8.0, 8.5 and 9.0 — and are designed to accommodate the range of individual differences found in sixth-grade classrooms. They also can be used in advanced fifth grades or slower seventh grades. Skills provided for include comprehension, retention, vocabulary, word attack and reading rate. A color scheme is used to designate difficulty levels. One student record book and one teacher's handbook are included. Replacement materials can be purchased. (For use with individual pupils or an entire classroom, potentially self-directive; $75.34.)

## SRA ELEMENTARY READING LABORATORY

These self-corrective materials are written on ten carefully graded reading levels — 2.0, 2.5, 3.0, 3.5, 4.0, 5.0, 6.0, 7.0, 8.0, 9.0 — and are designed to accommodate the reading needs of fourth, fifth and sixth grades. They also can be used for remedial work in grades seven and important aspects of understanding: finding main ideas, recognizing details, evaluating what has been read and applying what has been read. A color scheme is used to designate difficulty levels. One student record book and one teacher's handbook are included. Replacement materials can be purchased. (For use with individual pupils or an entire classroom, potentially self-directive; $75.34.)

## SRA READING LABORATORY 3A

These self-corrective materials are written on ten carefully graded reading levels — 3, 4, 5, 6, 7, 8, 9, 10, 11 and 12 — and are designed to accommodate the reading needs of students in grades seven through nine. Exercises emphasize comprehension skills and test students' recognition of details and main ideas, their understanding of important relationships, perception of authors' tone and purpose, application of material read and evaluation of two or more conflicting reports. Word mastery is built through students' spelling a word, pronouncing it and understanding it. To get meanings, students learn to use context clues, prefixes, suffixes and roots. A color scheme is used to designate difficulty levels. One student record book and one teacher's handbook are included. Replacement materials can be purchased. (For use with individual pupils or an entire classroom, potentially self-directive; $79.34.)

## SRA DIMENSIONS IN READING SERIES

These self-corrective materials are designed for high school students who will enter the working world and are written on eight graduated levels from 3.5 to 7.4. The contents have been drawn from current books, magazines and trade and professional journals dealing primarily with masculine jobs. Topics fall into three broad categories: (1) conservation and the skills involved; (2) related facts of natural history, geology, botany, zoology, weather, conservation and mineralogy; (3) occupational skills such as those of the welder, carpenter, telephone repairman, soil scientist and electrician. Comprehension questions of different kinds follow each selection. A handbook for the teacher is available and replacement materials can be purchased. (For use with individual pupils or an entire classroom, potentially self-directive; $90.00.)

## SRA READING FOR UNDERSTANDING

These self-corrective materials are designed to develop the student's ability to grasp the full meaning of what is read by teaching him to analyze a sequence of ideas and make logical conclusions. It is excellent, too, for meaning vocabulary development. Exercises consist of a card bearing ten short paragraphs in areas such as education, politics, history, art, science, business, sports, agriculture and philosophy. The student reads the selection and chooses the best of four suggested conclusions implied in the selection but never stated directly. Correct conclusions are provided in the answer key. *Reading for Understanding* is available in three editions, each accommodating a number of grade levels: grades three through eight; grades eight through twelve; grades five through college. Each of the three units includes four hundred lesson cards arranged in order of difficulty. Each student works independently, recording his responses in his Record Book, checking his own work and charting his progress. (For use with individual pupils or an entire classroom, potentially self-directive; $46.00 for each edition.)

THE EDL STUDY SKILLS-LIBRARY FOR SCIENCE

These self-corrective materials are written on six levels of difficulty: Kit D (fourth grade), Kit E (fifth grade), Kit F (sixth grade), Kit G (seventh grade), Kit H (eighth grade) and Kit I (ninth grade). The major study skills developed include interpretation (detecting author's purpose, drawing conclusions, making comparisons, making inferences, visualizing); evaluation (judging relevancy, noting significance, recognizing validity, verifying accuracy); organization (finding main ideas, selecting details to support main ideas, outlining, classifying, determining sequential order); and reference (using alphabetical order, using parts of a book, using reference material, using library facilities). (For use with individual pupils or an entire classroom, potentially self-directive; $10.50 per kit.)

THE EDL STUDY SKILLS-LIBRARY FOR SOCIAL STUDIES

These self-corrective materials are written on six levels of difficulty: Kit DD (fourth grade), Kit EE (fifth grade), Kit FF (sixth grade), Kit GG (seventh grade), Kit HH (eighth grade) and it II (ninth grade). The major study skills developed include interpretation (detecting author's purpose, drawing conclusions, making comparisons, making inferences, visualizing); evaluation (judging relevancy, noting significance, recognizing validity, verifying accuracy); organization (finding main ideas, selecting details to support main ideas, outlining, classifying, determining sequential order); and reference (using alphabetical order, using parts of a book, using reference material, using library facilities). (For use with individual pupils or an entire classroom, potentially self-directive; $10.50 per kit.)

THE EDL STUDY SKILLS-LIBRARY FOR REFERENCE

These self-corrective materials are written on six levels of difficulty: Kit DDD (fourth grade), Kit EEE (fifth grade), Kit FFF (sixth grade), Kit GGG (seventh grade), Kit HHH (eighth grade) and Kit III (ninth grade). The major study skills developed include interpretation (detecting author's purpose, drawing conclusions, making inferences, visualizing); evaluation (judging relevancy, noting significance, recognizing validity, verifying accuracy); organization (finding main ideas, selecting details to support main ideas, outlining, classifying, determining sequential order); and reference (using alphabetical order, using parts of a book, using reference material, using library facilities). (For use with individual pupils or an entire classroom, potentially self-directive; $10.50 per kit.)

## The Literature Sampler, Junior Edition*

These materials take the form of a boxed kit of one hundred twenty book previews consisting of excerpts from books that appeal to pupils in the intermediate grades. Reading difficulty varies between the second and ninth-grade levels. (A senior edition also is available.) A "how" and "why" question card follows each selection and is accompanied by a discussion card which informs the pupil which answer is best and why it is best. (For use with individual pupils or a group of pupils; $45.00.)

## Building Word Power†

These self-corrective materials are designed to help students identify the meaning of unknown words through context clues, establish the meaning of a whole word if the base word is known through structural analysis and assist students in developing their comprehension skills by learning to find the main idea or central thought of a paragraph. The kit is designed for use by any student reading on or above the fifth-grade level. (For use with individual pupils or an entire classroom, potentially self-directive; $35.00.)

## Word-Analysis Practice‡

These materials consist of three sets of thirty cards each for intermediate grade levels. Level A cards contain seven hundred twenty words and can be used with pupils of low fourth-grade reading ability. Levels B and C cards contain 1,200 words each and can be used respectively with average pupils of fourth to low fifth and average fifth to low sixth grade reading ability.

The pupils are required to read words and decide under which of three suggested categories the words are to be classed. Pupils then write each word on paper under its proper classification. To accomplish this, the individual pupil, according to the author, must first read and recognize each word. If the word is not in his reading vocabulary, his first attack is phonetic. Since he knows the word must fit one of the category headings, he has a meaning clue he can apply to verify or reject the result of his phonetic analysis. He therefore gets practice in combining

---

*Encyclopedia Britannica Press, Inc., 425 N. Michigan Ave., Chicago, Ill.
†Charles E. Merrill Books, Inc., 1300 Alum Creek Drive, Columbus, Ohio 43216.
‡By Donald Durrell et al., comes in three 7 by 10 inch envelopes and is published by Harcourt, Brace & World, Inc.

phonetic analysis with context clues. (For use with individual pupils, potentially self-directive; three sets, $2.40 each.)

## Multilevel Books and Workbooks

### Specific Skill Series*

This series consists of twenty-three workbooks with accompanying answer sheets. The latter permits optional self-correction. A complete breakdown of the series is as follows:

Using the Context, Levels 1 to 6 (Books A, B, C, D, E, F) ...............$5.69
Working with Sounds, Levels 1 to 4 (Books A, B, C, D) ..................$3.89
Following Directions, Levels 1 to 4 (Books A, B, C, D) ..................$3.89
Locating the Answer, Levels 1 to 4 (Books A, B, C, D) ..................$3.89
Getting the Facts, Levels 1 to 5 (Books A, B, C, D, E) ...................$4.74

If worksheets are purchased, the need for annual reordering of workbooks is eliminated. (100 worksheets, $1.25)

## Lessons for Self-Instruction in Basic Skills (Reading)†

These programmed lessons consist of sixteen books with difficulty levels ranging from third through ninth grade. Although designed primarily for intensive review, the materials are useful in strengthening the reading skills of weaker students. A complete breakdown of the series is as follows:

| | |
|---|---|
| Following Directions | Each of these categories has four |
| Reference Skills | books with the following difficulty |
| Reading Interpretations I | levels: A-B (3 to 4th grade level); |
| Reading Interpretations II | C-D (5th to 6th grade level); E-F (7 to 8th grade level); G (ninth grade level and above). |

(For use with individual students working alone or in a group, potentially self-directive; each booklet, $1.00.)

## Developmental Reading Series‡

Unique among basal readers is Bond's *Developmental Reading Series* for grades one through eight. Each reader has a "Classmate" edition

---

*Available through Barnell Loft Ltd., 111 South Center Ave., Rockville Center, N.Y.

†Available through California Test Bureau, Monterey, California.

‡*The Developmental Reading Series* by Guy L. Bond is published by Lyons & Carnahan, Chicago, Illinois.

which presents the identical stories with the same page numbering and illustrations. The latter, however, is a simplified version and has difficulty level about one grade below the regular reader. This permits a teacher to differentiate her instruction more effectively when working with two groups of pupils who vary in reading ability. (For use with individual pupils or a group of pupils; readers 1 to 8, Classmate — Simplified edition — $2.24 to $3.80, each.)

## Programmed Learning

The terms "teaching machine" and "programmed learning" are used interchangeably by many people. Actually, they are not the same. The program is the important thing. The machine merely acts as a vehicle for presenting the program.

A learning program consists of a carefully ordered and organized sequence of material to which a student responds. His response takes the form of filling in a space, selecting one of a number of multiple-choice answers, indicating agreement or disagreement and so forth. Immediately after a student has made a choice or answered a question, he is permitted to see the correct answer so he knows whether an error was made.

At the present time programs are available on many grade levels and with a variety of subjects. Spelling, geography, arithmetic, algebra, biology, psychology, political science, logic, engineering, foreign languages and reading are among the areas covered.

Some of the specific principles that characterize successful programs are as follows:

1. *Logical Sequence of Small Steps*: Subject matter is broken down into information fragments and is presented one step at a time so it can be easily understood. The sequence is orderly, and the difficulty increment narrow. This permits steady student progress uncomplicated by undue frustration.

2. *Immediate Feedback*: Since nothing succeeds like success, it is important that the program provides an immediate appraisal of each response. The theory of reinforcement emphasizes that a student profits from the consequences of his responses. Since a student is constantly appraised for how well he is doing, there is little danger he will go far astray.

3. *Self-pacing*: The student engaged in programmed-learning activity can work at his own rate. He is not held back by other students who do not comprehend readily or who lack the drive to persist. On the other

hand, the student is not discouraged by others capable of working at a more rapid rate than he. The programmed learning process is completely individualized.

4. *Teacher Evaluation*: The teacher can easily evaluate a student's progress by checking the nature of the responses made to the items involved. Thus the kind of special help a student needs is easy to pinpoint.

Some available programmed materials which do not require teaching machines are the following:

a. Charles E. Merrill Books, Inc., 1300 Alum Creek Drive, Columbus 16, Ohio
   *Building Word Power*
   (meaning vocabulary and comprehension; fifth grade and above)
b. McGraw-Hill Book Company, 330 West 42nd St., New York
   *Programmed Reading*
   (letter sounds, words; 14 programs for grade one)
c. Institute of Educational Research, 2226 Wisconsin Ave., N.W., Washington, D.C.
   *Basal Progressive Choice Reading Program*
   (letter forms, sounds, words; primary grades)
d. Center for Programmed Instruction, 365 West End Ave., New York
   *Phonetic Analysis* and *Structural Analysis*
   (primary grades and remedial work)
e. Honor Products Co., 20 Moulton St., Cambridge, Massachusetts
   *Word Clues: Be a Word Detective*
   (context clues program for intermediate grades)
f. Coronet Instructional Films, 65 East South Water St., Chicago 1, Illinois
   *How to Improve Your Vocabulary*
   (developmental reading skills for seventh-grade reading level)
   *David Discovers the Dictionary*
   (programmed text for fourth grade)
   *Maps: How We Read Them*
   (programmed text for the sixth grade)
g. The Macmillan Company, 60 5th Ave., New York
   *How to Use the Dictionary*
   (intermediate grades)
   *Spectrum of Skills*
   (vocabulary, word attack skills and comprehension; intermediate grades)
h. California Test Bureau, Monterey, California
   *Lessons for Self-Instruction in Basic Skills*
   (vocabulary, following directions, reference skills, interpretation; grades three to nine)

i. Science Research Associates, 258 E. Erie St., Chicago, Illinois
   *Lift-Off to Reading*
   (phonics, comprehension; grades one to six)
   *Words*
   (vocabulary; grades seven to eight)
   *Reading in High Gear*
   (basic reading skills; for culturally deprived and nonreaders; grades seven to twelve)

The following are among the programmed materials requiring suitable teaching machines:

a. Cenco Center, 2600 S. Kostner Ave., Chicago, Illinois
   *Vocabulary Building I* and *Vocabulary Building II*
   (elementary and secondary)
b. General Education, 96 Mt. Auburn St., Cambridge, Massachusetts
   *Studentutor Library of Matching Exercises*
   (readiness; primary level)
c. Publishers' Co., 1106 Connecticut Ave., N.W., Washington, D.C.
   *Reading: Word Recognition*
   (primary level)
d. Honor Products, 20 Moulton St., Cambridge, Massachusetts
   *Word Clues: Be a Word Detective*
   (context clues; intermediate grades)
   *Fun with Words*
   (homonyms; intermediate grades)
e. Learning Inc., 1317 West 8th St., Tempe, Arizona
   *Synonyms, Antonyms, Homonyms*
   (intermediate grades)
f. E-Z Sort Systems, 45 Second St., San Francisco, California
   *Beginning Sight Vocabulary*
   (primary grades)

Chapter

9

# Reading Improvement Program in Practice

Elementary school teachers and administrators usually are aware of the large number of pupils who fail to reach expected goals in reading every year but may not always avail themselves of appropriate corrective measures. The extensive retardation in reading found in most schools is the millstone that prevents raising the level of teacher and pupil efficiency and the basis for much of the criticism directed at the schools by the public. In order to resolve the reading problem the school must become acquainted with underlying causes or learning deficiencies and accept responsibility for their improvement and correction. The school must show concern for individual learning problems and provide a school environment that compensates for an underprivileged or unwholesome out-of-school life. When reading difficulties are permitted to accumulate and become more severe each year, when reading problems are tolerated but not diagnosed and corrected and when pupils handicapped in reading are struggling with instructional material on the frustration level of difficulty, problems in reading will continue to flourish.

The learning process is unique. Each pupil and the methods best suited to him differ widely. There is no best method of teaching all pupils to read effectively. The question to be resolved is not whether phonics or look and say is the most effective method of teaching word perception. It is not whether systematic instruction using basal readers is superior to wide reading and incidental learning. The problem before the teacher is this: What combination and emphasis on phonics, look and say, systematic developmental instruction, individualized correction and recreational reading will best meet the needs of the individual and teach him to become an efficient reader? (1)

This book maintains that a complete mastery of the basic reading skills of word recognition and word analysis at each grade level is an essential prerequisite to independence in reading. While a mastery of the mechanics of reading is but a means to the end, it is vital to the attainment of competence in reading comprehension. Pupils in the third grade who have not attained the status of an independent reader should be given individualized corrective instruction. The authors emphasize the importance of doing this before pupils enter the fourth grade. By the same token, disabled readers already in the middle and upper grades first should be studied for deficiencies in the basic skills of word recognition and word analysis. If these deficiencies exist, they must be met before improvement of comprehension skills is undertaken. The basic reading skills are foundational to all high-level reading.

Considerable space and emphasis are given to the need for individualized correction of reading difficulties through the use of self-directed material. The instructional material described in this volume is designed to correct reading difficulties and improve the reading status of all pupils on the elementary school level. Because the material is largely self-directive it enables the teacher to meet individual needs with relative ease.

Independent readers above the primary grades may experience difficulty in their reading because of deficiencies in meaning vocabulary, comprehension and study skills associated with textbooks in the content fields. Teachers must become aware of these difficulties as soon as they arise. The self-directive aids described in Chapter 7 prove valuable in meeting the needs of these pupils.

The authors feel that recreational reading has great value for improving the reading status of normal and accelerated readers. If books are properly selected and evaluated it proves a valuable supplement to individualized practice for retarded readers; however, a recreational reading program without an individual study of hazards to learning, without an awareness of individual reading levels, specific difficulties or individual interests, is largely ineffective with retarded readers.

In summary, the essentials of reading improvement as set forth by the authors and reflecting their philosophy and experiences are as follows:

1. Child study which discovers individual hazards to learning and adjustment. Such a child study program will provide a better understanding of children and will facilitate planning a wholesome and more effective school environment.

2. Functional and systematic evaluation that is designed to discover individual reading levels, specific reading difficulties and reading potentials. This program would employ intelligence tests, silent reading tests, oral reading tests, teacher observation, interviews and cumulative records.
3. A developmental instructional program in reading which (a) provides both group and individual balance, (b) provides instructional material on multilivels of difficulty, (c) provides systematic and sequential instruction in the reading skills, (d) avoids frustration levels of difficulty, (e) prevents an accumulation of reading difficulties, (f) promotes total mastery of reading skills, (g) has independent reading status as a goal for all pupils at the end of the primary grades.
4. A corrective program which uncovers and diagnoses reading difficulties and utilizes self-directed instructional material designed to eliminate individual reading difficulties.
5. A wide reading program designed to provide all pupils with additional practice and stimulation. Such a program would use specially adapted books and materials for retarded readers. Included, too, would be supplementary readers and materials on many levels of difficulty that would interest and appeal to average and accelerated readers.

## In-Service Reading Programs

Many teachers enter service with minimal professional training in reading and are unable to cope with the problems they face in their classrooms. Other teachers received their training and teaching credentials so long ago that they feel the necessity of familiarizing themselves with more modern approaches to reading instruction. It is evident, therefore, that the principle of individual differences is as applicable to teachers as it is to the children they teach. Any in-service training program must take cognizance of this by being broad enough to meet the needs of the neophyte teacher as well as those of the veteran staff member who has had years of experience. The program must begin where each teacher is and move toward the goal of maximum teaching effectiveness for all. Such a program is most effective if centered around specific problems which both new and experienced teachers encounter. To be a genuine success, planning should grow out of a cooperative effort of both administration and staff. Teachers tend to reject an in-service training program imposed from above.

## In-Service Training Practices

Preschool and postschool workshops, orientation weeks, teacher institutes and teachers' meetings are scheduled by many schools as part of an in-service training program. Consultants in reading from nearby colleges and universities may be used for these purposes, although on occasions individuals with little professional training in reading attempt to provide leadership. In any event, these one shot attempts seldom provide any lasting benefits since more than momentary teacher enthusiasm is needed to sustain a program throughout the year.

More permanent benefits are achieved when school districts employ consultants who make classroom visits and carry out on-the-spot demonstrations of effective techniques and approaches for the teachers. Often such consultants give additional assistance to counselors, nurses, administrators and parents.

Some schools have experienced success by initiating an intraschool visitation plan whereby new teachers are given opportunities to observe experienced teachers at work with children. Informal, small group discussions according to grade level may continue throughout the year. These may be led by experienced teachers. The groups devote attention to the causes of reading retardation, classroom grouping techniques, methods that are helpful in overcoming specific weaknesses and problems, interpreting test scores, utilizing school records and so forth.

Teachers should be encouraged to take advantage of extension courses, summer courses and extended workshops in the reading area. Alert administrators should hold conferences with teachers and bring to their attention specific courses which will be of benefit to them and will strengthen the staff as a whole. Teachers availing themselves of prescribed opportunities for professional growth should be given opportunities to share their learnings with other interested teachers.

Larger districts can encourage teachers to contribute practical ideas for the publication of an inexpensive bulletin which might bear the title, "It Worked for Me" or "Here's How I Did It."

Material centers which house the latest devices and materials can be organized for teacher use. A section of the school library or a shelf in the teacher's room may be set aside for books and magazines which constitute an up-to-date professional library in reading. Copies of reading and language arts bulletins which have been purchased with school funds may also be displayed. Teachers are invited to check out such materials for study away from school.

Some school districts encourage teachers to carry out individual and group research projects and experiments. These projects are not only of benefit to teachers who participate in them directly but benefit all teachers in the district with whom the results can be shared.

A few city school systems have developed reading clinics which are used as training centers for teachers who, after a semester's work in the clinic, go back into their classrooms bristling with new insights and competencies. Such a plan has been employed in the St. Louis schools for a number of years. A group of select teachers is trained in the clinic under close supervision. After a full year in the clinic, the teachers are returned to the classroom. Dr. Kottmeyer states, "Although the efficiency of the clinic program is no doubt curtailed, the values of the in-service training for many teachers justify the policy." (2)

## Professional Library

Teachers can build a library of professional books in reading which will enable them to keep abreast of current trends. (See Appendix F1 for a listing of recommended books.) Although teachers have access to public, university and college libraries they are not absolved of the responsibility of accumulating a personal library of authoritative books that deal with a process as important to learning as reading. Indeed, one would be suspicious of a medical doctor or lawyer who practiced his profession without the finger-tip accessibility of literature relating to his work. (3) As a matter of fact, functional books and manuals such as the following should be kept on the teacher's desk for ready reference.

KOTTMEYER, WILLIAM, *Teacher's Guide for Remedial Reading*, St. Louis: Webster Publishing, 1959.

RUSSELL, DAVID and ETTA KARP, *Reading Aids Through the Grades* rev. ed., Bureau of Publications, Teachers College, Columbia University, 1951.

Teachers should join professional organizations such as the International Reading Association and subscribe to professional magazines which devote space to studies and articles in the area of reading. Periodicals particularly valuable in this respect are *The Reading Teacher, Journal of Reading, Education, Elementary English* and the *Elementary School Journal*.

Teachers can keep a file of advertising materials which lists the names and addresses of companies, along with the latest teaching aids available in the reading field. Another file can be devoted to free and inexpensive materials (booklets, charts, posters, filmstrips, etc.) which innumerable industrial, governmental and business firms will send to any teacher who makes a request. Hundreds of such sources are to be found in the booklet titled *Free Teaching Aids.** This booklet will prove invaluable to teachers at all grade levels.

---

*Available through Gordon and Sheridan, Post Office Box 943, Riverside, California.

Lastly, teachers should not overlook but should exploit to the fullest all available school resources. For example, manuals accompanying basal and supplementary readers furnished by the school should be studied carefully to glean all value from them. Certainly, too, the counsel of any available reading consultants, psychologists and other specialists should be sought in an effort to implement an instructional program in reading that is geared to individual needs.

## Suggestions for Initiating a Reading Improvement Program

When an objective assessment of the school's present reading program is undertaken, consideration should be given to the presence of any of the following vulnerable factors:

1. Failing to discover or alleviate individual hazards to learning
2. Failing to be concerned with the reading difficulties of pupils who receive low scores on a silent reading test
3. Using instructional material on a single level of difficulty in each grade
4. Permitting reading difficulties to accumulate and assigning new material on the frustration level of difficulty
5. Permitting pupils to enter the fourth grade before they have become independent readers
6. Failing to use oral reading for diagnostic purposes
7. Failing to utilize a systematic and diagnostic approach to discover reading difficulties
8. Failing to utilize self-directed instructional material for corrective reading
9. Failing to provide systematic practice in reading through a program of recreational reading

What evolves from a school's efforts to initiate and maintain a reading improvement program will vary from school to school. These differences will in large measure determine the emphasis the improvement program should take; however, factors such as the following must not be overlooked.

1. An enthusiastic and conscientious principal who has a sympathetic understanding of the reading problem and who wishes to see something done about it. Such a principal will assume responsibility for the following:

   a. Obtaining the kinds of materials needed to implement the program. (For example, commercially made materials such as the SRA reading laboratories, workbooks and other self-directive materials). In addition, teachers may request special materials that are needed to build their own files of learning aids.

b. Supporting and encouraging an in-service training program in reading. Use may be made of teachers' meetings, workshops, institutes, preschool conferences, postschool conferences and extension classes which could be given at the school by a neighboring college or university.

c. Acquiring the trained personnel needed to carry out an efficient program in reading. Personnel needed would include remedial teachers, speech therapists, school psychologists and a reading consultant.

2. All teachers must work together in evolving the program. Librarians, counselors and school nurses also should share responsibility. If this is done, each individual will feel that the program's success is dependent on him. Another advantage stemming from group participation is that the principles, aims and purposes around which the program is built will be better understood by all.

3. Periodic evaluations of the improvement program should be made. And when modifications seem necessary, they should be introduced without hesitation. As the program develops, parents need to be informed of the progress taking place.

4. Particular attention should be given to developing a program that is coordinated at all levels. This means that intermediate grade and junior-high teachers should understand what primary teachers are seeking to accomplish. By the same token, primary teachers should be interested in knowing how best they can prepare children for the grades lying ahead.

## Inventory of Instructional Practices in Reading

When the school staff is ready to initiate an improvement program in reading, the problem of its organization and implementation is of immediate concern. One useful approach to the problem is to undertake a survey or evaluation of the present reading program in terms of pupil achievement. It is also important to ascertain if the prevailing practices are wholesome and efficient. The *Inventory of Instructional Practices in Reading* suggests an over-all evaluation which may be applied to the entire school or to a particular grade. This *Inventory* may serve as a guide to a committee that is organized to evaluate the reading program.

1. Child Study

a. Describe the activities of the school involving home visitation and parent conferences during the year. Indicate the reasons for the visits and the conferences and the results obtained.

b. List the names of the children in each grade who have been identified as having impaired health, hearing and vision and indicate the corrective steps taken by the parents and the school.

c. List the names of the children in each grade who are socially and emotionally maladjusted, indicating the nature of the maladjustment in each case. What corrective measures have been taken by the school?

d. Are cumulative records used and kept up to date?

2. Reading Readiness in the First Grade

a. List the reading readiness tests and the intelligence test used, indicating date each test was administered.

b. List the names of the children receiving low ratings on each of these tests.

c. What part did teacher judgment play in determining children's reading readiness?

d. What part did visual maturity play in the reading readiness program?

e. Indicate the materials used and the types of experiences provided in the reading readiness program. What was the length of this period?

f. List the names of the children retained in the reading readiness program for a longer period, indicating the length of the second period.

g. Evaluate the reading readiness materials used.

3. Reading in the First Grade

a. When and how was phonics introduced?

b. What percent of the children in the first grade mastered the first-grade reader?

c. What percent mastered only the preprimers and primers?

d. What percent mastered only the preprimers?

e. Identify the children with an inadequate mastery of a first-grade sight vocabulary.

4. Oral Reading (grades 1 to 4)

a. What percent of time devoted to instruction in reading is spent on oral reading in class? Oral reading to the teacher?

b. How do the instructional activities in oral reading for retarded readers differ from the activities for nonretarded readers?

c. Describe the purposes, frequency and extent of pupil-teacher oral reading.

d. Describe the nature and frequency of audience reading.

5. Analysis of Reading Difficulties (grades 1 to 8)

a. Check the methods and materials listed below which were used to identify individual reading problems.

| | |
|---|---|
| ___Observation | ___Oral reading to the teacher |
| ___Oral reading in class | ___Word recognition tests |
| ___Silent reading test | ___Standardized oral reading test |
| | ___Other |

b. Check the reading difficulties such as those listed below which are most prevalent.

| | |
|---|---|
| ___Word recognition | ___Comprehension |
| ___Word Analysis | ___Study skills |
| ___Faulty reading habits | ___Rate of comprehension |

6. Word Recognition
   a. What materials and techniques were used to develop skill in word recognition?
   b. What sight vocabulary was used in developmental teaching?
   c. How was mastery in word recognition evaluated?
   d. What level of mastery in word recognition did the nonretarded readers attain?
   e. What level of mastery in word recognition did the retarded readers attain?
   f. What level of mastery in word recognition is required of retarded readers before more difficult reading material is undertaken?
7. Word Attack
   a. What elements of phonetic and structural analysis are emphasized with retarded readers?
   b. Check the instructional materials and procedures listed below which are used to develop skill in word attack.

   ___Oral reading in class
   ___Oral reading to the teacher
   ___Developmental exercises in word analysis
   ___Phonics workbooks
   ___Word analysis games
   ___Others
8. Meaning Vocabulary (grades 4 to 8)
   a. What percent of the children in the grade are retarded in meaning vocabulary as measured by a meaning vocabulary test?
   b. Describe the materials and procedures used to develop a more effective meaning vocabulary.
9. Comprehension (grades 4 to 8)
   a. What percent of the children in the grade are retarded five or more months in reading comprehension?
   b. What materials and procedures are used to help retarded readers improve their comprehension?
10. Recreational Reading
    a. How and by whom are books for recreational reading selected?
    b. What records are kept of the recreational reading done by the pupils?
    c. How are retarded readers motivated to engage in recreational reading?
    d. How extensive is the recreational reading done by retarded readers?
    e. How many books adapted for retarded readers are there in the room or library?
11. Individualization
    a. Is the corrective work in reading individualized? If so, describe the materials and procedures used.
12. Summary
    a. List the names of the children in each grade who are retarded five or more months in silent reading and indicate the amount of retardation for each.

b. List the names of the children in each grade who are retarded five or more months in oral reading and indicate the amount of retardation for each.
c. What percent of the children in each grade who are retarded in reading have failed to reach their full reading potential?
d. What percent of the children in each grade who are not retarded in reading have attained their full reading potential?
e. What percent of the children in the fourth grade find the text too difficult?
f. List the instructional practices believed to be most helpful in preventing retardation in reading.
g. List the instructional practices believed to be most helpful in correcting difficulties in reading.

### SUPPLEMENTARY PROBLEMS FOR ORAL AND WRITTEN DISCUSSION

1. Examine the teacher's manual accompanying a series of basic readers for a specific grade:

   a. Summarize the suggestions given for the diagnosis and correction of difficulties in word analysis and word recognition.
   b. Summarize the suggestions given for the diagnosis and correction of difficulties in comprehension.
2. Determine the reading status of a class in the intermediate or upper grades in terms of oral and silent reading skills:

   a. Indicate specific tests utilized.
   b. Identify the pupils who are retarded in oral reading.
   c. Identify the pupils who are retarded in silent reading.
   d. Indicate the amount of retardation for each pupil.
   e. Make a list of each pupil's reading difficulties in need of correction.
3. Select and organize a program of self-directed corrective material in reading for a specific grade.
4. Describe the in-service program in reading provided by a school system of your choice or as reported in a magazine.
5. Obtain the aid of a teacher in-service. Summarize her reading program by using the Inventory of Instructional Practices appearing in this chapter.

### REFERENCES

1. ALBERT J. HARRIS, *Effective Teaching of Reading* (New York: David McKay Co., Inc., 1962), p. 166.
2. WILLIAM KOTTMEYER, *Teacher's Guide for Remedial Reading* (Manchester, Mo.: Webster Publishing, 1959), p. 243.
3. DELWYN G. SCHUBERT, "Do Teachers Read About Reading?" *California Journal of Educational Research* (March, 1960).

# Appendixes*

## APPENDIX A
## ELEMENTS AND PRINCIPLES OF PHONICS

A fluent reader will have mastered the skills of phonics along with underlying principles. Appendix A provides an outline of elements and principles involved in this area for ready reference. These are drawn from manuals accompanying widely used basal reader series.

## Elements and Principles of Phonics†

CONSONANTS

I. A consonant is a letter which is produced by stopping or interrupting the breath by a speech organ. Those consonants that are produced with no vocal cord vibration are called voiceless consonants. Examples are *p, t, s*. Consonants that involve vocal-cord vibration in their production are known as voiced consonants. Examples are *g, l, m*. When consonants are sounded in isolation, teachers should do their best to minimize the *uh* sound which inescapedly must be added to some of them.

---

*Any material appearing in these appendixes may be reproduced by teachers for their own use.

†For more definitive information about this subject see William S. Gray, *On Their Own in Reading* and Albert J. Harris, *How to Increase Reading Ability* (See Appendix D) Also, T. Clymer, "The Utility of Phonic Generalizations in the Primary Grades," *The Reading Teacher* (January, 1963) and C. Winkley, "Which Accent Generalizations Are Worth Teaching?" *The Reading Teacher* (December, 1966).

A. Some consonants represent several sounds.
  1. Most often *c* sounds like *k*: cone, candy, cup. Once children generalize this principle, the following rhyme can be employed.

> When *c* comes before *o, u,* and *a*
> It sounds exactly like a *k*.

  a. When the letter *c* precedes the vowels *i, e* or *y*, usually it has the sound of *s*. Examples are cent, cigar, cyclone. Once children generalize this principle, the following rhyme can be employed.

> When *c* comes before an *i, y* or *e*,
> It makes a hissing sound for me.

  2. Most often *g* has a hard sound: go, game, gun.
  a. When the letter *g* precedes the vowels *i, e* or *y*, usually it has the sound of the letter *j*. Examples: gist, gem, gym. (Exceptions to this rule are fairly prevalent.)
  3. When *y* begins a word it acts as a consonant. Examples are yes, yard, yoke.
  a. When *y* ends a one syllable word it sounds like a long *i*. Examples: by, cry, sly.
  4. The letter *x* usually has the sounds of *ks*. Examples: box, tax, six.
  a. When *x* begins a word it never has the *ks* sound. Examples: X-ray, xylophone.
  5. The letter *s* usually has the sound of *s* when it follows a voiceless sound. Examples: boats (*t* is voiceless), rips (*p* is voiceless).
  a. The letter *s* usually has the sound of *z* when it follows a voiced sound. Examples are: cars (*r* is voiced), hums (*m* is voiced).
B. Consonant blends are combinations of two or three letters which when pronounced give credence to each letter. The first letter blends into the second: *gr*apes, *st*ick, *bl*ack. Blends also may appear in terminal positions. Examples: fir*st*, cha*sm*, cla*sp*.
C. Consonant digraphs are two letter sounds. Examples: *ch*icken, *sh*oe, *th*umb, *th*at, wi*ng*, *ph*one, *wh*ere, rou*gh*. (It is important for the child to learn that each letter loses its individual sound when the letters are working together to make a new sound.)
D. When two consonants appear together, one of them may be silent.
  1. When *b* follows *m*, the *b* usually is silent: lamb, comb.
  2. When *t* follows *b*, the *b* usually is silent: doubt, debt.
  3. When a vowel follows *gh*, the *h* usually is silent: ghost, ghastly.
  4. When a vowel precedes *gh*, the *gh* usually is silent: taught, light, weigh.
  5. When *d, m* or *k* follow *l*, the *l* is usually silent: would, talk, palm.

6. When *s* follows *p*, the *p* usually is silent: psalm, psychic.
7. When *r* follows *w*, the *w* usually is silent: wrench, write.
8. When *ch* follows *t*, the *t* usually is silent: witch, watch.

## VOWELS

I. A vowel is a sound which is produced with little or no narrowing or obstructing of the speech organs. Phonetically, single vowels are the most inconsistent letters in the English alphabet. Each vowel — a, e, i, o, u (sometimes y and w) — has a number of sounds. Fortunately, however, these sounds seem to fall roughly into two broad categories. These are the long and short sounds. Examples of the long and short vowel sounds are ate, at; even, elephant; iron, ink; old, ox; unicorn, uncle.

A. As stated previously, when *y* begins a word it acts like a consonant, but when *y* ends a one syllable word it has a long *i* sound.
1. When *y* ends a two syllable word it may sound like a short *i* or a long *e*. A difference of opinion exists among lexicographers. Actually, the sound of the *y* in these instances seems to be somewhere between a short *i* and a long *e*. Examples: slowly, lovely.

B. In words like crow, blow and know, the *w* acts as a vowel so the *o* says its name.

C. Vowel diphthongs involve a slurring of two vowels; that is, one vowel glides or slides into the other. Examples are b*oy*, *oil*; c*ow*, h*ouse*. (It should be noted that the double vowel rule does not apply to diphthongs.)

D. Following are principles that aid in determining vowel sounds:
1. When a word has one vowel and that vowel is at the end of the word, usually it has a long sound. Examples: go, me.
2. When a word has one vowel and that vowel is *not* at the end of the word, usually it has the short vowel sound. Examples: at, in, cut, hot, bet.
3. When there are two vowels together in a word, usually the first says its name and the second one is silent. Examples: boat, feet, seal. When children generalize this principle, it can be turned into the following rhyme.

When two vowels go walking
The first one does the talking

4. When there are two vowels in a word, one of which is a final *e*, the first vowel says its name and the *e* is silent. Examples: fine, home, tune. Children like to call this principle the "Magic E Rule."
5. If a single vowel in a word is followed by an *r* the sound of the vowel usually is controlled by the sound of *r*. Examples: bird, hurt, work, hard.

a. When *r* follows *e, i* or *u,* only the *r* sound is heard: her, fur, sir.
b. When *r* follows *a* or *o,* the vowel and the *r* are pronounced. The *a* has an *ah* sound and the *o* sounds like *aw*: Far, car, order, north.
6. When the only vowel in a word is an *a,* followed by *l* or *w,* the *a* usually has neither the long nor short vowel sound.

## Principles that Aid in Understanding Accent

1. When two syllable words end in a consonant followed by *y,* the first syllable is accented. Examples: lovely, slowly.
2. When the first syllable of a word is *de, re, be, ex* or *in,* the accent involves the last syllable. Examples: depress, return, beware, expect, inspect.
3. When the final syllable of a word ends in *le,* the syllable preceding it usually is accented. Examples: table, little.
4. When endings form syllables they usually are unaccented. Examples: foxes, tallest, tested.
5. When a word ends in a suffix, the accent usually falls on the root word. Examples: sneeze, sneezing; fool, foolish.
6. When words end in *ity, ic, ical, ian, ial* and *ious,* the primary accent usually involves the syllable preceding the suffix. Examples: publicity, artistic, typical, musician, official, religious.
7. When words end in *ate,* the primary accent usually falls on the third syllable from the end. Examples: intermediate, depreciate.

## Generalizations that Apply in Attacking Compound, Inflected or Derived Forms

1. Root words, prefixes and suffixes are meaning units in words.
2. Doubling the final consonant, changing a final *y* to *i* or dropping a final *e* before an ending or suffix usually does not change the sound of the root word.
3. When an ending or a suffix is preceded by a single vowel letter followed by a single consonant, the root word usually ends in *e.*
4. When an ending or a suffix is preceded by the letter *i,* the root word usually ends in *e.*
5. Inflectional variants can be formed by adding an ending or suffix without changing the root word. Examples: hunting, talked, foxes, shorter.
6. When root words end in a single consonant, the consonant is usually doubled before an ending is added. Examples: hitting, running.
7. When root words end in *e,* the *e* usually is dropped before adding an ending that begins with a vowel. Examples: wiping, strangest.
8. When root words end in *y,* the *y* usually is changed to *i* before an ending or suffix is added. Examples: fried, replied.

9. When root words end in *f*, the *f* usually is changed to *v* before an ending is added. Examples: wharves, calves.

## Principles that Aid in Determining Syllables in Words

1. When the first vowel in a word is followed by a double consonant, the word is divided between the consonants. Examples: rabbit, chipmunk. (This is not true, however, when the digraphs *sh, ch, th, wh,* and *ph* are involved.)
2. When the first vowel in a word is followed by a single consonant, that consonant usually begins the second syllable. Examples: above, pupil.
3. When a word ends in *le* the consonant preceding the *le* begins the last syllable. Examples: circle, able.
4. When the ending *ed* is preceded by *d* or *t*, it usually forms a separate syllable. Examples: padded, fitted.
5. When the various endings *less, ment, cion* and *sion* appear they usually form separate syllables. Examples: careless, government, suspicion, decision.

## APPENDIX A1
## WORD ANALYSIS GLOSSARY*

ACCENT: The stress given a certain syllable of a word to make it stand out over the other syllables of the word.

ACCENT, PRIMARY: The syllable receiving the main emphasis in the pronunciation of a given word.

ACCENT, SECONDARY: A stress weaker than the primary accent and one falling upon a different syllable of a given word.

AFFIX: That which is added to a root of a word; a suffix or prefix.

ANALYSIS, PHONETIC: A method of analyzing a printed word to determine its pronunciation through the use of consonant and vowel sounds, blends, syllables, etc.

ANALYSIS, STRUCTURAL: A method of analyzing a printed word to determine its pronunciation by identifying meaningful parts — roots, inflectional endings, syllables, prefixes and suffixes — which in turn may be blended into the sound of the word.

ANALYSIS, WORD: Analyzing an unfamiliar printed word for clues to its sound and/or meaning. Synonym: word attack.

ANTONYM: A word which is directly opposite in meaning to another word, for example, *small* is the antonym of *large.*

BLEND: The fusion of two or more letter sounds in a word without the identity of either sound being lost. A blend may consist of two or more consonant letters (*st, bl, st*) or one or more consonants and a vowel (*bi* as in *big*).

---

*From D. Schubert, *A Dictionary of Terms and Concepts in Reading* (Springfield, Ill.: Charles C Thomas, Publisher, 1964.)

BLEND, CONSONANT: See definition of blend.

BLEND, FINAL: The fusion of two or more letter sounds at the end of a word with each sound maintaining its identity.

BLENDING, SOUND: The fusion of two or more letter sounds without losing the identity of either sound, for example, *t* and *r* in *train*.

BREVE: A curved mark placed over a vowel to indicate the short sound, for example, bĭg.

CLUE, CONFIGURATION: A clue to word analysis based on the general shape or pattern of a printed word.

CLUE, CONTEXT: Utilizing surrounding words, phrases or sentences as an approach to word recognition and meaning.

CLUE, PICTURE: A picture related to a unit in reading that provides a useful clue to its meaning.

CONSONANT: A letter representing a speech sound characterized by a closure or very strongly modified narrowing of the mouth or throat, for instance, *b, t, s.*

CONSONANT, FINAL: A consonant which appears at the end of a word.

CONSONANT, INITIAL: A consonant appearing as the first letter of a word.

CONSONANT, MEDIAL: A consonant appearing inside a word.

CONSONANT, VOICED: A consonant sound which when produced is accompanied by vocal-cord vibration, for instance, *b, d, g.*

CONSONANT, VOICELESS: A consonant sound which when produced is not accompanied by vocal-cord vibration, for instance, *f, h, s.*

DERIVATIVE: A word composed of a root plus a prefix and/or suffix, for example, unhappy, happiness, unhappiness. Synonym-derived form.

DIACRITICAL MARK: A symbol placed over a letter to indicate the pronunciation.

DIGRAPH, CONSONANT: Two consonants which lose their individual identity and go together to represent a single sound, for example, *ch* as in *chicken*.

DIGRAPH, VOWEL: Two vowels that together make one sound, for example, *oa* in *boat*.

DIPHTHONG: A union of two vowels to make a gliding sound, as *oy* in *boy* or *ow* in *owl*.

GRAPHEME: A letter of the alphabet; the sum of all written letters and letter combinations that represent one phoneme.

HETERONYM: A word spelled the same as another but having a different pronunciation and meaning, for example, *lead* (to conduct) and *lead* (a metal).

HOMOGRAPH: One of two or more words identical in spelling but different in derivation and meaning, as *bow* (a tie) and *bow* (to bend).

HOMONYM: A word having the same pronunciation as another but differing from it in origin, meaning, and often, in spelling, for example, *bare* and *bear*.

HOMOPHONE: Words that are spelled differently but pronounced alike, for instance, *to, too, two*.

INFLECTED FORM: A word to which an inflectional ending has been added, for example, *s* may be added to the root word *fight*.

INFLECTIONAL ENDING: Designating or pertaining to an affix used in inflection, for example, John's sings, played, longer.

MORPHEME: The smallest meaningful unit in the structure of words (a root word, a prefix, a suffix or an inflectional ending), for instance, *rainy* consists of two morphemes, the root *rain* and the suffix *y*.

PHONEME: A speech sound or group of variants of one speech sound.

PHONETICS: The science of speech sounds, including their pronunciation, the action of the larynx, tongue and lips in sound production and the symbolization of sounds.

PHONICS: The study of sound-letter relationships in reading and spelling and the use of this knowledge in recognizing and pronouncing words.

PHONOGRAM: A letter or group of letters representing a speech sound.

PREFIX: A letter, syllable or group of syllables placed at the beginning of a word to modify or qualify its meaning.

ROOT, WORD: The basic form from which words are developed by the addition of prefixes, suffixes and inflectional endings.

SCHWA: A term borrowed from Hebrew phonetics, designating an indistinct vowel, one represented by the letters *a, e, i, o* and *u* in unaccented syllables, for example, April, problem; represented in phonetic script by an inverted *e*.

SIGHT WORD: A word recognized because of its shape or configuration rather than by the blending of parts into the whole.

SUFFIX: A letter or syllable added at the end of a word or root to modify its meaning, such as the *ment* in *agreement*.

SYLLABICATION: Synonym of syllabification.

SYLLABIFICATION: The act of forming or separating words into syllables.

SYLLABLE: A unit of pronunciation consisting of a vowel sound alone or with one or more consonant sounds and pronounced with one impulse of the voice.

SYLLABLE, CLOSED: A syllable ending with a consonant, for example: set.

SYLLABLE, OPEN: A syllable ending in a vowel, for example, we.

SYNONYM: A word that expresses the same idea as another word but usually differs from it in some shade of meaning.

TRIGRAPH, CONSONANT: A combination of three consonants, for example, *str*.

VOWEL: A single, open vocal sound in which there is no audible friction or stoppage.

WORD, COMPOUND: A word composed of two or more elements, themselves usually words: *housetop, bluebird*.

WORD, MONOSYLLABIC: A one syllable word.

WORD, POLYSYLLABIC: A word having two or more syllables.

WORD-ATTACK SKILLS: Synonym of word analysis.

# APPENDIX B
## KINESTHETIC METHOD IN READING

Pupils vary widely in their response to and acceptance of different instructional methods. The pupil who has been in school several years but is a nonreader should be exposed to new and novel instructional methods and materials. The kinesthetic method involving the visual, auditory and motor senses is frequently a most effective way of teaching the nonreader. A summary of this method appears on the following page. Teachers seeking to employ the kinesthetic method should consult the original source by Fernald. (See Appendix D1 for title and publisher.)

## The Kinesthetic Method

Explain to the child that we have a new way of learning words and that many bright people who have had the same difficulty as he have learned easily by this method. Let *him* select any *words he wants to learn*. Teach him the words in this manner:

1. Teacher writes the word in manuscript with crayon.
2. Child traces the word with his finger and says each part of the word as he traces it.
3. Child writes the word without looking at the copy and then compares his effort with the copy.
4. If he has made an error, he continues to trace the copy until he can write it correctly.

After the child has learned several words in this manner and has discovered that he can learn, he begins to write stories about any subject he chooses. The following procedure is used:

1. The child asks the teacher to write any word which he needs in his story.
2. He learns the word by tracing it and saying the parts as he does so.
3. He writes the word first on scrap paper and then in his story.
4. He files the word.
5. Teacher types the story.
6. The child reads the story to the teacher or to the group.

Cautions to the teacher:

1. Be sure the child always writes the word in the story without looking at the copy.
2. Be sure the child's finger actually touches the paper as he traces the word.
3. The word should always be written as a unit and should never be patched up by erasing or substituting.
4. Emphasize success. Call attention to the new words he has learned.

# Reading Readiness: Group

| Name of Test | Grade Level | Abilities Measured | Number of Forms | Working Time Minutes | Publisher |
|---|---|---|---|---|---|
| American School Reading Readiness Test | 1 | Vocabulary, discrimination of letter forms, recognition of words, discrimination of geometric forms, following directions, memory for geometric shapes | 1 | 45 | Public School Publishing Co. |
| Binson-Beck Reading Readiness Test | Kg-1 | Picture vocabulary, visual discrimination, following directions, memory for story, motor control | 1 | 40 | Acorn Publishing Co., Inc. |
| Gates Reading Readiness Test | 1 | Picture directions, word matching, word-card matching, rhyming | 1 | 50 | Bureau of Publications, Teachers College, Columbia University |
| Harrison-Stroud Reading Readiness Profiles | Kg-1 | Using symbols, visual discrimination, using the context, auditory discrimination, naming letters | 1 | 76 | Houghton, Mifflin Company |
| Lee-Clark Readiness Test | K-1 | Discrimination of letter forms and word forms | 1 | 20 | California Test Bureau |
| Metropolitan Readiness Tests | K-1 | Visual perception, similarities, copying, vocabulary, sentences, numbers, information | 2 | 60 | Harcourt, Brace & World, Inc. |
| Murphy-Durrell Diagnostic Reading Readiness Test | 1 | Auditory perception, visual perception, rate of learning | 1 | 72 | Harcourt, Brace & World, Inc. |
| Reading Readiness Test (M. J. Van Wagenen) | 1 | Information, perception of relations, vocabulary, memory span, word discrimination, word learning | 2 | 30 | U. S. Educational Test Bureau |

## Oral Reading: Individual

| Name of Test | Grade Level | Abilities Measured | Number of Forms | Working Time Minutes | Publisher |
|---|---|---|---|---|---|
| Diagnostic Reading Tests Lower Level, Section IV Oral Reading. Frances Triggs et al. | 4-6 | Accuracy and comprehension of oral reading | 2 | 20 | Committee on Diagnostic Reading Tests |
| Durrell Analysis of Reading Difficulty | 1-6 | Accuracy and comprehension of oral reading, word analysis, phonetics, spelling | 1 | 50 | Harcourt, Brace & World, Inc. |
| Gilmore Oral Reading Test | 1-8 | Accuracy, comprehension, and rate of oral reading | 2 | 20 | Harcourt, Brace & World, Inc. |
| Gray's Oral Reading Paragraphs | 1-6 | Accuracy of oral reading | 1 | 10 | The Psychological Corporation |
| Leavell Analytical Oral Reading Test | 1-8 | Accuracy and comprehension | 2 | 20 | U. S. Educational Test Bureau |

## Oral and/or Silent Reading: Individual

| Name of Test | Grade Level | Abilities Measured | Number of Forms | Working Time Minutes | Publisher |
|---|---|---|---|---|---|
| Diagnostic Reading Scales, Spache | 1-6 | Individual diagnosis of reading difficulties | 1 | 45 | California Test Bureau |
| Durrell Analysis of Reading Difficulty | 1-6 | Individual diagnosis of reading difficulties | 1 | 30-90 | Harcourt, Brace & World, Inc. |
| Gates-McKillop Reading Diagnostic Tests | 1-8 | Individual diagnosis of reading difficulties | 2 | 60-90 | Bureau of Publications, Teachers College, Columbia University |

| Name of Test | Grade Level | Abilities Measured | Number of Forms | Working Time Minutes | Publisher |
|---|---|---|---|---|---|
| Monroe Diagnostic Reading Examination | 1-6 | Individual diagnosis of reading difficulties | 1 | 45 | C. H. Stoelting Co. |
| Wide Range Achievement Test (Individual) | 1-12 | Individual test of word recognition (spelling and arithmetic) | 1 | Untimed | The Psychological Corporation |

## Silent Reading (Diagnostic): Group

| Name of Test | Grade Level | Abilities Measured | Number of Forms | Working Time Minutes | Publisher |
|---|---|---|---|---|---|
| The Botel Reading Inventory | 2-12 | Phonics mastery, word recognition, word meaning, listening | 1 | Untimed | Follett Publishing Company |
| Diagnostic Reading Tests | | | | | Committee on Diagnostic Reading Tests |
| Booklet I, Section IV | | | | | |
| Part I, Oral | 4-6 | Word attack | 2 | Untimed | |
| Part II, Silent | 4-6 | Word attack | 2 | Untimed | |
| Booklet II, Section IV | | | | | |
| Part I, Oral | 7-12 | Word attack | 2 | Untimed | |
| Part II, Silent | 7-12 | Word attack | 2 | Untimed | |
| Doren Diagnostic Reading Test | 3-8 | Eleven word-recognition skills | 1 | Untimed | U. S. Educational Test Bureau |
| Diagnostic Reading Test of Word Analysis Skills (Roswell-Chall) | 2-8 | Five word-analysis skills | 2 | Untimed | Essay Press |
| Durrell-Sullivan Reading Capacity Tests | | Ability to understand spoken language | | | Harcourt, Brace & World, Inc. |
| Primary | 2.5-4.5 | | 2 | 45 | |
| Intermediate | 3-6 | | | | |

| Name of Test | Grade Level | Abilities Measured | Number of Forms | Working Time Minutes | Publisher |
|---|---|---|---|---|---|
| Learning Methods Test Robt. E. Mills | | Proficiency in learning auditory, kinesthetic, visual | 1 | | Author Fort Lauderdale, Florida |
| McCullough Word Analysis Test | 4-12 | Seven types of word analysis skills | 1 | Untimed | Ginn and Company |
| Roswell-Chall Auditory Blending Test | 1-4 | Auditory blending | 1 | 5 | Essay Press |
| Scholastic Diagnostic Reading Tests | 1-9 | Word recognition, vocabulary, comprehension, study skills | 2 | | Scholastic Testing Service, Inc. |
| Silent Reading Diagnostic Test (Bond, et al.) | 3-8 | Twenty scores in word recognition | 2 | Two 45-Minute Periods | Lyons & Carnahan |
| Step Listening Tests Form 4A Form 3A | 4-6 7-9 | Skill in understanding, interpreting, applying and evaluating spoken language | 4 | 35 | Cooperative Test Division |
| Stroud-Hieronymous Primary Reading Profile | 1-2 | Reading aptitude, auditory association, word recognition, word attack, comprehension | 1 | | Houghton Mifflin Company |
| Test of Study Skills | 4-9 | Use of references, graphs, tables, maps, critical inference | 2 | 60 | Steck-Vaughn Company |

## Silent Reading (Survey): Group

| Name of Test | Grade Level | Abilities Measured | Number of Forms | Working Time Minutes | Publisher |
|---|---|---|---|---|---|
| California Reading Tests Elementary Junior High | 4-6 7-9 | Meaning vocabulary comprehension | 2 | 20 to 50 Minutes | California Test Bureau |

| Name of Test | Grade Level | Abilities Measured | Number of Forms | Working Time Minutes | Publisher |
|---|---|---|---|---|---|
| The Developmental Reading Tests (Bond, Clymer, Hoyt) 3 parts | 3-6 | Word recognition, comprehension, study skills | 1 | Two 45-Minute Periods | Lyons & Carnahan |
| Iowa Every-Pupil Test of Basic Skills Test B Work-Study Skills Elementary Advanced | 3-5 5-9 | Reading maps, graphs, charts and tables; use of references, index and dictionary | 4 | Two 45-Minute Periods | Houghton Mifflin Company |
| Garvey Primary Reading Test | 1-3 | Recognition of form, sight vocabulary and comprehension | 2 | 40 | California Test Bureau |
| Gates Basic Reading Tests Type A Type B Type C Type D | 3-8 3-8 3-8 3-8 | General significance Predicting outcomes Understanding directions Noting details | 4 4 4 4 | 6-8 6-8 8-10 8-10 | Bureau of Publications, Teachers College, Columbia University |
| Gates Primary Reading Tests | 1-2 | Word recognition, sentence meaning, paragraph meaning | 3 | 55 | Harcourt, Brace & World, Inc. |
| Gates Advanced Primary Reading Tests | 2-3 | Word recognition, paragraph meaning | 3 | 55 | Harcourt, Brace & World, Inc. |
| Gates Reading Survey | 3-10 | Meaning vocabulary, comprehension, speed and accuracy of reading | 2 | 60 | Bureau of Publications, Teachers College, Columbia University |
| Ingraham-Clark Diagnostic Reading Tests Primary Intermediate | 1-3 4-8 | Meaning vocabulary, comprehension, speed and accuracy of reading | 2 | 40 | California Test Bureau |

| Name of Test | Grade Level | Abilities Measured | Number of Forms | Working Time Minutes | Publisher |
|---|---|---|---|---|---|
| Iowa Every-Pupil Tests of Basic Skills in Silent Reading Comprehension | | Meaning vocabulary, comprehension; noting details, organization, total meaning | | | Houghton Mifflin Company |
| Elementary | 3-5 | | 4 | 46 | |
| Advanced | 5-9 | | 4 | 68 | |
| Iowa Silent Reading Test Elementary | 4-8 | Rate of reading, meaning vocabulary, comprehension, work-study skills | 4 | 49 | Harcourt, Brace & World, Inc. |
| Nelson Silent Reading Test | 3-9 | Meaning vocabulary, comprehension; general significance, details, prediction of outcomes | 3 | 30 | Houghton Mifflin Company |
| Sangren-Woody Silent Reading Test | 4-8 | Word meaning, rate, fact material, total meaning, central thought, following directions, organization | 2 | 27 | Harcourt, Brace & World, Inc. |
| Traxler Silent Reading Test | 7-10 | Rate, story comprehension, word meaning, paragraph comprehension (Additional tests contained in test batteries) | 4 | 46 | Public School Publishing Co. |

# Group Intelligence Tests

| Name of Test | Grade Level | Abilities Measured | Number of Forms | Working Time Minutes | Publisher |
|---|---|---|---|---|---|
| California Test of Mental Maturity | | Language and nonlanguage tests of memory, spatial relationships, logical reasoning and vocabulary | | | California Test Bureau |
| Pre-Primary Series | K-1 | | 1 | 90 | |
| Primary Series | 1-3 | | 1 | 90 | |
| Elementary Series | 4-8 | | 1 | 90 | |
| Intermediate Series | 7-10 | | 1 | 90 | |

| Name of Test | Grade Level | Abilities Measured | Number of Forms | Working Time Minutes | Publisher |
|---|---|---|---|---|---|
| California Short-Form Test of Mental Maturity | | Language test of numerical quantity, inference and vocabulary; nonlanguage tests of sensing right and left, manipulation of areas and similarities | | | California Test Bureau |
| Pre-Primary Series | K-1 | | 1 | 45 | |
| Primary Series | 1-3 | | 1 | 45 | |
| Elementary Series | 4-8 | | 1 | 45 | |
| Intermediate Series | 7-10 | | 1 | 45 | |
| Chicago Non-Verbal Examination | 1-12 | Designed to measure the intelligence of deaf and foreign-born children and children who are handicapped in the language area | 1 | 25 | The Psychological Corporation |
| Davis-Eells Test of General Intelligence or Problem Solving Ability | | Ability to solve problems common to all urban cultural groups | | | Harcourt, Brace & World, Inc. |
| Grade | 1 | | 1 | 60 | |
| Grade | 2 | | 1 | 90 | |
| Elementary | 3-6 | | 1 | 120 | |
| Goodenough Intelligence Test | K-1 | Based on spontaneous drawings of the children | 1 | | Harcourt, Brace & World, Inc. |
| Hennon-Nelson Tests of Mental Ability (self-marking) | 3-8 | Vocabulary, number completion, analogies | 3 | 30 | The Psychological Corporation |
| Kuhlmann-Anderson Intelligence Tests | K-8 | Separate booklet for each grade | 1 | 30 | Educational Test Bureau |
| Otis Quick-Scoring Test of Mental Ability | | Revision of the Otis Self-Administering Intelligence Test | | | Harcourt, Brace & World, Inc. |
| Alpha Test | 1-4 | | 2 | 25 | |
| Beta Test | 4-9 | | 2 | 30 | |
| Pintner General Ability Tests—Verbal Series Primary | K-2 | Seven tests composed entirely of pictures | 3 | 25 | Harcourt, Brace & World, Inc. |

| Name of Test | Grade Level | Abilities Measured | Number of Forms | Working Time Minutes | Publisher |
|---|---|---|---|---|---|
| Elementary | 2-4 | Scale 1, picture content; Scale 2, reading content | 2 | 45 | |
| Intermediate | 4-9 | Verbal content; reasoning, vocabulary, logical selection, etc. | 2 | 45 | |
| Pintner General Ability Tests—Non-language Series | 4-9 | Mental functions independent of word knowledge and facility | 2 | 50 | Harcourt, Brace & World, Inc. |
| SRA Primary Mental Abilities, Ages 5-7 | K-2 | Verbal meaning, quantitative, space, perceptual, speed, motor | 1 | 35 | Science Research Associates |
| Ages 7-11 | 2-6 | Verbal meaning, space, reasoning, perception, numbers | 1 | 35 | |
| Ages 11-17 | 6-12 | Verbal meaning, space, reasoning, number, word fluency | 1 | 26 | |

# APPENDIX C1

## What Do Diagnostic Reading Tests Diagnose? Skills Included in Six Analytical Reading Measures*

| | Botel Reading Inventory | Developmental Reading Tests Silent Reading Diagnostic Tests | Durrell Analysis of Reading Difficulty | Gilmore Oral Reading Test | Diagnostic Reading Scale | Gates-McKillop Reading Diagnostic Tests |
|---|---|---|---|---|---|---|
| Silent Reading Comprehension | | | X | | X | |
| Oral Reading Comprehension | | | X | X | X | |
| Oral Reading Accuracy | | | X | X | X | X |
| Oral Reading Rate | | | X | X | X | |
| Listening Comprehension | | | X | | X | |
| Word Recognition (oral) | X | | X | | X | X |
| Word Recognition (silent) | | X | | | | |
| Word Recognition in context (silent) | X | | | | | |
| Phrase Reading (oral) | | | | | | X |
| Recognition of phonetic word elements (oral) | X | | | | X | X |
| Recognition of phonetic word parts (silent and listening) | | X | X | | | |
| Root Words (silent) | | X | | | | |
| Rhyming Words (listening or silent) | X | X | | | | |
| Word Opposites (listening and/or silent) | X | | | | | |

*M. Trella, "What Do Diagnostic Reading Tests Diagnose? Skills Included in Six Analytical Reading Measures," *Elementary English Journal* 43, 370-372, April, 1966. Used by permission of author and the National Council of Teachers of English.

| | Botel Reading Inventory | Developmental Reading Tests — Silent Reading Diagnostic Tests | Durrell Analysis of Reading Difficulty | Gilmore Oral Reading Test | Diagnostic Reading Scale | Gates-McKillop Reading Diagnostic Tests |
|---|---|---|---|---|---|---|
| Word Blending (silent) | | X | | | | |
| Word Blending (oral) | | | | | X | X |
| Saying Syllables | | | | | X | X |
| Number and accent syllables (listening) | X | | | | | |
| Syllabication (silent) | | X | | | | |
| Identifying Letter Sounds (listening) | | X | X | | | X |
| Identifying Beginning Word Sounds (listening) | X | X | | | | X |
| Identifying Word Endings (listening) | | | X | | | X |
| Saying Letter Sounds | | | X | | X | |
| Identifying consonant blends and/or digraphs (listening) | X | | | | X | |
| Saying consonant blends and/or digraphs | | | X | | X | |
| Identifying long and short vowels (oral) | | | | | X | X |
| Identifying long and short vowels (listening) | X | | | | | X |
| Naming capital and lower case letters (oral) | | | X | | | X |
| Spelling (listening) | | | X | | | X |
| Spelling (oral) | | | X | | | |
| Reversible Words (silent) | | X | | | | X |
| Visual memory of words (silent) | | | X | | | |

# APPENDIX D
## READING READINESS CHECK LIST

Evaluation of
Factor Involved

Vision:

| | | | | | |
|---|---|---|---|---|---|
| Acuity at near point | 1 | 2 | 3 | 4 | 5 |
| Acuity at far point | 1 | 2 | 3 | 4 | 5 |
| Binocular skill | 1 | 2 | 3 | 4 | 5 |
| Eye-hand coordination | 1 | 2 | 3 | 4 | 5 |
| Directional sense | 1 | 2 | 3 | 4 | 5 |

Hearing:

| | | | | | |
|---|---|---|---|---|---|
| Auditory acuity | 1 | 2 | 3 | 4 | 5 |
| Auditory discrimination | 1 | 2 | 3 | 4 | 5 |
| Clarity of enunciation | 1 | 2 | 3 | 4 | 5 |

Speech:

| | | | | | |
|---|---|---|---|---|---|
| Absence of baby talk | 1 | 2 | 3 | 4 | 5 |
| Absence of a lisp | 1 | 2 | 3 | 4 | 5 |
| Absence of stuttering | 1 | 2 | 3 | 4 | 5 |
| Overall clarity of speech | 1 | 2 | 3 | 4 | 5 |

General Health:

| | | | | | |
|---|---|---|---|---|---|
| Absence of fatigue | 1 | 2 | 3 | 4 | 5 |
| Well-nourished body | 1 | 2 | 3 | 4 | 5 |
| Bodily coordination | 1 | 2 | 3 | 4 | 5 |
| Freedom from physical defects | 1 | 2 | 3 | 4 | 5 |

Social and Emotional Status:

| | | | | | |
|---|---|---|---|---|---|
| Leadership ability | 1 | 2 | 3 | 4 | 5 |
| Ability to work with others | 1 | 2 | 3 | 4 | 5 |
| Ability to carry on independently | 1 | 2 | 3 | 4 | 5 |
| Absence of infantile behavior | 1 | 2 | 3 | 4 | 5 |
| Feelings of security | 1 | 2 | 3 | 4 | 5 |

Home Environment:

| | | | | | |
|---|---|---|---|---|---|
| Quality of English spoken in home | 1 | 2 | 3 | 4 | 5 |
| Parental interest in books | 1 | 2 | 3 | 4 | 5 |
| Parental sharing of books with child | 1 | 2 | 3 | 4 | 5 |
| Parental harmony | 1 | 2 | 3 | 4 | 5 |
| Parental agreement on disciplinary measures | 1 | 2 | 3 | 4 | 5 |
| Parental acceptance | 1 | 2 | 3 | 4 | 5 |
| Travel opportunities | 1 | 2 | 3 | 4 | 5 |

Language Skill:

| | | | | | |
|---|---|---|---|---|---|
| Listening skill | 1 | 2 | 3 | 4 | 5 |
| Speaking vocabulary | 1 | 2 | 3 | 4 | 5 |
| Use of complete sentences | 1 | 2 | 3 | 4 | 5 |
| Ability to tell a story | 1 | 2 | 3 | 4 | 5 |

Intelligence:

Ability to recognize relationships .................................... 1   2   3   4   5
Ability to think sequentially ........................................ 1   2   3   4   5
Ability to memorize with ease ...................................... 1   2   3   4   5
Ability to sustain attention ......................................... 1   2   3   4   5
Ability to make good judgments .................................. 1   2   3   4   5

## APPENDIX E
## LETTER TO PARENTS OF DISABLED READERS

Dear_____:

A parent can do a great deal to help his child with his reading. Here is a list of some practical suggestions:

1. Have your child receive an annual physical examination which gives particular attention to his vision, hearing and general health. *Make sure the vision specialist to whom you go is interested in how well your child's eyes function at reading distance.* If you have a child about to enter first grade, a before school visual examination is good insurance.

2. Should the teacher or nurse observe symptoms of problems that require referral to another medical specialist (neurologist, psychiatrist, endocrinologist, etc.) do your best to cooperate. The specialist may report that nothing is wrong, but it is unwise to take a chance when your child's welfare is at stake.

3. Make sure your child gets enough sleep and a hot breakfast in the morning. A youngster who is tired finds it difficult to remain alert in school; a child who is hungry finds concentration a chore.

4. Provide a healthy home atmosphere. A child is more likely to do poorly in reading when parents are inconsistent in their discipline, when they reject the child or are overly solicitous or when they subject him to unfavorable comparisons with other children. As parents, it is important to build your child's confidence and feelings of self-worth. Give him plenty of love and accept him as an individual. Above all, do not resort to threats and bribes.

5. Enrich your child's language experiences by providing him with a rich background. Since reading involves bringing meaning to printed symbols, taking him on picnics, trips and excursions and explaining the "what," "how" and "why" of situations or happenings proves invaluable.

6. Provide a comfortable and inviting atmosphere for reading at home. Set aside a period for reading to and with your child. If he wishes to share with you something he has read, take the time to listen. And that means giving your undivided attention. More is needed than an "uh-huh."

7. Set a good example. Actions speak louder than words. If you wish your child to develop a love of reading, you have to do a lot of reading yourself. Soon he will begin thinking, "Gee, Dad and Mom like to read. Reading must be fun. I want to do it, too."

8. Help your child develop the library habit. Take him to the neighborhood library and get to know the librarian. Perhaps she can show him around before she gives him his own library card.

9. Provide a place for whatever books your child acquires. Perhaps you can give him a special shelf in the family bookcase. Even a drawer in a dresser or the kitchen cupboard is better than no place at all. Having a place for his books and other reading material will help your child develop pride in his library and an interest in reading.

10. Help your child evolve a television-viewing schedule that will not interfere with his reading and school work. Allowing him to choose with your help a select number of programs he wishes to view each week is a good democratic approach. In any event, an hour of television viewing daily should be sufficient. This means, of course, curtailing your own viewing of television on school nights. A child can't concentrate on books when others are watching television.

11. Don't negate what is being done by the school. Get to know your child's teacher and find out what you can do to help. She may provide you with a list of books that have high-interest appeal and are not too difficult. She also may recommend some reading game activities that are ideally suited to your child's needs. Many good books and reading games are available for purchase. They make fine birthday or Christmas gifts. But if your child has a severe reading problem, neither should be purchased without professional guidance.

12. Acquaint yourself with books that will help you understand the school's reading program and how to assist your child. Some recommendations follow:

ARTLEY, A. STERL, *Your Child Learns to Read,* Chicago: Scott, Foresman & Company, 1953.

CASEY, SALLY L., *Ways You Can Help Your Child with Reading,* Evanston, Ill.: Row, Peterson and Co., 1950.

GOLDENSON, ROBERT M., *Helping Your Child to Reading Better,* New York: Thomas Y. Crowell Company, 1957.

LARRICK, NANCY, *A Parent's Guide to Children's Reading,* Garden City, N.Y.: Doubleday & Company, Inc., 1958.

13. If the school your child attends has no remedial specialist, avail yourself of a college or university reading clinic should one be in the community. Reading clinics often have a team of specialists who can diagnose your child's reading problem and provide him with proper instruction. Sometimes, too, remedial reading specialists are available outside the school; but choosing a good one isn't a simple matter. Reading specialists vary greatly in their background. If possible, select one who has had experience and training in a college or university reading clinic. And most important, make sure the individual is the kind of person who is capable of establishing a good relationship with your child. Whether your child likes or hates his reading lesson is dependent on whether he likes his teacher.

14. Tutoring your own child is not recommended. As a parent you are emotionally involved and it is almost impossible to sustain the patience that is needed in a learning situation. Although there is no danger in furnishing your child with a word when he is stymied, it would be hazardous to attempt formal reading instruction involving phonics. Most parents

not only lack the patience needed to teach word-attack skills but the knowledge as well.

# APPENDIX F
## BIBLIOGRAPHY OF PROFESSIONAL BOOKS AND OTHER MATERIALS IN READING

As an aid to teachers and administrators in selecting useful books for their personal library and for the school library as well, Appendix F has been prepared. Teachers as professional workers cannot afford to neglect their professional library if they are to maintain professional status. Appendix F1 will help them in selecting worthwhile professional books and materials. Appendix F2 gives a list of sources of books adapted for retarded readers. An ample supply of these books is essential in every grade if retarded readers are to be provided with books for recreational reading that are of appropriate difficulty and interest.

## APPENDIX F1

### Selected Professional Books and Pamphlets

ARBUTHNOT, MAY, *Children and Books*, Chicago: Scott, Foresman & Company, 1947.

ARTLEY, STERL, *Your Child Learns to Read*, Chicago: Scott, Foresman & Company, 1953.

BARBE, WALTER, *Personalized Reading Instruction*, Englewood Cliffs, N. J.: Prentice-Hall, Inc., 1961.

BETTS, EMMETT, *Foundations of Reading Instruction*, New York: American Book Company, 1946.

—————, *The Prevention and Correction of Reading Difficulties*, Evanston, Ill.: Row, Peterson and Co., 1936.

BLAIR, GLENN, *Diagnostic and Remedial Teaching* rev. ed., New York: The Macmillan Company, 1956.

BLOOMER, RICHARD, *Skill Games to Teach Reading*, Dansville, N.Y.: F. A. Owen Co., 1961.

BOND, GUY and MILES TINKER, *Reading Difficulties, Their Diagnosis and Correction* 2nd ed., New York: Appleton-Century-Crofts, 1967.

BOTEL, MORTON, *How to Teach Reading*, Chicago: Follett Publishing Company, 1962.

BRUECKNER, LEO and GUY BOND, *The Diagnosis and Treatment of Learning Difficulties*, New York: Appleton-Century-Crofts, 1955.

COHN, JACK and STELLA COHN, *Teaching the Retarded Reader*, New York: The Odyssey Press, Inc., 1967.

COLE, LUELLA, *The Improvement of Reading*, New York: Holt, Rinehart & Winston, Inc., 1938.

DARROW, HELEN and VIRGIL HOWES, *Approaches to Individualized Reading*, New York: Appleton-Century-Crofts, 1960.

DAWSON, MILDRED and HENRY BAMMAN, *Fundamentals of Basic Reading Instruction*, New York: David McKay Co., Inc., 1959.

DECHANT, EMERALD V., *Improving the Teaching of Reading*, Englewood Cliffs, N. J.: Prentice-Hall, Inc., 1964.

DEBOER, JOHN and MARTHA DALLMAN, *The Teaching of Reading* rev. ed., New York: Henry Holt and Company, Inc., 1964.

DOLCH, EDWARD, *Methods in Reading*, Champaign, Ill.: Garrard Press, 1955.

————, *Psychology and Teaching of Reading* rev. ed., Champaign, Ill.: Garrard Publishing Co., 1951.

FERNALD, GRACE, *Remedial Techniques in Basic School Subjects*, New York: McGraw-Hill Book Company, 1943.

FRIES, CHARLES C., *Linguistic and Reading*, New York: Holt, Rinehart & Winston, Inc., 1963.

GATES, ARTHUR, *The Improvement of Reading*, New York: The Macmillan Company, 1947.

GETMAN, G. N. and ELMER R. KANE, *The Physiology of Readiness*, Minneapolis, Minn.: P.A.S.S., Inc., 1964.

GRAY, LILLIAN, *Teaching Children to Read* 3rd ed., New York: The Ronald Press Company, 1963.

GRAY, WILLIAM, et al., *Developing Children's Word-Perception Power*, Chicago: Scott, Foresman & Company, 1954.

————, *On Their Own in Reading* rev. ed., New York: Scott, Foresman & Company, 1960.

HARRIS, ALBERT, *Effective Teaching of Reading*, New York: David McKay Co., Inc., 1962.

————, *How to Increase Reading Ability* rev. ed., New York: David McKay Co., Inc., 1961.

HEGG, THORLEIF, *Remedial Reading Drills*, Ann Arbor, Mich.: George Wahr, 1953.

HEILMAN, ARTHUR W., *Principles and Practices of Teaching Reading*, Columbus, Ohio: Charles E. Merrill Books, Inc., 1961.

HILDRETH, GERTRUDE, *Teaching Reading*, New York: Henry Holt and Company, 1958.

KOTTMEYER, WILLIAM, *Teacher's Guide for Remedial Reading*, Manchester, Mo.: Webster Publishing, 1959.

MARKSHEFFEL, NED D., *Better Reading in the Secondary School*, New York: The Ronald Press Company, 1966.

MIEL, ALICE, *Individualizing Reading Practices*, Bureau of Publications, Teachers College, Columbia University, 1958.

MCKIM, MARGARET, *Guiding Growth in Reading in the Modern Elementary School*, New York: The Macmillan Company, 1955.

MONROE, MARION and BERTIE BACKUS, *Remedial Reading*, Boston: Houghton Mifflin Company, 1937.

————, *Growing into Reading*, Chicago: Scott, Foresman & Company, 1951.

ORTON, SAMUEL, *Reading, Writing and Speech Problems in Children*, New York: W. W. Norton & Company, Inc., 1937.

ROBINSON, HELEN, *Why Pupils Fail in Reading*, Chicago: University of Chicago Press, 1946.

RUSSELL, DAVID, *Children Learn to Read* rev. ed., Boston: Ginn and Company, 1961.

————, *et al.*, *Reading Aids Through the Grades*, Bureau of Publications, Teachers College, Columbia University, 1956.

SCHUBERT, DELWYN G., *A Dictionary of Terms and Concepts in Reading*, Springfield, Ill: Charles C Thomas, Publisher, 1964.

SCHUBERT, DELWYN G., *Reading Games That Teach*, Santa Fe Springs, Calif.: Creative Teaching Press, Inc., 1965.

SCOTT, LOUISE and JAMES THOMPSON, *Phonics in Listening, in Speaking, in Reading, in Writing*, Manchester, Mo.: Webster Publishing, 1962.

SPACHE, GEORGE, *Good Reading for Poor Readers* rev. ed., Champaign, Ill.: Garrard Publishing Co., 1966.

————, *Reading in the Elementary School*, Boston: Allyn & Bacon, Inc., 1964.

————, *Toward Better Reading*, Champaign, Ill.: Garrard Publishing Co., 1963.

STAUFFER, RUSSELL, *Individualizing Reading Instruction*, University of Delaware, School of Education, 1957.

STRANG, RUTH, *Diagnostic Teaching of Reading*, New York: McGraw-Hill Book Company, 1964.

————, and DOROTHY BRACKEN, *Making Better Readers*, Boston: D. C. Heath & Company, 1957.

————, CONSTANCE MCCULLOUGH and ARTHUR TRAXLER, *The Improvement of Reading* 3rd ed., New York: McGraw-Hill Book Company, 1961.

TINKER, MILES A. and C. M. MCCULLOUGH, *Teaching Elementary Reading*, New York: Appleton-Century-Crofts, 1962.

WILSON, ROBERT M., *Diagnostic and Remedial Reading*, Columbus, Ohio: Charles E. Merrill Books, Inc., 1967.

WITTY, PAUL, *Reading in Modern Education*, Boston: D. C. Heath & Company, 1949.

WITTY, PAUL and DAVID KOPEL, *Reading and the Educative Process*, Boston: Ginn and Company, 1939.

ZINTZ, MILES V., *Corrective Reading*, Dubuque, Iowa: Wm. C. Brown Company Publishers, 1966.

## Selected Publications of the National Society for the Study of Education*

Twentieth Yearbook, 1921, Part II — *Report of the Society's Committee on Silent Reading*, M. A. Burgess *et al.*

Twenty-fourth Yearbook, 1925, Part I — *Report of the National Committee on Reading*, W. S. Gray, Chairman.

---

*Published by Scholastic Magazines, 33 W. 42nd St., New York 36, N.Y. (The official organ of the International Reading Association is *The Reading Teacher*, 5454 South Shore Drive, Chicago 15, Illinois.)

Twenty-fourth Yearbook, 1925, Part II — *Adapting the Schools to Individual Differences,* report of the Society's Committee, Carleton W. Washburne, Chairman.

Thirty-sixth Yearbook, 1937, Part I — *The Teaching of Reading,* prepared by the Society's Committee, W. S. Gray, Chairman.

Forty-third Yearbook, 1944, Part II — *Teaching Language in the Elementary School,* prepared by the Society's Committee, M. R. Trabue, Chairman.

Forty-eighth Yearbook, 1949, Part II — *Reading in the Elementary School,* prepared by the Society's Committee, Arthur I. Gates, Chairman.

Sixtieth Yearbook, 1961, Part I — *Development in and through Reading,* prepared by the Society's Committee, Paul A. Witty, Chairman.

Sixty-first Yearbook, 1962, Part I — *Individualizing Instruction,* prepared by the Society's Committee, Fred T. Tyler, Chairman.

## International Reading Association Conference Proceedings*

*Better Readers for Our Times,* W. S. Gray and Nancy Larrick, editors, 1956.

*Reading in Action,* Nancy Larrick, editor, 1957.

*Reading for Effective Living,* J. Allen Figural, editor, 1958.

*Reading in a Changing Society,* J. Allen Figural, editor, 1959.

*New Frontiers in Reading,* J. Allen Figural, editor, 1960.

*Changing Concepts of Reading Instruction,* J. Allen Figural, editor, 1961.

*Challenge and Experiment in Reading,* J. Allen Figural, editor, 1962.

*Reading as an Intellectual Activity,* J. Allen Figural, editor, 1963.

*Improvement of Reading Through Classroom Practice,* J. Allen Figural, editor, 1964.

*Reading and Inquiry,* J. Allen Figural, editor, 1965.

*Vistas in Reading,* J. Allen Figural, editor, 1966.

*Forging Ahead in Reading,* J. Allen Figural, editor, 1967.

## Supplementary Educational Monographs†

| Vol. I | *Recent Trends in Reading,* William S. Gray, editor, 1939. |
| Vol. II | *Reading and Pupil Development,* William S. Gray, editor, 1940. |
| Vol. III | *Adjusting Reading Programs to Individuals,* William S. Gray, editor, 1941. |
| Vol. IV | *Cooperative Efforts in Schools to Improve Reading,* William S. Gray, editor, 1942. |
| Vol. VI | *Reading in Relation to Experience and Language,* William S. Gray, editor, 1944. |

*Published by the University of Chicago Press, 5750 Ellis Ave., Chicago 37, Ill.
†The Supplementary Educational Monographs which have been published since 1939 include the Proceedings of the Annual Conference on Reading held each year at the University of Chicago as well as other reports pertaining to the subject of reading. These monographs are published by the University of Chicago Press, 5750 Ellis Ave., Chicago 37, Illinois.

| | |
|---|---|
| Vol. VII | *The Appraisal of Current Practices in Reading*, William S. Gray, editor, 1945. |
| Vol. VIII | *Improving Reading in the Content Fields*, William S. Gray, editor, 1946. |
| Vol. IX | *Promoting Personal and Social Development through Reading*, William S. Gray, editor, 1947. |
| Vol. X | *Basic Instruction in Reading in Elementary and High Schools*, William S. Gray, editor, 1948. |
| Vol. XI | *Classroom Techniques in Improving Reading*, William S. Gray, editor, 1949. |
| Vol. XII | *Keeping Reading Abreast of the Times*, William S. Gray, editor, 1950. |
| Vol. XIII | *Promoting Growth Toward Maturity in Interpreting What is Read*, William S. Gray, editor, 1951. |
| Vol. XIV | *Improving Reading in All Curriculum Areas*, Helen Robinson, editor, 1952. |
| Vol. XV | *Corrective Reading in Classroom and Clinic*, Helen Robinson, editor, 1953. |
| Vol. XVI | *Promoting Maximal Reading Growth Among Able Learners*, Helen Robinson, editor, 1954. |
| Vol. XVII | *Oral Aspects of Reading*, Helen Robinson, editor, 1955. |
| Vol. XVIII | *Developing Permanent Interest in Reading*, Helen Robinson, editor, 1956. |
| Vol. XIX | *Materials for Reading*, Helen Robinson, editor, 1957. |
| Vol. XX | *Visual Perceptual Abilities and Early Reading Progress*, Helen Robinson, editor, 1958. |
| Vol. XXI | *Reading Instruction in Various Patterns of Grouping*, Helen Robinson, editor, 1959. |
| Vol. XXII | *Sequential Development of Reading Abilities*, Helen Robinson, editor, 1960. |
| Vol. XXIII | *Controversial Issues in Reading and Promising Solutions*, Helen Robinson, editor, 1961. |
| Vol. XXIV | *The Underachiever in Reading*, Helen Robinson. Helen Robinson, editor, 1962. |
| Vol. XXV | *Reading and the Language Arts*, Helen Robinson. Helen Robinson, editor, 1963. |
| Vol. XXVI | *Meeting Individual Differences in Reading*, Helen Robinson, editor, 1964. |
| Vol. XXVII | *Recent Developments in Reading*, Helen Robinson, editor, 1965. |
| Vol. XXVIII | *Reading: Seventy-Five Years of Progress*, Helen Robinson, editor, 1966. |

## APPENDIX F2

## Publications Which Contain Bibliographies of Books for Retarded Readers

BLAIR, GLENN, *Diagnostic and Remedial Teaching* rev. ed., New York: The Macmillan Company, 1956, pp. 180-198.

BOTEL, MORTON, *How to Teach Reading*, Chicago: Follett Publishing Company, 1962, pp. 117-120.

CARPENTER, HELEN, *Gateways to American History: An Annotated Graded List of Books for Slow Learners in Junior High School*, New York: H. W. Wilson Co., 1942.

CARTER, HOMER and DOROTHY McGINNIS, *Learning to Read*, New York: McGraw-Hill Book Company, 1953, pp. 115-118.

DAWSON, MILDRED and HENRY BAMMAN, *Fundamentals of Basic Reading Instruction* 2nd ed., New York: Longmans, Green and Co., 1963.

DUNN, ANITA *et al.*, *Fare for the Reluctant Reader*, Albany, N.Y.: State University of New York, 1952.

EAKIN, MARY, *Library Materials for Remedial Reading, bibliography*, No. 4, Instructional Materials Bulletin, May, 1959, Cedar Falls, Iowa: Iowa State Teachers College Library.

FRY, EDWARD and WARREN JOHNSON, "Books for Remedial Reading," *Elementary English* 35: 373-379, 1958.

HARRIS, ALBERT, *How to Increase Reading Ability*, New York: Longmans, Green and Co., 1961, pp. 594-607.

HILL, MARGARET, *A Bibliography of Reading Lists for Retarded Readers*, Extension Bulletin. College of Education Series, No. 37, Iowa City: State University of Iowa, 1953.

HOBSON, CLOY and OSCAR HAUGH, *Materials for the Retarded Reader*, Kansas State Department of Public Instruction, 1954.

HOWARD, VIVIAN, *Books for Retarded Readers*, Illinois State Library, 1954.

KOTTMEYER, WILLIAM, *Teacher's Guide for Remedial Reading*, Manchester, Mo.: Webster Publishing, 1959, pp. 189-201.

KRESS, ROY, *A Place to Start: A Graded Bibliography for Children with Reading Difficulties*, Reading Center, Syracuse University, 1963.

KUGLER, LORNA *et al.*, *Choosing the Right Book*, California Library Association, 1955.

LAZAR, MAY, ed., *The Retarded Reader in the Junior High School*, Bureau of Educational Research Bulletin No. 31, New York Board of Education, 1952.

ORR, KENNETH, *Selected Materials for Remedial Reading*, Division of Special Education, Indiana State Teachers College.

ROSWELL, FLORENCE and JEANNE CHALL, *Selected Materials for Children with Reading Disabilities* rev. ed., The Remedial Reading Service of the City College Educational Clinic, New York, 1959.

RUE, ELOISE, *America Past and Present*, New York: H. W. Wilson Co., 1948.

SLATER, RUSSELL, *Books for Youth Who Dislike Reading*, Columbus, Ohio: Ohio State University, 1941.

SPACHE, GEORGE, *Good Reading for Poor Readers* rev. ed., Champaign, Ill.: Garrard Publishing Co., 1960, pp. 108-115.

STRANG, RUTH *et al.*, *Gateways to Readable Books* 3rd ed., New York: H. W. Wilson Co., 1958.

WOOLF, MAURICE and JEANNE WOOLF, *Remedial Reading*, New York: McGraw-Hill Book Company, 1957, pp. 385-394.

# APPENDIX G
## PUBLISHERS OF TESTS AND OTHER READING MATERIAL

### List of Publishers or Manufacturers of Reading Tests, Textbooks, Materials and Devices

The following alphabetically arranged list contains the names and addresses of all the publishers or manufacturers of reading tests, textbooks, materials and devices mentioned in this book.

| | |
|---|---|
| Acorn | Acorn Publishing Company, Inc., Rockville Centre, New York |
| Allyn | Allyn & Bacon, Inc., 410 Atlantic Ave., Boston, Mass. 02110 |
| American | American Book Company, 55 Fifth Ave., New York, N.Y. 10003 |
| Appleton | Appleton-Century-Crofts, 440 Park Ave. S., N.Y. 10016 |
| Audio Center | Audio Visual Center, 270 Willow St., San Jose, Calif. 95100 |
| Audio Research | Audio Visual Research, 523 S. Plymouth Court, Chicago, Ill. 60605 |
| Barnell Loft | Barnell Loft Ltd., 111 S. Centre Ave., Rockville Centre, N.Y. |
| Beckley | Beckley-Cardy Co., 1900 N. Narragansett Ave., Chicago, Ill. 60639 |
| Bell | Bell & Howell Co., 7100 McCormick Road, Chicago, Ill. 60645 |
| Ben | Ben-G-Products, 462 Sagamore Ave., East Williston, N.Y. |
| Bobbs | The Bobbs-Merrill Co., Inc., 4300 W. 62nd St., Indianapolis, Ind. 46206 |
| Bradley | Milton Bradley Co., 74 Park St., Springfield, Mass. 01102 |
| Bureau | Bureau of Publications, Teachers College, Columbia University, New York, N.Y. 10027 |
| California | California Test Bureau, Monterey, Calif. 93940 |
| Cenco | Cenco Educational Aids, 2600 S. Koster Ave., Chicago, Ill. 60623 |
| Chicago | University of Chicago Press, 5750 Ellis Ave., Chicago, Ill. 60637 |
| Committee | Committee on Diagnostic Reading Tests, Mountain Home, North Carolina 28758 |
| Cooperative | Cooperative Test Division, Educational Testing Service, Princeton, N. J. 08540 |
| Craig | Craig Research Inc., 3410 S. La Cienago Blvd., Los Angeles, Calif. 90016 |
| Dictaphone | Dictaphone Corporation, 2224 W. Olympic Blvd., Los Angeles, Calif. 90016 |

| | |
|---|---|
| Educational | Educational Cards, Inc., 1302 Industrial Bank Bldg., Detroit, Mich. 48200 |
| Educational Aids | Educational Aids, 845 Wisteria Drive, Fremont, Calif. 94538 |
| Educational Laboratories | Educational Developmental Laboratories, 75 Prospect, Huntington, N.Y. 11746 |
| Educational Associates | Educational Research Associates, 2223 S. Olive, Los Angeles, Calif. |
| Educational Bureau | Educational Test Bureau, 720 Washington Ave., S. E., Minneapolis, Minn. 55414 |
| Encyclopedia | Encyclopedia Britannica Press, Inc., 425 N. Michigan Ave., Chicago, Ill. 60611 |
| Essay | Essay Press, Box 5, Planetarium Station, New York, N.Y. 10024 |
| Fearon | Fearon Publishers, Inc., 2263 Union St., San Francisco, Calif. 94100 |
| Follett | Follett Publishing Company, 1010 W. Washington Blvd., Chicago, Ill. 60607 |
| Garrard | Garrard Publishing Co., 1607 N. Market St., Champaign, Ill. 61820 |
| Ginn | Ginn and Company, P. O. Box 191, Boston, Mass. 02117 |
| Hale | E. M. Hale and Company, 1201 S. Hastings Way, Eau Claire, Wisc. 54701 |
| Hammond | Hammond Incorporated, 515 Valley St., Maplewood, N. J. 07040 |
| Harcourt | Harcourt Brace & World, Inc., 757 Third Ave., New York, N.Y. 10017 |
| Harper | Harper & Row, Publishers, 49 E. 33rd St., New York, N.Y. 10016 |
| Heath | D. C. Heath & Company, 285 Columbus Ave., Boston, Mass. 02116 |
| Holiday | Holiday Games, P. O. Box 2565, Bell Gardens, Calif. |
| Holt | Holt, Rinehart & Winston, Inc., 383 Madison Ave., New York, N.Y. 10017 |
| Houghton | Houghton Mifflin Company, 2 Park St., Boston, Mass. 02107 |
| Ideal | Ideal School Supply Co., Chicago, Ill. 60620 |
| Imperial | Imperial Productions, Inc., 247 W. Court St., Kankakee, Ill. 60901 |
| Iroquois | Iroquois Publishing Co., Syracuse, N.Y. 13200 |
| Kenworthy | Kenworthy Educational Service, 45 N. Division St., Buffalo, N.Y. 14203 |
| Keystone | Keystone View Co., Meadville, Pa. 16335 |
| Kohner | Kohner Brothers, 155 Wooster St., New York, N.Y. 10012 |

| | |
|---|---|
| Judy | The Judy Co., 310 N. Second St., Minneapolis, Minn. 55401 |
| Lafayette | Lafayette Instrument Co., Lafayette, Ind. 47901 |
| Lippincott | J. B. Lippincott Co., E. Washington Square, Philadelphia, Pa. 19105 |
| Learning | Learning Through Seeing, Sunland, Calif. 91040 |
| Longmans | See McKay |
| Lyons | Lyons & Carnahan, 407 E. 25th St., Chicago, Ill. 60616 |
| Macmillan | The Macmillan Co., 866 Third Ave., New York, N.Y. 10022 |
| McCormick | McCormick-Mathers Publishing Co., Inc., Box 2212, 1440 E. English St., Wichita, Kansas 67201 |
| McGraw | McGraw-Hill Book Company, 330 W. 42nd St., New York, N.Y. 10036 |
| McKay | David McKay Co., Inc., 750 Third Ave., New York, N.Y. 10017 |
| Owen | F. A. Owen Publishing Co., Dansville, N.Y. 14437 |
| Oxford | Oxford University Press, Inc., 200 Madison Ave., New York, N.Y. 10016 |
| Parker | Parker Brothers Inc., Salem, Mass. 01971 |
| Perceptual | Perceptual Development Laboratory, St. Louis, Mo. 63105 |
| Primary | Primary Playhouse, Sherwood, Ore. 97140 |
| Psychological | The Psychological Corp., 304 E. 45th St. New York, N.Y. 10017 |
| Psychotechnics | Psychotechnics, Incorporated, 105 W. Adams St., Chicago, Ill. 60603 |
| Public | Public School Publishing Co., 204 W. Mulberry St., Bloomington, Ill. 61701 |
| Putnam | G. P. Putnam's Sons, 200 Madison Ave., New York, N.Y. 10016 |
| Reader's | Reader's Digest Services, Inc., Educational Division, Pleasantville, N.Y. 10570 |
| Remedial | Remedial Education Center, 1321 W. Hampshire Ave., Washington 6, D. C. |
| Rinehart | See Holt |
| Ronald | The Ronald Press Company, 79 Madison Ave., New York, N.Y. 10016 |
| Row | See Harper & Row |
| Scholastic | Scholastic Testing Service, Inc., 3774 West Devon Ave., Chicago, Ill. 60645 |
| Science | Science Research Associates, Inc., 259 E. Erie St., Chicago, Ill. 60611 |
| Scott | Scott, Foresman & Company, 1900 E. Lake Ave., Glenview, Ill. 60625 |
| Society | Society for Visual Education, Chicago, Ill. 60614 |
| Steck | Steck-Vaughn Company, Box 2028, Austin, Tex. 78767 |
| Stoelting | C. H. Stoelting Co., 424 N. Homan Ave., Chicago, Ill. |

| | |
|---|---|
| Syracuse | Syracuse University Press, Box 8, University Station, Syracuse, N.Y. 13210 |
| Teachers' Supplies | Teachers' Supplies, 6571 Beach Blvd., Buena Park, California 90620 |
| Three | Three Dimension Co., Chicago, Ill. 60641 |
| Visualcraft | Visualcraft, 2636 W. Union St., Blue Island, Ill. 60406 |
| Wahr | George Wahr Publishing Co., 316 S. State St., Ann Arbor, Mich. 48106 |
| Webster | Webster Publishing, Manchester Rd., Manchester, Mo. 63011 |
| Winston | See Holt, Rinehart & Winston |
| World | World Book Company, see Harcourt |

# Author Index

# Subject Index